TRUMP / RUSSIA

TRUMP/RUSSIA

A DEFINITIVE HISTORY

SETH HETTENA

MELVILLE HOUSE
BROOKLYN
LONDON

Trump / Russia

First published in 2018 by Melville House
Copyright © Seth Hettena, 2018
All rights reserved
First Melville House Printing: May 2018

Melville House Publishing
46 John Street
Brooklyn, NY 11201
and
Suite 2000
16/18 Woodford Road
London E7 0HA

mhpbooks.com
facebook.com/mhpbooks
@melvillehouse

ISBN: 978-1-61219-739-5
ISBN: 978-1-61219-740-1 (eBook)

Designed by Richard Oriolo

Printed in the United States of America
10 9 8 7 6 5 4 3 2 1

A catalog record for this book is available from the Library of Congress

FOR MY SONS, RYAN AND EVAN

"There are three ways of influencing a person: blackmail, vodka, or the threat of murder."

—VLADIMIR PUTIN, AS QUOTED IN *SOVERSHENNO SEKRETNO*, FEBRUARY 1, 2000

"Man is not what he thinks he is, he is what he hides."

—ANDRÉ MALRAUX

CONTENTS

INTRODUCTION

VLADIMIR LENIN IS OFTEN CREDITED WITH coining the phrase "useful idiot" to describe the shallow thinkers in the West who did the Communist Party's bidding without realizing it. During the Cold War, liberals consistently lived down to the stereotype that they were Soviet dupes, too gullible and weak-minded to see they were buying the rope that would hang them, as Lenin put it. With each passing day, it becomes more and more difficult to avoid the conclusion that the current president of the United States, Donald J. Trump, is either hiding something when it comes to the Kremlin, or simply one of its useful idiots. Neither conclusion is comforting.

In the halls of Congress and in the office of Special Counsel Robert Mueller, investigations are underway to determine whether Trump or members of his campaign and administration colluded with Russia to influence the 2016 presidential election. The answer appears more and more likely to be a resounding yes. A hoax or fake news, counters Trump, who peddles a shameless conspiracy theory that it was all cooked up by a "deep state" trying to stage a quiet coup and expel a president democratically elected by angry voters who sent him to burn the corrupt Washington establishment to the ground. The GOP-led House Intelligence Committee's 14-month investigation found no collusion; the Senate's investigation and the special counsel's roll on. Hyped by the press, diminished by the president's defenders, and analyzed by legions of armchair pundits and self-styled investigators, the Russia issue has split the country right down the middle, with half of all Americans believing that the Trump campaign did collude with Russia.

So divisive is this issue that it obscures the very real and very alarming fact that Vladimir Putin directed an information warfare campaign aimed at influencing the outcome of the 2016 presidential election. This is grave stuff, not fake news, but rather the sobering conclusion of the heads of the FBI, CIA, and NSA, as well as Special Counsel Mueller's crack team of prosecutors. Acting on Putin's orders, Russian intelligence broke into the networks of the Clinton campaign and the Democratic Party and stole thousands of emails, which were then released to WikiLeaks. At the same time, a shadowy Internet group based in St. Petersburg, Russia, directed employees to pose as Americans online and use social media to help Trump's chances and manipulate the 2016 election.

The battle is engaged. America is under attack by a foreign adversary, and for the first time in its history, this country has not responded. With more attacks sure to come in the 2018 midterm elections and the 2020 presidential election, government response of some kind is required, yet the commander in chief remains either unable or unwilling to do anything about it. President Trump rails on about witch hunts and hoaxes, and mocks the very intelligence agencies tasked with figuring out how to repel this assault on American democracy.

Despite Trump's pugilism, however, there has been one man he has not crossed: Vladimir Putin. Their relationship can be distilled to quiet admiration from afar. "I think [Trump] is an experienced person, a businessman with very extensive experience," Putin told NBC News personality Megyn Kelly during an interview in March 2018, "and he understands that if you need to partner with someone you must treat your future or current partner with respect, otherwise nothing will come of it. I think this is a purely pragmatic approach."[1]

Trump for his part has not been shy about his admiration for Russia's longtime president, whom he has called "a leader far more than our president [Obama] has been." Just a few months before Putin's NBC News interview, Trump acknowledged his belief that Putin and Russia did not interfere with the 2016 elections: "[Putin] said he didn't meddle. He said he didn't meddle. I asked him again. You can only ask so many times. Every time he sees me, he says, 'I didn't do that.' And I believe, I really believe, that when he tells me that, he means it. I think he is very insulted by it."[2]

Trump's friendly history with Russia stretches back decades, to when Trump Tower first began taking on tenants after opening in 1983. From the beginning, the Russian Mafiya made Trump Tower a base for their skulduggery, a trend that continued when Trump built his Taj Mahal casino in Atlantic City. When that venture failed, and Trump spent the latter part of the 1990s bankrupt, he turned again to the Russians, hoping to sell them on a Trump Tower in Moscow. The Russian capital became such a favored travel and business destination for the Trump family that Eric Trump once quipped to a friend of the family, who reported it later, "We have all the funding we need out of Russia . . . [W]e go there all the time."[3]

That affinity has long gone both ways. Russian oligarchs, criminal masterminds, and Kremlin-linked officials have been drawn to Trump and his properties for years. But prior to the 2016 presidential election, those connections, nearly all of them shady, remained behind a curtain. With Trump's candidacy came more audacious attempts by high-powered Russians to assist him in his run, by reaching out with numerous offers of secret back channels, dirt, and hacked emails. While this book does not deeply dive into some of the more recent examples (the Seychelles meeting between Trump and Putin associates to establish a back channel between the two presidents) or more obscure intrigues now being dredged up (Trump's phone call to Putin congratulating him on his election victory), it does lay out a comprehensive historical narrative of this relationship. The problem with this story isn't that there's a lack of material. Rather, there's far too much of it to go into every aspect in great detail, with new items of interest emerging at a breakneck pace. As I write this, news that Trump has dismissed Secretary of State Rex Tillerson (via Twitter, of course) is making the rounds, only a day after Tillerson had broken ranks with the administration to blame Russia for the poisoning of an ex–Russian spy in England. So is news that the Trump administration has finally announced Russia sanctions on the Moscow-based Internet Research Agency team for their election interference, the first time Trump, in his role as U.S. president, has ever punished Russia for meddling in the 2016 presidential election. At some point, my editor and I agreed that, barring revelations like these that we felt were groundbreaking, we would need to cease adding new items. To write a "definitive history" that is still writing itself may seem ambitious, but what most people need to know right now is how all this was even able to happen. What this book represents, then, is a primer that accounts for all the essential information anyone curious about this subject would need to know about the Trump-Russia scandal, as well as many of the side-stories that have formed along its periphery.

The Trump-Russia story keeps advancing at such a pace that it's easy to forget all that happened in the first year of the Trump presidency: a former national security advisor pleaded guilty to federal charges of lying to the FBI about his contacts with the Russian ambassador; the president fired his FBI director, James Comey; the very next day, he told the same Russian ambassador in the White House that firing Comey relieved great pressure that the FBI's Russia investigation had placed on him; a campaign aide pleaded guilty to lying about contacts with people connected to the Russian government who told him that Russia had "dirt" on Hillary Clinton and "thousands of emails"; and we learned another campaign aide was the subject of a year-long secret surveillance warrant because the FBI suspected that he was acting as a foreign agent for Russia.

At the time of this writing, while the House has wrapped up its investigation, Mueller's investigation is ongoing, and there are many reasons to believe that we have a long way to go before any final conclusions are reached. The collusion narrative is far from dead. The evidence continues to build. Russian intelligence has an indisputable reputation for their expertise in the black arts of espionage, which has often been used to acquire *kompromat* ("compromising material") for blackmailing. Trump's boorish behavior has made him uniquely vulnerable to blackmail and extortion, as was shown by the $130,000 hush payment made in the weeks before the election to porn star Stormy Daniels to silence her from speaking out about their affair. Members of Trump's campaign and his own son, Don Jr., showed a willingness to collude with offers of "dirt" or hacked emails stolen by Russia, a foreign adversary. There were numerous efforts, including some by Trump's campaign chairman and Trump's son-in-law, to set up private communication channels with politically connected Russians. This behavior deserves condemnation; whether it rises to the level of a crime is another matter.

At the very least, this behavior fits the narrative of collusion perfectly. It's certainly not the actions of the falsely accused. Innocent parties use the facts to show how they don't fit the conclusion. Members of Trump's team, when confronted with the facts, have reflexively lied, even to the FBI, and destroyed evidence, while at the same time attacking anyone who might hold them accountable as haters and Clinton stooges. Still, the questions persist. Why would a presidential nominee trying to appeal to jingoists in the reddest states in America be working equally as hard to stay friendly with the Kremlin? There has been no answer to this question.

Trump has emphatically insisted that he has no business in Russia. "Russia has never tried to use leverage over me," he declared on Twitter. "I HAVE NOTHING TO DO WITH RUSSIA—NO DEALS, NO LOANS, NO NOTHING!"[4] While Trump would have the American public take him at his word, there is much about Trump's businesses and his personal affairs that he does not want us to know. This, after all, is the first president to withhold his tax returns since Watergate.

Trump also refused to put his businesses into a blind trust, handing the Trump Organization over to his sons, who have participated in varying degrees in his administration. People with stories to tell have been paid or ordered to keep quiet. Much like his campaign, the president behaves like a man with something to hide.

The material gathered in this book is based on more than 100 interviews I have conducted since Trump's presidential campaign began. It includes conversations with many state and federal law enforcement agents, some of whom have never spoken on this subject before. In addition, I have reviewed thousands of pages of court documents, business records, congressional hearings, FBI files, and other records obtained under the Freedom of Information Act to tell the story of Trump's murky business dealings to bring Russian money into his pockets. Some of this material I previously posted on my website trump-russia.com. As long as this investigation continues and more material is uncovered, I will continue to document it even after this book goes to press.

＿

ONE CRITICAL FACTOR IN THE Trump-Russia scandal is the role the Russian Mafiya played within it. While various media outlets have touched upon these relationships, I have further detailed them here to give readers a chance to understand just how tightly this shadowy web of intrigue entangles. To provide a taste of what I mean, take the case of how two Russian gun rights enthusiasts worked their way into Trump's inner circle. It begins with Alexander Porfirievich Torshin, the 54-year-old silver-haired deputy of the Central Bank of Russia and former chairman of Russia's upper house of parliament, the Federation Council. Torshin was a suspected boss of the Taganskaya Mafiya organization. A lengthy investigation carried out by José Grinda, the famed Spanish anti-corruption prosecutor and bête noire of the Russian Mafiya, found Torshin used his connections in the political, financial, and criminal worlds to help amass an ill-gotten fortune.[5]

On wiretaps, Grinda's team of Spanish investigators discovered that members of the Taganskaya referred to Torshin as "Godfather." Grinda's investigators also overheard Torshin and a Mafiya-affiliated former oil executive discuss how to coerce a Russian bank director into approving the transfer of millions of dollars into Mallorcan real estate. Not only did Torshin have links to the Russian Mafiya, but he was tied to Russian security services. He served on the country's National Anti-Terrorism Committee, a government council that included the director of the Federal Security Service (FSB), the Russian intelligence service that succeeded the KGB. He was best known in Russia for leading the official inquiry into the 2004 Beslan school siege that left 334 dead, more than half of them children. Torshin's review blamed terrorists for the deaths. An independent review by the European Court of Human Rights contradicted that finding by concluding that Russian authorities overreacted by using tanks and flamethrowers to storm the school.

Torshin exemplified the typical corrupt politician who was more concerned with bettering his financial standing than bettering the lives and safety of his country's citizens. Where he comes into the orbit of Trump is a bizarre connection to the National Rifle Association (NRA), itself representative of a new breed of dupe for Russia: the useful idiots of the American right. Not long after Trump's election to the office of the American presidency, two *Washington Post* journalists published an investigation into the common cause between right-wing American movements and their Russian equivalents, including same-sex marriage opponents, Christian fundamentalists, and gun-rights enthusiasts. Among the individuals highlighted by the article was George Kline Preston, a Nashville-based lawyer who had a long history of conducting business in Russia and who kept in his office both a white porcelain bust of Russian president Vladimir Putin and a portrait by a Russian painter of George Washington.[6]

Preston's interest in Russia led him to Torshin, who had done some pro–gun rights lobbying around Moscow. Wanting to help Torshin's cause, Preston introduced the Mafiya Godfather to David Keene, the NRA's president and former chairman of the American Conservative Union. Delighted by his new Russian friend, Keene published an editorial in his newspaper written by Torshin, who revealed that he was an NRA "Life Member" and extolled the virtues of the late Russian creator of the AK-47.

The following year, Keene traveled to Russia for a conference hosted by The Right to Bear Arms, a new Russian group dedicated to gun rights formed by a woman named Maria Butina, an attractive 25-year-old gun enthusiast with striking red hair. Having the head of the NRA pay a visit to their smaller, nascent, almost insignificant Russian counterpart was like Steve Jobs's famed 1985 visit to the Soviet Union where he hoped to sell Macs. It was "like an answer from one side," Butina said.[7] In 2014, Butina and Torshin brought a politically connected NRA figure named Paul Erickson to speak at an open forum in Moscow. Erickson "had participated in every GOP presidential primary campaign since 1980," former Reagan official Ralph Benko wrote, "and was Pat Buchanan's presidential campaign manager in 1992. He is a sort of 'secret master of the political universe' known almost exclusively to the cognoscenti."[8] Butina became friendly with Erickson, and they went into business together.[9] Butina brought a delegation of NRA members to Moscow, where they met up with Dmitry Rogozin, the deputy prime minister in charge of Russia's defense industry, and a subject of U.S. sanctions, to shoot guns.

In Las Vegas in July 2015, Butina attended the Trump FreedomFest rally where she addressed the mogul candidate herself, and took the opportunity to ask about his foreign policies toward Russia. "Do you want to continue the politics of sanctions that are damaging both economies?" Butina asked. Trump replied: "I know Putin, and I'll tell you what, we'll get along with Putin . . . I believe I would get along very nicely with Putin, OK? I mean, where we have the strength. I don't think you'd need the sanctions. I think that we would get along very, very well."[10]

Torshin, meanwhile, used his years of accumulated contacts to make a push into the Trump campaign in 2016. A top campaign aide received an email informing him that Torshin had proposed a meeting between Vladimir Putin and Trump. The subject line of the email, turned over to Senate investigators, read, "Russian backdoor overture and dinner invite." The proposal reached senior levels of the Trump campaign before Jared Kushner, the president's son-in-law, rejected it. "Pass on this," Kushner said, according to his attorney's letter to the Senate Judiciary Committee. "Most likely these people then go back home and claim they have special access to gain importance for themselves. Be careful."[11]

That should have shut the door on Torshin, Butina, and Erickson's efforts to cozy up to Trump. Instead Erickson wrote a different email to Rick Dearborn, a Trump campaign veteran and future White House Deputy Chief of Staff for Policy. In the email, titled "Subject: Kremlin Connection," Erickson wrote that Russia was "quietly but actively seeking a dialogue with the U.S.," and would use the NRA's annual convention in Louisville, Kentucky, to make "first contact." The email did not name Torshin, but described him as "President Putin's emissary on this front." "Putin is deadly serious about building a good relationship with Mr. Trump," Erickson continued. "He wants to extend an invitation to Mr. Trump to visit him in the Kremlin before the election. Let's talk through what has transpired and Senator Jeff Sessions's advice on how to proceed." (Sessions has said he does not recall the outreach.)[12]

Torshin shared a dinner table with the president's son Don Jr. at the NRA convention in Louisville, Kentucky, in May 2016. Don Jr. is an avid hunter and the two are said to have chatted about guns. Several Trump campaign consultants attended Butina's costume-party birthday celebration in Washington, DC, and she was on hand at the invitation-only Freedom Ball to celebrate Donald Trump's swearing-in as president of the United States. Torshin and Butina were finally to get their chance to meet the newly sworn-in president in February 2017 at the National Prayer Breakfast. At the last minute, however, their hopes were dashed when an alert White House national security aide noticed Torshin's name and flagged him for his suspected ties to organized crime.

Torshin and Butina likely wouldn't even have gotten to that kind of proximity to Trump if it weren't for their connections to the NRA, which spent $30 million to support Trump in the 2016 elections, three times as much as the gun-rights group gave to Republican Mitt Romney four years earlier. In January 2018, *McClatchyDC* reported that the origin of the NRA's suddenly swollen bank account was an item of interest in Special Counsel Mueller's investigations into the Russian scandal.[13] The FBI is reportedly investigating whether money for the NRA's donations to the Trump campaign came from Torshin himself, which, if true, would make the NRA guilty of the criminal act of taking foreign money for election campaign funds. Guilty, that is, of collusion.

—

TRUMP ISN'T THE ONLY PRESIDENT to have ties to organized crime or to have Mafiosi attempt an acquaintanceship. Recently unearthed documents revealed that President Nixon's close friend Charles "Bebe" Rebozo was described by the FBI as a "non-member associate of organized crime figures" and reportedly ran a Mob-linked bank. John F. Kennedy shared a mistress with Sam Giancana, the boss of the Chicago syndicate. The woman, Judith Campbell Exner, said she arranged meetings between the two men both before and after Kennedy's election to the White House, and carried envelopes of their correspondences back and forth. But the critical difference between presidents past and the current one is that Trump may be the only president to have been helped by criminals with ties to prominent officials within a foreign power.

Just as the CIA conspired with the American Mafia to try to kill Fidel Castro, the Russian state has used its gangsters when it suited them. In Soviet days, criminals were kept in the shadows, but the chaos that followed the collapse of the USSR saw Russia's gangsters emerge into the daylight and take their place in the new ruling class of the country. This new power structure, a loose and shifting network of alliances among bureaucrats, spies, oligarchs, and criminals, may be difficult for Americans to understand, but in Russia the lines blur between business, politics, and crime far more than they do in the West.

José Grinda, the Spanish anti-corruption prosecutor who uncovered Alexander Torshin's status as a Godfather, said in a closed-door briefing that he considered Russia to be a virtual "Mafia state." In Russia, he said, one cannot tell the difference between the activities of the government and those of its organized-crime groups. Grinda believed that organized crime in Russia is controlled by the country's security services. Unlike terrorists who want to eliminate the state, Russian organized crime seeks to complement it.[14]

The Russian Mafiya and the role it plays in the country's affairs are critical to understanding both the allegations of collusion levied against the Trump campaign and Russia's meddling in the U.S. election. Russia's political culture is very much one of opportunism. Just as his Soviet predecessors did, Vladimir Putin saw the Russian Mafiya as an asset that could be used to his advantage in his country's adventures abroad. At the same time, the Russian Mafiya was also on the lookout for opportunities to impress the inner circles of power surrounding Vladimir Putin. "If you can get a line into the Trump campaign and the slightest crack in the sanctions regime, then you will curry favor with the political leadership," Mark Galeotti, a senior researcher at the Institute of International Relations in Prague and one of the foremost experts on the Russian Mafiya, told me.

It is the Russian Mafiya's connections to both the Kremlin and now the White House that are at the heart of the Trump-Russia collusion scandal. This is not a book of conspiracy theories—clear evidence of attempted collusion, such as the June 2016 meeting at Trump Tower with the president's son and a "Russian government lawyer" who had "dirt" on Hillary Clinton, actually happened. That meeting was only able to occur through the many connections the Trumps had to Russia, connections that are suspected to have led to Donald Trump's ascendancy to the American presidency. And it all began at the same place that launched Trump's career into the stratosphere: Trump Tower.

PART I

EARLY AFFILIATIONS

1.

THE WORLD'S MOST TALKED ABOUT ADDRESS

THE *NEW YORK TIMES* HEADLINE GAVE away nothing of what was to come: "Bonwit Teller Building to Be Sold."[1] The real estate article, published on January 26, 1979, a Friday, was big enough Manhattan news to be included on the front page. The luxury department chain had been a fixture in the city since the turn of the century. For nearly 50 years, it had been headquartered in a Midtown building celebrated for its art deco design, including a 15-foot limestone relief depicting dancing nymphs. But despite varying degrees of success, including launching the career of designer Christian Dior, financial woes had caused the store to change owners. When it could no longer afford its mortgage, Bonwit Teller was forced to sell its celebrated flagship store to avoid bankruptcy. But while the deal, which included "the building, the leases on the land underneath, and the rights to use the name Bonwit Teller in New York City," set the sun on an era for the seller, it dawned one anew for its buyer, a 32-year-old up-and-coming real estate developer named Donald J. Trump.

It was not his first appearance in the *Times* (a profile of Trump had been published by the paper in 1973),[2] but it did foreshadow much about the dealings of a businessman who would only grow in notoriety: "Mr. Trump was reported by sources close to the deal to be considering replacing the present building with mixed-use structure similar to the Olympic Tower at 51st Street and Fifth Avenue, though probably larger, containing luxury condominiums, offices and boutiques." As the *Times* noted, it was the latest in a spate of purchases by Trump, or as they termed it, "a series of dramatic maneuvers" that included, within a year, the purchase and remodeling of the city's historic Commodore Hotel into the Grand Hyatt, and a senior role in helping the city select a site for a new convention center on the western terminus of Thirty-Fourth Street. The article noted how Trump was "considering" keeping the Bonwit Teller building.

Instead, the building was demolished. In a snub to the Metropolitan Museum of Art, to whom Trump had promised to donate the fresco of the dancing nymphs, he had them jackhammered instead. Despite the outcry, a spokesman identified as a vice president of the Trump Organization named John Baron claimed that the reliefs had been declared to be "without artistic merit," after having thrice been appraised. Baron was later discovered to be a pseudonym that Trump used to pen the rebuttal himself.

Shortly after it opened to the public in 1983, I went with my mother to visit Trump Tower on the corner of Fifty-Seventh Street and Fifth Avenue, about as close to the heart of Manhattan as you could get. At that time, I was 13 years old and knew little about the tower's namesake, save that he was a born-and-raised New Yorker like myself. Trump, who tore down the architecturally celebrated 12-story Bonwit Teller building to construct his staggering 58-story skyscraper, was far from an urban conservationist. But for a lifelong New Yorker like my mother, who could remember when other classic New York buildings, such as Penn Station, had been demolished for more contentious and hideous construction, this zigzagging dark glass edifice was something new, exciting even.

We arrived on a winter day, stepping through the entrance doors pulled open for us by livery-clad doormen. They looked like the Queen's Guard at Buckingham Palace, minus the bearskin hats. We gawked at the six-story atrium, an enormous public space replete with its own artificial waterfall and lined with orange Italian marble that gave off a warm, inviting glow. We rode up and down the escalators and peered in the windows of shops offering Cartier watches and Buccellati jewelry. Like the baubles on display, the building was a place that anyone could visit but few could afford, which seemed to be the point. Trump spent $2 million promoting Trump Tower as the Manhattan pied-à-terre for the global superrich, pulling off a master class in media manipulation, sending out lavish brochures that proclaimed Trump Tower "the world's most talked about address" and placing ads listing its premier tenants as the "World's Great Merchants." He also told *New York* magazine, in confidence, that Trump Tower had drawn the interest of the British monarchy. Prince Charles and his new bride, Princess Diana, were said to be mulling the purchase of a $5 million, 21-room apartment in Trump Tower. "They're negotiating, and they want to put money in Trump Tower down," *New York* quoted a "source" as saying. "I was told it would be for their use when they visit this country."[3] As Trump revealed in his half-personal, half-business, co-written memoir *The Art of the Deal*, the whole tale was made up. Rather than attracting the likes of Prince Charles, however, Trump Tower attracted buyers of a different sort: those who preferred to keep the source of their incomes hidden.

—

WHILE TRUMP WAS BREAKING GROUND in Manhattan, bread was being broken across the East River, in Brooklyn. On a Saturday morning in the fall of 1980, a 24-year-old, up-and-coming member of the Colombo crime family named Michael Franzese entered a Brooklyn gas station for a meeting prearranged by one of his henchmen. Franzese—the intel-

ligent and business-savvy son of underboss John "Sonny" Franzese—
had recently entered the murky wholesale gasoline trade. He joined up
with Lawrence Iorizzo, a 400-pound Long Island merchant who was
masterminding a scam to cheat the government out of tax revenue from
the sale of gasoline.

Franzese's newfound business interests could not have been better
timed.[4] A trio of Russian business partners who were operating their
own gas-tax scheme at several stations, and who needed help collecting debts and restoring their recently revoked wholesaler license, had
approached his enforcer, who informed Franzese. Sensing an opportunity, Franzese agreed to meet them, though he had to stifle a laugh when
the three Russian business partners walked in. One of them looked, as
he put it later, "like a rug salesman who had just hit the lottery."[5]

But as they talked, Franzese could tell that he was dealing with
some cunning operators, including a scrawny, Woody Allen lookalike
named David Bogatin. Franzese listened as the Russians described their
operation, known as a daisy chain scam. Loopholes allowed corrupt distributors to defraud the government out of gas-tax revenue by moving
money from one dummy petroleum handling company to the next right
before declaring bankruptcy, creating a nightmare of a paper trail. It
was similar to the operation Franzese and Iorizzo were running, but
the Russians had figured it all out within a few years of arriving in a
new country. While 27 cents was supposed to be paid to the government
as excise tax fees, most of that money instead went into the pockets of
Bogatin and his associates. And because they were able to sell gas at such
a high volume, they could make a ton of money. Several former prosecutors and investigators told me that, conservatively, the scam generated a
million dollars a week.

But it was not an easy racket to maintain. The Russians were having
trouble getting people to pay debts. Shakedown artists were trying to
get a cut of their operation and Bogatin was struggling to get his wholesaler license restored. As Franzese later told the U.S. Senate, Bogatin and
his partners were eager to align themselves with someone who could

make their problems go away. "Because of my association with organized crime, they believed me to be that person," Franzese testified. "As it turned out, I was."

Franzese proposed a deal. The Colombo family would provide Bogatin and his associates with protection from rival mob-run distributors and shakedown artists while lending them the muscle needed to collect on their debts. In addition, Franzese knew a guy in the State House in Albany who could get them their wholesaler gasoline license. Since the Colombo family would be taking most of the risk, Franzese wanted 75 percent of the illegal proceeds. Bogatin and his partners accepted the terms, cementing one of the most profitable partnerships between Russian organized criminals and one of New York's original five Mafia families. Franzese made a fortune from the deal and became something of a tabloid celebrity. His sharp wardrobe and good looks earned him the nickname "the Yuppie Don."[6]

A meeting between members of Russian and Italian organized crime was an indication of the times. During the 1970s, Brighton Beach—a neighborhood on the outer fringes of New York City, not far from Coney Island—became home to tens of thousands of Russian Jewish families after the Soviet Union allowed their emigration. The plight of Jews trapped in the Soviet Union, with its echoes of the Biblical tale of Jews in Egypt, had awakened the American Jewish establishment. The result was the Jackson-Vanik Amendment, which linked trade with Russia to freedom of emigration for Soviet Jews.

The streets of Brighton Beach soon became lined with Russian meat markets and restaurants, as well as nightclubs that catered to the neighborhood's newest and sizable demographic. By the mid-1980s, an estimated 80,000 people from the Soviet Union had moved in, earning the neighborhood the nickname "Little Odessa." (An earlier generation of Soviet Jews escaping the Holocaust had settled in Ocean Hill, Brooklyn, including Rae Kushner, grandmother to Jared Kushner.) The Trump name was well known to many Russians in Brighton Beach. Trump's father, Fred, had built Trump Village, a seven-building complex in west

Brighton Beach. (While other buildings in New York were removing the Trump name after their namesake was elected president, Trump Village residents were proud to be associated with him.)

The great majority of these new arrivals were hard-working, law-abiding citizens grateful for the opportunity to put their talents to work in the capitalist system. However, there was speculation in the U.S. intelligence community that the Kremlin began emptying its prisons in 1975 in order to rid the country of criminals, including many who still had ties to the black market back home. The FBI estimated that out of the 200,000 Soviet immigrants who arrived in the 1970s and 1980s, roughly 2,000 had served time in Soviet prisons.[7] It was an idea that caught on—around the time Franzese was meeting with Bogatin and his men, Fidel Castro was sneaking similar state-punished malefactors onto the Mariel Harbor boatlift.

"They sent over all their shit," said William Moschella, an FBI investigator who tracked the Russian Mafiya in the 1980s. "The Russians started emptying their prisons in 1975. The Cubans with the Mariel boatlift wasn't for another few years." Moschella then reiterated something the U.S. intelligence community would also claim, "I think before the Soviet Union hosted the 1980 Olympics, they wanted them gone."[8]

Among those with a Soviet criminal record was Bogatin. Born into a Jewish family at the end of World War II in Saratov, a Soviet city on the Volga River, Bogatin later told an American reporter that his grandfather was a Talmudic scholar who had been imprisoned in the 1930s for his religion and was later murdered by fellow inmates. Bogatin's father, who continued to practice his religion in private, spent 18 years in prison in Siberia. Bogatin himself had spoken to the reporter from a jail in Poland. But while incarceration ran in the family, Bogatin portrayed himself, like all Russian gangsters did, as a humble, hardworking businessman. He had served in the Soviet army for three years and spent 1966 as a military advisor for the North Vietnamese army before returning to Saratov, where he took on a job as a printer. In the mid-1970s, Bogatin, by then married with children, said he lost his job when he agreed to print clandestine material for Jewish dissidents. He told Franzese he had spent time in a Soviet prison before arriving in the United States in 1977 with only three dollars in his pocket.[9]

Criminals like Bogatin brought sophistication to the Russian immigrant underworld. The first stirrings of a Russian organized-crime element in 1970s New York were, by comparison, almost childlike in their simplicity. A group of Ukrainians from the Odessa region became known as the "Potato Bag Gang" after they set up a scamming operation in New York's harbors. Posing as merchant seamen whose ships had just arrived in port, gang members would approach Soviet immigrants and show them what appeared to be antique gold rubles. Those who fell for it were sold what turned out to be a sack of potatoes.

Over the next few years, Franzese got to know Bogatin and his partners quite well. They were much more loosely organized than the Colombo family, clannish even, and would not hesitate to use violence against one of their own. Because Bogatin had done time in the hellish Soviet prison system, he was unintimidated by U.S. law enforcement. Soviet prison cells were dark, cold, spare of food and water, but abundant in abuse and torture; no American prison could measure up alongside any gulag. At the same time, Bogatin and his associates also seemed a bit in awe of the American Mafia and enjoyed the status their partnership brought them. The Russians admired money and deferred to the person they knew could bring them lots of it. "I found them to be intelligent, possessing remarkable business instincts that they would not hesitate to use for illegal gain," Franzese said. For instance, when investigators came looking for the gas-tax money owed by Shoppers Marketing Inc., the gasoline wholesaler Bogatin and his associates fronted under, they were only able to locate a single owner: a drunken Polish immigrant who worked as a gas station attendant and spoke little English. He subsequently disappeared.

Every week, the Russians would deliver Franzese his share of the proceeds in paper bags that reeked of gasoline. Together the Russians and Lawrence Iorizzo skimmed a fortune that Iorizzo estimated at around a billion dollars.[10] "To give you an idea how lucrative the gas tax business was," Franzese told the Senate committee in a 1996 hearing on

Russian organized crime, "it was not unusual for me to receive $9 million in cash per week from the Russians and Iorizzo." With success, however, came new problems. Bogatin needed a place to launder all his newfound wealth. He eventually hit upon the idea of investing in expensive Manhattan real estate. And the property that attracted him most was the newly built Trump Tower.

ONE-THIRD OF THE TRUMP TOWER units sold were held in the names of foreign corporations, many of them registered in tax havens such as Panama and the Netherlands Antilles.[11] Trump rolled out the welcome mat for such buyers. In fact, Trump Tower was one of only two buildings in New York City that allowed anonymous buyers (the other being the neighboring Olympic Tower).[12] Jim E. Moody, a former deputy assistant director of the FBI, told me: "Trump Tower allowed people who wanted to hide their money to buy there because their names were never really published." As a result, a rogue's gallery of embezzlers and money launderers had no problem buying up units. One of Trump's earliest buyers was Gino A. G. Bianchini, who was wanted in Italy on criminal charges of illegal export of currency and was pursued by several Italian banks for millions of dollars in outstanding loans. Another was Roberto Polo, a Cuban-born financier who had purchased six Trump Tower apartments under the names of offshore corporations, and was later the subject of a five-week international manhunt after being convicted, in multiple countries, of swindling investors out of $130 million.[13] The Haitian dictator Jean-Claude "Baby Doc" Duvalier owned a $1.625 million condo in Trump Tower purchased under a Panamanian shell company.[14] This was to be the foundation of Trump's business model for the rest of his career: as long as your money gave him a fig leaf of plausible deniability, he would take it with no questions asked.

These allowances are likely what drew the newly wealthy Bogatin to one of Manhattan's most audacious pieces of real estate. Michael Markowitz, Bogatin's Romanian-born partner in the gas-tax scam, explained to the FBI that "Bogatin was having problems with his wife and wanted to have an apartment should they separate." Bogatin left behind a wife in Russia. In America, he married a tall, blond dominatrix, an ex-model from the Soviet Union who kept embarrassing him in front of his gangster friends. Markowitz then added a surprising detail: Bogatin had made the acquaintance of Donald Trump, who "talked him into purchasing five apartments in Trump Towers as an investment."[15]

Bogatin purchased three condos in Trump Tower—45B, 52K, and 53B—on October 10, 1984, and acquired two more units—47A and 45A—shortly before Halloween. At one point, Franzese was considering buying condos in Trump Tower himself, and although he eventually passed, the two agreed it was a good investment. Bogatin's five condos cost him more than $5.8 million, the equivalent today of $14.1 million. "What do you need five for?" asked Roger Berger, a former criminal investigator with the New York State Department of Taxation and Finance who worked on the gas-tax scam case and investigated the Russian Mafiya. "The only reason is: You're selling the apartments or renting them. The other reason is that you're doing a favor for the owner. I'm 90 percent sure they were doing Trump a favor." The FBI, however, never questioned Trump. "In retrospect we should have been looking in that direction," said Ronald Noel, a former FBI agent who worked the case.

How Trump might have met the Russian mobsters isn't clear, but former FBI agent William Moschella said it wouldn't have been hard. "There were several Russian organized crime guys friendly with political guys, there were links to the Jewish community, and it's easy to see them being introduced to Donald Trump," Moschella told me. "I think there were even connections to the mayor's office. New York City is a small community when you are talking about money guys. They go to the same clubs, same restaurants, golf courses, and everyone wants to be the guy that introduced the guy that makes them money. Everyone eats from the crumbs of the rich guy's table." One of those clubs that attracted both Trump and the "money guys" in the 1970s was a New York social hangout called Le Club. It was there, Trump wrote in *The Art of the Deal*, where he met "the sort of wealthy people, particularly Europeans and South Americans, who eventually bought the most expensive apartments in Trump Tower and Trump Plaza."

Helping Bogatin wash his dirty money clean was Marvin E. Kramer, a New York attorney who assisted gasoline scam artists in evading millions of dollars in taxes. Lining the shelves of his Coney Island office were black binders filled with paperwork for dummy corporations. Crooks like Bogatin could walk in and purchase shell companies, literally off the shelf.[16] Of the five apartments Bogatin purchased in Trump Tower, only one, 53B, was acquired in his own name. The rest were purchased with four New York shell companies, which had been formed on the same day using Kramer's name. Kramer was never prosecuted for his role in the gas-tax scam business.[17]

It was painfully obvious to prosecutors that Bogatin had purchased the condos to launder money and hide assets. "We didn't think he was living in five apartments," Ronda Lustman, a former assistant New York attorney general, told me. Kenneth McCallion, a former prosecutor who worked out of the Brooklyn office of the Justice Department's Organized Crime Strike Force in the 1980s, told me that Bogatin was running prostitutes out of his Trump Tower apartments.

Trump, however, didn't appear to have a problem with this 39-year-old Russian immigrant, who despite having no apparent means of support was spending nearly $6 million to buy five Trump Tower apartments under five different entities. In fact, far from bothering him, Trump is said to have personally attended the closing of the deal, where he met with Bogatin and his lawyer.[18]

In 1985, things began to unravel for Bogatin and Franzese. Not long after Bogatin became the owner of five Trump Tower condos, Franzese was indicted on 14 counts of racketeering, counterfeiting, and extortion and, after pleading guilty to two counts, sentenced to 10 years and ordered to pay $14 million in restitution. Franzese's arrest and imprisonment effectively ended the relationship between Bogatin and the Colombo family. Bogatin was indicted in Albany and pleaded guilty to evading millions of dollars in state fuel taxes in what state officials called one of the largest gasoline-bootlegging operations in the nation.

He posted a $500,000 bond and hired David Clayton, a Mob lawyer who helped him strike a deal with New York attorney general Robert Abrams. In hopes of remaining a free man, Bogatin agreed to a plea, the terms of which he would later challenge as a misunderstanding. Among the terms were a $3 million payment to New York state and county prosecutors, as well as $1.75 million to the federal government. To guarantee payment on the tax bills, Bogatin pledged his five Trump Tower condos as collateral. He flew into Albany on a private jet to make it official.

Not only was Trump making inroads with Russians in New York, he was also making contacts in the Soviet Union. In 1986, at a luncheon hosted by Leonard Lauder, son of the cosmetic mogul Estée Lauder, Trump was seated next to the then Soviet ambassador to the United States, Yuri Dubinin. The story Trump told in *The Art of the Deal* was that Dubinin's daughter had been impressed by Trump Tower and the ambassador struck up a conversation. Dubinin's daughter, Natalia, told a slightly different story that seems more in line with her father's reputation as a shrewd, savvy Soviet operative. She said that her father had won Trump over by telling him his building was the first he saw in New York. "Trump melted immediately," she told *Moskovskij Komsomolets* in 2016. "He is an emotional man, sometimes impulsive. He needs acceptance and, of course, he is happy receiving it. For him, my father's visit was like honey for the bee."

The conversation led to an official invitation. On July 4, 1987, Trump and his Russian-speaking wife, Ivana, flew on an all-expenses-paid visit to Moscow where he was wined and dined, all in the interest of having him erect another of his towers in the Russian capital. Trump's trip had an official blessing, for he met high-ranking officials of the *nomenklatura*, the most powerful posts of the Soviet Union's ruling Communist Party.

It was, however, a strange move for the Russians to bring a millionaire into Moscow, especially one who attracted publicity like Trump. Trump wasn't by a long shot the only wealthy American the Soviets flattered, pampered, and graced with official VIP treatment. But these sorts of visits were not publicly showcased in a country that was still run by the Communist Party. The very idea of a millionaire was anathema to Soviet propaganda, which still depicted capitalists as cartoonish fat cats in top hats. Why publicize a deal that, if successful, would earn a millionaire like Trump even more money?

Intourist, the Soviet travel agency infiltrated by the KGB, arranged the trip, and there is little doubt that Trump's every move in Russia was photographed and documented. Standard operating procedure when "welcoming" a foreign visitor, from diplomats to journalists to tourists to businessmen and students, was to monitor them closely and collect information on them to use later as leverage should the need arise. We have no idea whether Trump was approached by Russian intelligence, but he certainly would have made a juicy target for recruitment. "Egocentric people who lack moral principles—who are either too greedy or who suffer from exaggerated self-importance. These are the people the KGB wants and finds easiest to recruit," said Yuri Bezmenov, a former KGB officer who defected to Canada.[19]

Donald and Ivana stayed in Lenin's suite at the National Hotel, and Trump said he was impressed with the ambition of the Soviet officials seeking to make a deal. Trump was shown more than half a dozen potential building sites; none were across the street from the Kremlin, as he had hoped one would be. Of course, Trump might have been able to learn all this without ever leaving Trump Tower. There were trade organizations like the US-USSR Trade and Economic Council in New York that were set up to facilitate exactly this sort of negotiating and initial deal prospecting. Trump traveled to Russia for a deal that never materialized, but was that the real purpose of the trip?

A few months later, on September 2, 1987, Trump spent more than $94,000 to run a full-page ad in three major newspapers, arguing that America should stop paying to defend countries that can afford to defend themselves. The letter, addressed to the American people, began with the declaration: "For decades, Japan and other nations have been taking advantage of the United States." Trump argued that Japan had grown wealthy on the backs of American taxpayers who subsidized the island nation's defense.[20]

The message, which Trump would echo for the next 30 years, certainly would have been welcome in the Kremlin in the 1980s. Despite glasnost and perestroika, premier Mikhail Gorbachev's efforts to open the country, the Cold War was, if anything, heating up at the time. President Reagan increased defense spending to combat what he called the Soviet "evil empire." The USSR boosted its subversive efforts to undermine the "main enemy," and Trump's message meshed perfectly with a campaign the KGB was running in Japan.

Stanislav Levchenko, a former KGB major stationed in Tokyo who defected to the United States, said one of the key goals of Russian intelligence was to weaken Japan's military alliance with the United States. Testifying in 1982 before the House Intelligence Committee, Levchenko listed the major objectives of what he called the Soviet "active measures" campaign in Japan: "First, to prevent further deepening of political and military cooperation between Japan and the United States. Second, to provoke distrust between Japan and the United States in political, economic, and military circles."[21]

The New York Times published a story that ran the same day as Trump's full-page ad. The story began with the opening paragraph, "Donald J. Trump, one of New York's biggest and certainly one of its most vocal developers, said yesterday that he was not interested in running for political office in New York, but indicated that the Presidency was another matter." An advisor said the 41-year-old real estate developer was planning a trip to New Hampshire, the site of the first presidential primary. The article also noted that Trump had recently traveled to Moscow "where he met with the Soviet leader, Mikhail S. Gorbachev." (This wasn't true, as a correction the following day made clear, although he did meet Gorbachev in Washington later that year.) "The ostensible subject of their meeting was the possible development of luxury hotels in the Soviet Union by Mr. Trump," the *Times* wrote. "But Mr. Trump's calls for nuclear disarmament were also well-known to the Russians."[22] Trump was indeed deeply concerned about a nuclear holocaust, but once again, nuclear disarmament was a major target of Soviet active measures.

When Gorbachev visited New York in 1998 for a meeting at the United Nations, a visit to Trump Tower appeared on the former Soviet premier's itinerary. He and his wife were to share a private meal with Donald and Ivana. On the eve of the trip the idea was nixed, and Trump was fooled into shaking hands on the street in front of Trump Tower with a Gorbachev impersonator.

—

BOGATIN'S PARTNER, MICHAEL MARKOWITZ, ALSO flew into Albany on a private plane and pleaded guilty to tax-evasion charges. Federal officials were also looking at adding racketeering charges, which would have added 12 years to his sentence, so Markowitz began cooperating. He met with the FBI more than 20 times, but he strung agents along. "Wise guys always thought that Markowitz provided a lot of useful information, that he was a real help. He wasn't," James Rodio, a former assistant U.S. attorney who prosecuted the case, told me. "Everything he gave us was useless." By working the system, Markowitz got off easy. He was sentenced to six months' home detention and ordered to pay $5 million in restitution. Rodio said he recalled that Markowitz served out his home detention in Trump Tower, where he may have had two apartments of his own.

Word got back to "Frankie the Bug" Sciortino that Markowitz had pleaded guilty to state tax evasion charges and was cooperating with the federal government. The penalty La Cosa Nostra imposed on informants was death, and the job of assassinating Markowitz fell to Frankie the Bug. "Sciortino told his associate that Markowitz was a rat and talking to the Feds," Ronald Noel, the former FBI agent, told me, "and had to be taken out."

Sciortino was a "capo" or captain in the Colombo crime family, the same New York Mafia family to which Franzese belonged. He was a short, middle-aged fireplug of a man with a violent temper, a larger-than-life version of the character played by Joe Pesci in the movie *Goodfellas*. He earned his nickname because he was as crazy as a bedbug,

Noel said. Sciortino's associate, whom Noel called "Big John," became a cooperating witness for the government, entered the witness protection program, and told the FBI about the comedy of errors that unfolded next outside Trump Tower. Trump's dealings with Bogatin and Marko-witz brought two would-be assassins to the doorstep of his celebrated creation and it was only sheer ineptitude that spared his celebrated tower from being the scene of a gangland slaying.

Frankie the Bug and Big John staked out Markowitz at his Trump Tower apartment. Trump Tower does not have a parking garage, and Markowitz garaged his car, a large silver-and-maroon Rolls-Royce, nearby. The two Mafiosi found a suitable place where they could catch Markowitz as he walked to his garage one morning. Sciortino and Big John arrived at the scene at 7 AM, but found Markowitz had already left. The two Mafiosi decided to try again. They returned to the scene within the next few days around 5 AM.

This time, Markowitz's car was still parked in the garage. The trap was set. Markowitz would get his due. Sciortino and Big John had brought along handguns, but what the two would-be hit men lacked was patience. Frankie the Bug woke up in the car and realized, to his horror, that he and Big John had both fallen asleep. The Rolls was gone. Markowitz had come and left. Furious, Sciortino took his rage out on Big John for failing to wake him up. He slapped him, cursed him, and blamed him for the screwup.

"On the next and last attempt to kill Markowitz," Noel told me, "Sciortino and his crime partner got there at around 4 AM and decided to take turns at watch while the other slept. While Sciortino slept, Big John saw blinking lights at a nearby bagel store and could not resist the temptation, so he left to get some. Upon his return, Sciortino awoke and asked if Markowitz had left. Big John said he did not see him. After a search of the garage they found that the car was gone and Sciortino blew up, slapping and cursing his inept associate."

Markowitz's luck ran out in May 1989. While driving his Rolls-Royce home from a poker game in south Brooklyn, Markowitz was shot three times in the chest with a rapid-fire shotgun. He lived long enough to crash into two parked cars, stagger out, and collapse.[23] "MOB CANARY SLAIN: Had testified in bootleg gas probes," read the headline in the next day's *Daily News*. (Franzese said he was reasonably certain that the Colombo family authorized the hit, but it may have been the Russians who pulled the trigger.) An attempt was also made on the life of another of Bogatin's partners, Lev Persits, who was permanently disabled by the attack and confined to a wheelchair.

Bogatin may have sensed that things were heating up in New York. He began making a series of business trips to Austria, where he and Franzese had squirreled away nearly $100 million in gas-tax proceeds in the Vienna-based Creditanstalt-Bankverein. (Austrian banks have long been important to the Russian Mafiya because they accepted anonymous accounts.) Bogatin later stated that his trips helped him be closer in proximity to family that he wanted to help leave the Soviet Union, including his brother Jacob. On his fourth such trip, only two months after being indicted for the gas-tax scam, Austrian authorities arrested him on currency and counterfeiting charges. Bogatin was also wanted on fraud charges in Britain. Until he was cleared of charges months later, he was made to hold tight in a Vienna hotel. The U.S. Justice Department's Organized Crime Strike Force met with Bogatin to discuss bringing him back to the States, possibly in exchange for becoming an FBI informant, but he refused.[24] He may have known that he had bigger things to fear back home.

When Bogatin left Austria, he did not return to the United States, but struck out for Poland. There he managed to keep his criminal past under wraps until the Warsaw-based newspaper *Gazeta Wyborcza* exposed it in early 1992. By then, Bogatin had become a notable entrepreneur, launching one of the country's first chains of commercial banks. He had even teamed up with fugitive commodities trader Marc Rich on a plan to rebuild the Polish port city of Gdansk.[25] And even though hundreds of depositors immediately closed out their accounts, many others kept theirs open after Bogatin offered to start a lottery system for apartments and cars for anyone who stuck by him. Along with some of his clientele, Bogatin's bodyguards turned out to be equally loyal. When Polish authorities took him into custody after a brief standoff, Bogatin's body-guards refused to leave his side, following him in a caravan as he was escorted to prison.[26] To the surprise of prosecutors, he was extradited back to New York and sentenced to eight years in Attica state prison.

The New York Attorney General's office considered seizing Bogatin's five Trump Tower condos, but in the end decided it wasn't worth the effort. The properties were so over-leveraged as to be virtually worthless. One of the banks that held a $1.5 million mortgage on the apartments was the Bank of Credit and Commerce International, dubbed "the Bank of Crooks and Criminals" by other bankers when its dealings with arms merchants, drug dealers, and money launderers came to light after the bank collapsed in 1991. Another of Bogatin's apartments had three mortgages on it, including one split into two $600,000 loans made not by a financial institution, but by individuals. After fleeing to Austria, Bogatin assigned the mortgages in his Trump Tower apartments to an associate in the Genovese crime family, whereupon they were liquidated and the funds moved through a Mafia-controlled bank in Chelsea.[27]

It didn't help that prosecutors weren't really sure if Bogatin's condos actually belonged to him. "It was never really clear whether they were his or whether they represented money from someone else," Ronda Lustman, the former New York state prosecutor, told me, nodding to the idea that Bogatin could have been the puppet of a bigger force. It sent up a flag that nobody recognized. "People didn't know a lot about the Russian Mob back then," Lustman said. "These guys were sort of the first Russians we encountered." In hindsight, all the elements that would appear again and again in the years to come were present in this early case: Russian mobsters with piles of cash, money laundering in expensive Trump properties, connections to powerful Mafiya groups, even Austrian banks. The only thing that would change going forward is that subsequent real estate transactions would be conducted at arm's length. Looking back, Lustman realized that investigators had missed what turned out to be the first signs of the growing power and sophisti-cation of Russian organized crime in America.

—

THE PURCHASE OF FIVE CONDOS by a Russian organized criminal and Trump's supposed appearance at the closing came up again just as Trump was seeking a renewal of his license for the Taj Mahal casino in New Jersey. First alleged in a book published in 1992 by the late reporter Wayne Barrett, the item was noteworthy because it wasn't required of Trump to witness his new tenants signing their deeds.[28] This is likely why Barrett's reporting caught the eye of the Division of Gaming Enforcement (DGE), the agency that carefully monitored New Jersey casinos for any hint of an organized-crime connection. At the time, New Jersey gambling regulators were considering Trump's application to renew his casino license for his troubled casino, the Taj Mahal, and any association with the Mafia would be grounds for revoking the license. An investigative memo recommended that Trump be questioned under oath about his relationships with the Russian Mafiya, including his presence at the Bogatin closing. At my request, Steven Perkins, a former investigator with the DGE, consulted his notes from a 1992 sworn interview with Trump (the transcript of which has never been made public), and I was surprised to learn that the DGE never questioned the real estate mogul about Bogatin.[29] While the reasons why remain unclear, it may be that by the time of the interview, Trump had aroused so much suspicion over his ties with the Mob that Bogatin seemed like a mere footnote to pursue. Bogatin's name did not appear in the final report, and New Jersey casino regulators concluded that Trump's character was not negatively affected by the allegations in Barrett's book.

Someone else who dismissed any serious connections between Trump and Russian organized criminals like Bogatin was Michael Franzese. After he became a born-again Christian, Franzese left the Mafia and went on to launch a ministry, become a motivational speaker, and write several books about his experience, even securing movie rights to his memoirs. The investigation of Trump's ties to Russia struck him as a persecution by Democrats and Clintonites. Although Franzese said he is no Trump apologist, the whole affair seemed to him little more than a waste of government resources. Franzese told me he happened to know Rick Gates, the right-hand man of Paul Manafort, Trump's former campaign chairman. Gates pleaded guilty in February 2018 to financial fraud and lying to investigators in Special Counsel Robert Mueller's Russia investigation. "I know he had no connection at all to Trump/ Russia," Franzese wrote in an email. "Why Mueller indicted him is obvious to anyone who has had an ounce of experience with the Feds when they WANT to get you. And unfortunately, I have had a ton of experience in that regard. So, although I knew David [Bogatin] quite well, I would not be helpful to you in trying to establish the Russian connection with Trump because there was/is no *there* there."

Perhaps. It certainly would be easier to dismiss David Bogatin were he the only Russian criminal in Trump Tower. In fact, he was only the first in what would be a succession of Russian mobsters and Mob-linked figures who would find a home in Trump's properties in the years to come. One of the next to arrive would be one of Russia's most feared Mafiya bosses.

2.

MAFIYA TAJ MAHAL

ON A THURSDAY NIGHT IN APRIL 1990, a crowd gathered in Atlantic City, New Jersey, to celebrate Donald Trump's newest creation. Trump kicked off the festivities by rubbing a giant lamp that freed a genie named Fabu (short for Fabulous), who appeared on a massive screen. "Good evening, Master," the digital genie told Trump. "Is this not a magnificent house?" Fabu declared before intoning, "Open sesame." The entrance sign flashed on, a loudspeaker blared the theme from *Star Wars*, and the crowds thronged Trump's 39-story casino, the Taj Mahal.[1]

If Trump courted fanfare with Trump Tower, he flaunted it with his casino. Trump Taj Mahal was hailed by its braggadocious developer as "the eighth wonder of the world" and "the largest casino on the planet" when it opened (a claim disputed by the Las Vegas Riviera hotel). At an estimated cost of $1 billion, it remains one of the most expensive buildings ever built in the modern era. The Taj Mahal glistened with onion domes and minarets copied from St. Basil's Cathedral in Red Square, gilded columns, crystal chandeliers, and doormen in turbans.

Trump gloated over his new casino. "Nobody thought it could be built," he told *The New York Times* when the Trump Taj Mahal opened its doors. "That was the biggest risk—just getting it built. But I love proving people wrong."[2] It would turn out that the opening was the only thing about the 1,250-room casino hotel that he would be able to openly celebrate. Trump's massive casino was burdened with so much debt that it was doomed into a financial recession even before it opened its doors. In July of 1991, only 15 months after the Trump Taj Mahal opened, Trump filed for Chapter 11 bankruptcy protection in an effort to soften the casino's debt requirements. Even more alarming was that, during that time, an investigative unit of the Treasury Department reported that the Trump Taj Mahal casino broke anti–money laundering rules 106 times in its first year and a half of operation. In other words, Trump's eighth world wonder lost a wondrous amount of money even though it found a dedicated clientele of high rollers—the Russian Mafiya.

The Taj Mahal, like all casinos, was vulnerable to money laundering. A gambler could walk in with illicit funds, turn the money into a stack of chips, gamble a bit, and then cash out with clean money, which can be reported to the IRS as gambling profits. Kenneth McCallion, a former prosecutor who worked out of the Brooklyn office of the Justice Department's Organized Crime Strike Force, found Russian criminals were doing exactly that at the Taj Mahal. "Since we were in New York, we weren't the lead of any casino investigations but we were able to provide information about Russian organized criminals traveling back and forth with bags of money, cashing them into chips, and so forth," McCallion told me.

Most big casinos developed intelligence operations that rivaled the FBI's and instituted policies and practices designed to thwart money laundering. Casinos were required to file a currency transaction report (CTR) anytime a customer gambled more than $10,000 in a 24-hour period. But Trump's casino weakly enforced these rules, or didn't enforce them at all, which allowed money laundering to run rampant.

From the moment it opened, the Taj Mahal was a money-laundering concern. Documents released to me by the U.S. Treasury Department under the Freedom of Information Act show that the Taj Mahal repeatedly failed to implement rules designed to prevent potential money laundering. Treasury's Financial Crimes Enforcement Network (FinCEN) counted more than 100 instances in the casino's first 21 months of operation where the Taj Mahal had failed to file CTRs. The casino attributed it to start-up problems and challenged the findings for years until it finally agreed in 1998 to pay a fine of $477,000.[3] At the time, it was the biggest money-laundering fine ever levied against a casino

An early mistake could be forgiven, but the Taj Mahal stubbornly refused to clean up its operations. Four subsequent investigations by the U.S. Treasury found "repeated and significant violations" by the Taj Mahal of rules designed to prevent money laundering. Two separate reviews in 2010 and 2012 found that the Trump Taj Mahal "willfully violated" anti–money laundering rules of the Bank Secrecy Act. This finding, which meant the casino showed either "reckless disregard" or "willful blindness," bordered on criminal behavior. A $10 million civil penalty was imposed in 2015 while the casino was again in bankruptcy. "Like all casinos in this country, Trump Taj Mahal has a duty to help protect our financial system from being exploited by criminals, terrorists, and other bad actors," said FinCEN's director, Jennifer Shasky Calvery. "Far from meeting these expectations, poor compliance practices, over many years, left the casino and our financial system unacceptably exposed."[4]

The Taj Mahal not only failed to restrain criminal activity, it almost seemed to cater to it. While Trump railed to Congress about "rampant" organized crime in Indian casinos, his own gambling palace was becoming the favorite East Coast destination for Russian mobsters.[5] As one federal agent noted, "As long as these guys attract a lot of money or spend a lot of money, the casinos don't care."[6] High rollers were treated like royalty, receiving "comps" for up to $100,000 of free food, rooms, Champagne, cartons of cigarettes, and transportation in stretch limousines—all permissible under New Jersey law. "A lot of New York organized crime figures would go down there to gamble," Jim E. Moody, a former FBI assistant director, told me. "A lot of it's for show to make it look like they have lots of money. Even the lowest-level guy will gamble everything he has to make himself look like a big deal." An early 1990s powwow involving members of Italian and Russian organized-crime groups running a gas-tax scam was held in a Taj Mahal conference room that was bugged by the FBI.

One of the casino's connections to the underworld was Danny Leung, the vice president of Asian marketing at the Taj Mahal in its first three years of operation. In a 1992 hearing of the Senate's Permanent Subcommittee on Investigations, Leung was described by law enforcement as "an associate of the 14K Triad," an international heroin syndicate based in Hong Kong.[7] (Two informants later told the Division of Gaming Enforcement that Leung was a member of the Triad.) Leung, who also allegedly had contacts with Asian gangs in New York and Toronto, was brought into the casino business through William "Bucky" Howard, another Taj Mahal employee. (Howard was acquitted in an earlier case involving kickbacks to executives at the nearby Trump Castle casino in Atlantic City.) In addition to serving as a Taj Mahal executive, Leung had a separate contract to fly gamblers from Toronto to the casino.

The New Jersey Casino Control Commission held a lengthy hearing in 1995 to determine whether Leung's casino license should be revoked for his alleged association with organized crime. According to a report I obtained under a public records request, a Canadian detective testified that Leung brought in a group of Vietnamese gang members with criminal records for extortion and drug trafficking. (When questioned, Leung said he had more than 6,000 customers and could not recall the gang members.) According to the DGE's report, Leung also ran with a group of Italians from Canada later indicted in a $1 million credit scam at the Taj Mahal. The incident was never reported because Trump never filed charges. Trump also sent Taj Mahal president Danny Gomes to defend Leung at the 1995 Casino Control Commission hearing.[8] Over the objections of the DGE, the commission voted 3-1 to renew Leung's license.

It's likely that the Russian Mafiya may have frequented the casino not only because they were familiar with the Trump brand, but also because the Taj Mahal catered to a Russian clientele. The dancing bears and the acrobats of the Moscow Circus performed at the Taj Mahal a few months after the casino's grand opening, followed by "Moscow on Ice," featuring a Russian ice troupe dancing to the music of Janet Jackson. Trump also brought in Russian pop stars and singers. Russian pop diva Alla Pugacheva performed at a sold-out show at the casino in 1994 with her then husband, the flamboyant Philipp Kirkorov, who looked (and dressed) like a Las Vegas magician. Pugacheva is one of the few Soviet stars whose career survived the passing of the USSR, and she and her husband had connections on high with the former Soviet power elite, the people who became the oligarchs and ran the organized-crime networks of modern Russia.

The show was a success.[9] Trump presented Pugacheva and Kirkorov with a large trophy afterward for being the first Russian artists to play at the casino, and the real estate mogul kept in touch with Kirkorov over the years. Kirkorov was Trump's guest at a 1999 party at Mar-a-Lago, and he served as a juror at Trump's 2013 Miss Universe pageant.[10] "He was very often a guest of Russia, he loves Russia and Russians," Kirkorov said before Trump's election. "If Trump will be President, the relationship between our countries will be much closer. And I pray for that. Because we are two big countries, two big nations. We must be friends."[11]

▬

THOUGH MANY RUSSIAN CRIMINALS FREQUENTED the Taj Mahal, one particular patron stood out. According to FBI files, a man named Vyacheslav Ivankov was reported to have made 19 visits to the Taj Mahal between March and April 1993, reportedly gambling $250,000 during that time. Yet the CTRs submitted accounted for much less, a mere $103,000. This brazen gambling is all the more remarkable considering that, at the time, federal authorities had been tipped off by Russian officials to keep an eye out for him. Ivankov, it turned out, was a notorious and feared *vor v zakone* ("thief who follows the code"), a rough equivalent to a Mafia Godfather, and a rank that could only be obtained while doing hard time.

The tradition of the vor dated back to the Russian Revolution, and over time it had evolved into a position that commanded great respect and authority in the former Soviet underworld. A vor was above the law; he was his own law. A vor like Ivankov ruled on matters of "thieves' law" by settling disputes among groups and punishing violators. There was the rule of the Kremlin and there was the rule of the vor. Gatherings of the *vory* were called *skhodka*. Decisions were made on specific criminal activities, spheres of interest were redistributed, and responses to law enforcement operations were planned. New vory were crowned and punishment was meted out to those who violated the code. A vor could not marry, could not lie, and could never refuse a request from another vor. But Ivankov wasn't just any vor; he was one of the most highly regarded of them all, both within the criminal world and to the Russian public at large. Early on in his career, Ivankov developed a reputation for extorting ill-gotten wealth from corrupt Russian officials by leading a gang that dressed up as police and used bogus IDs and documents to search the homes of wealthy individuals and steal money and other valuables. "I am respected everywhere," Ivankov told a Russian journalist. "Absolutely. Because I have not given anyone the moral right to think badly of me. Every evening, I look into the mirror and account to my conscience. Believe me."[12]

Although Ivankov was a dapperly dressed middle-aged man on the smaller side of average, he was not someone to be taken lightly. His cruelty was the stuff of legends. Those who crossed him, it was said, were taken into the woods and tortured. One tale had him burying a Moscow restaurant manager alive and paving a road over him. A few weeks before departing for the United States, he was accused of killing two Turks in a Moscow restaurant. Ivankov was later quoted as saying, "Killing someone is as easy as lighting a cigarette."[13] Authorities eventually caught up with his banditry, and in a KGB sting, Ivankov was arrested and sentenced to 14 years' imprisonment.

Organized crime was nothing new in Russia. In the Soviet era, criminal groups and the black market long had an understanding with the Communist Party and the KGB. The criminals and the black market could operate as long as they stayed in the shadows and paid tribute to the authority of the state. As Ivankov sat in a Siberian labor camp, the old order gave way as the Soviet state crumbled. The nation was plunged into an abyss of poverty, rising inflation, and vast corruption. Honest citizens could barely make enough to feed their families. Even officers of the Moscow police reportedly were forced to resort to bribery or theft to keep food on the table, which led to a widespread distrust of law enforcement. By the late 1980s, corruption had reached such endemic levels that a criminal could bribe his way out of any law-breaking problem—even prison. If you were a businessman in the late 1980s, one Russian banker recalled, "you can either pay the mob, leave the country, or get a bullet through your brain."[14]

Ivankov's world of organized crime outlasted the Soviet Union, and without the choking hand of the state on its neck, the Russian Mafiya took its place at the center of power in the new, lawless Russia of the 1990s. It became impossible to run a profitable business without *krysha*, which were extortion payments meant to guarantee physical protection from organized-crime outfits. But krysha, or cover, or literally "roof," came to mean much more than physical protection in post-Soviet Russia; it meant protection from corrupt bureaucrats and investigators. Knowing someone's krysha was a way of keeping track of who was on the same team. Krysha was the key to the way things worked in the new Russia, a country where the crooks, spies, government, and business community were all under the same roof.

If there was any indication of how deeply tied to the Mob successful Russians of that era were, one needed only look at Joseph Kobzon, a bowl haircut crooner known as "Russia's Sinatra." The name was fitting in more ways than one. Along with being a staunchly loyal party member and the most decorated singer in Russian history, a fact confirmed by the *Guinness Book of World Records* (Russian edition), Kobzon, like his American counterpart, had ties to the Mob. FBI reports described Kobzon as the "spiritual leader"[15] of the Russian Mafiya in Moscow and noted the connections that he had to "the Government, the KGB, and the Moscow business community." Along with people like Kobzon behind him, Ivankov had another powerful friend. Semion Mogilevich, whom the FBI would later dub "The Brainy Don," bribed a judge on Russia's Supreme Court to secure Ivankov's release. In 1991, Russia's highest court commuted Ivankov's sentence to time served, freeing him four years ahead of schedule.

In March 1992, Ivankov landed incognito at John F. Kennedy International Airport. On his visa application, the vor listed the purpose of his business trip as "doing film negotiations" with Twelve LA Inc., a Russian film company with offices in Manhattan. After being admitted into the country, Ivankov was greeted at the airport by an Armenian vor who handed him a briefcase filled with $1.5 million in cash. Ivankov set up shop in Brighton Beach, where he recruited "two special brigades" made up of former Russian athletes and Special Forces veterans who had served in the Soviet-Afghan War.[16] According to the FBI, one brigade, whose second-in-command was a former KGB agent, carried out murders on Ivankov's behalf, including the killings of half a dozen top Russian Mafiya figures who "got in the way." Within months, Ivankov not only had a New York driver's license and a green card after a sham marriage, he had also become one of the most powerful heads of Russia's American Mafiya operations. As one Genovese family member put it, "When Ivankov came into town, I never saw such fear."[17]

INTERNATIONAL ORGANIZED CRIME, ESPECIALLY RUSSIAN, had become such a concern that in October of 1991, the United Nations held a multi-day conference on the issue. The International Seminar on Organized

Crime took place in Suzdal, a city located roughly 125 miles to the northeast of Moscow. Suzdal was old enough to have once been the capital of Russia, back when Moscow was still mostly cow pasture. Among those in attendance was special agent Jim E. Moody, the chief of the FBI's organized-crime section, who managed the bureau's programs targeting Mafia and drug trafficking. Though the UN invitation had originally been extended to the Department of Justice, the representative who accepted it, a DOJ attorney named Mike DeFeo, had extended the invitation to Moody. He not only received authorization to attend, but became the first, and possibly the last, FBI agent ever granted official permission by the Soviet Union to enter its borders.

The Soviet Union that Moody observed was not the mythic American foe he'd been raised to fear, but a third-world country so poor that it could barely feed its people. Moody noticed that some of the conference staff were selling food to people from out of the back of the kitchen. Food shortages weren't the only problem. Energy was so hard to come by that many people endured the brutal winters with only coats and blankets to warm them. Even the conference hallways were so feebly lit that Moody kept tripping on carpets and bumping into things. When a colleague later asked Moody if Russia still posed a threat to America, he simply replied, "As long as we don't invade them, no."

At the conference, Moody couldn't help but notice that Russian law enforcement took a particular interest in him. In official attendance in Suzdal were members of the MVD, Russia's Ministry of Interior Affairs, the country's federal law enforcement agency. Members of Russia's intelligence ministry, the KGB, were unofficial attendees. Moody later noted that KGB agents would come into the resort building where the conference was held during breaks in the proceedings and ask him specific questions that appeared as though they were fishing for classified information. "I asked how the acoustics were in the room," Moody said, making it clear that he understood that the Russian spy agency was eavesdropping. "They said they were really good."

Since Moody had come as a representative of the FBI, nearly everyone at the conference wanted to know how the bureau battled organized crime. Most of Moody's two decades in the bureau had been spent fighting the American-based families of La Cosa Nostra. At the FBI's huge bureau in New York, Moody led an investigation that resulted in the Mafia Commission Trial, what *Time* would call "the Case of Cases," as it resulted in the eventual prosecution of all five bosses of New York City's crime families, including the Genovese family boss Anthony "Fat Tony" Salerno. While in Suzdal, a KGB general invited Moody and DeFeo to a KGB-owned dacha situated in the middle of a game reserve right outside Suzdal. When Moody walked in, he came face to face with a large taxidermied wolf, an animal his hosts claimed had been shot just from the back porch of the dacha. A KGB colonel in charge of the Suzdal region and a KGB interpreter and others joined them for a meal of fresh venison in the cozy, wood-paneled dacha. The discussion once again turned to Russian organized crime. "What I found out when I was there was they had a huge organized crime problem," Moody said. "And they were afraid of it. They would deny it, but they were afraid of it."

Russia also had to contend with the deep corruption within its own ranks. This problem literally came knocking late one night at Moody's hotel room door, the source being the knuckles of an MVD officer whom he had met earlier at the conference. Accompanying him were seven other officers, each carrying a bottle of vodka. The MVD official explained that the seven officers were undercover—no one in the police department even knew who they were. "He told me he wanted me to meet these people to show me that there were officers in Russia that weren't corrupt," Moody said.

During his meetings in Russia, the KGB had asked Moody if it would be possible to set up a working relationship with the FBI to address organized crime. Moody turned them down, as the KGB had no jurisdiction and because they had been America's enemies for so many years. But Moody believed a relationship could be forged between the FBI and the MVD, the closest thing that Russia had to the FBI. Hollywood had even parodied such a relationship in the 1980s film *Red Heat*, starring Jim Belushi as a Chicago cop and Arnold Schwarzenegger as an MVD officer who team up to catch, what else, a Russian organized-crime kingpin.

Surely, the Cold War had thawed to the point where these kinds of partnerships weren't entirely in the realm of fantasy. Or so Moody thought.

Upon his return to Washington, Moody commissioned a survey of all of the FBI's 63,000 active cases, turning up 68 investigations involving members of the Russian Mafiya. In looking over these cases, Moody was surprised at the unorthodoxy of the Russian criminal mind. Because ethnic groups tend to cluster together in urban areas, a newly arrived immigrant criminal will typically prey on his fellow émigrés. Russian immigrant criminals behaved differently. "They ventured out *immediately* and set up relations with other organized-crime groups *immediately*," Moody said. This meant that Russian criminal interests were bafflingly widespread. While the FBI investigated crime by the nature of the offense—organized crime, drugs, gangs, white-collar crime, and so on—Russian organized criminals seemed to fall into all categories at once. Not only that, but crimes linked to the Russian Mafiya were popping up all over the world, from Europe to Asia to South America. "You name it, they were involved in it," Moody said. "Everything."

The Russian Mob had gone global, a problem that Moody knew would need international partnerships to successfully combat it. He began a quiet lobbying campaign inside the Justice Department. He briefed Janet Reno, then the attorney general, and the Attorney General's Organized Crime Council, an influential group of law enforcement officials from across the government. A year after his visit to the Soviet Union, the FBI received the bureaucratic blessing it needed to investigate Russian organized crime. It wasn't the highest priority. La Cosa Nostra, the Mafia in Italy, Mexican cartels, Asian gangs, Jamaican drug gangs, all were seen as more pressing, but at least it was on the radar.

The holdup was that Moody couldn't talk to the Russians. The FBI's foreign counterintelligence personnel, who had long viewed Russia as the enemy, had come in and denied him permission on national-security grounds. Moody would get permission to talk, only to be overruled again. Back and forth it went. "This went on for too damn long," he said. That is, until one day, when he found himself in a meeting of fairly high-ranking FBI officials. It was at this point that Moody's counterpart in FBI counterintelligence made a critical mistake. He asked Moody how many cases he had worked on with the Russians.

"None. I'm not allowed to talk to them," he replied.

An assistant FBI director thought that was crazy.

"That's exactly what I've been saying," replied Moody. And just like that, he was finally given the green light to pursue a relationship with Russian law enforcement.

In the winter of 1993, a redheaded, freckle-faced MVD deputy general named Mikhail Yegorov flew over from Siberia to spend a week at the FBI headquarters. To focus efforts on fighting organized crime, Yegorov had been assigned an army of 25,000 officers, and was keen to put them to use. After a night spent pounding back vodkas, Moody and Yegorov agreed on the terms for a working relationship between the FBI and the MVD, which would include teaming up with the German Federal Criminal Police, the BKA, which was dealing with the huge wave of crime unleashed by the fall of the Berlin Wall and the reunification of Germany.

Later that year, Moody returned to Russia, along with an agent named Ray Kerr. Bodyguards provided by the MVD protected them at all times. And it was during that visit that Moody first heard the name of someone he would compare to Professor Moriarty, the fictional nemesis of Sherlock Holmes. What made Professor Moriarty such a dangerous criminal, as Holmes explains to Dr. Watson, is that no one has ever heard of him. General Yegorov explained that a major Russian organized-crime boss had just set up a base of operations in the United States. In Russia, he was known as the "grandfather of the Soviet racketeers," but he dabbled in drug trafficking, and murder. In fact, according to MVD information, while Moody was in Moscow, this crime boss was in Denver to arrange a hit on a Russian Mafioso. Just as Dr. Watson had never heard of Professor Moriarty, Moody had never heard of Vyacheslav "Yaponchik" Ivankov.

—

MOODY'S EFFORTS TO DIRECT THE FBI's attention and resources toward Russian organized crime meant that Ivankov's days as a free man were numbered. In May 1994, under the leadership of Director Louis Freeh, the FBI set up the first squad, known internally as C-24, dedicated to fighting Russian organized crime in New York. This was not only a crucial step but a pragmatic one as well. Previously, Russian organized-crime investigations had been run out of a squad that also handled Asian gangs and anything else that wasn't La Cosa Nostra. Director Freeh had investigated organized crime in his days as a special agent and knew too well how the bureau's complacency had allowed La Cosa Nostra to establish itself. He was not about to repeat the same mistake with the Russian Mafiya. Thanks to Moody, the FBI not only had an open channel to Moscow, but even opened a legal attaché office in Moscow, staffed with Russian-speaking agents like Michael di Pretoro, whose job it was to work in partnership with Russian law enforcement. Ray Kerr, who had traveled to Moscow with Jim Moody, was named head of the squad. And target Number One was Vyacheslav Ivankov.

As the FBI investigation progressed, the agents came to learn that Russian criminal bosses had sent Ivankov to America with a mission. War between rival Russian gangs had broken out in Brighton Beach, where gun battles and car bombings were occurring with startling regularity. It was cheaper to have someone killed than to pay off a debt, as a Russian language newspaper in New York put it. The violence between Russian gangs on the streets of Brighton Beach was bad for business, and Ivankov was sent to put an end to it. A Moscow law enforcement official quoted in the FBI files summed up how much faith Russia's crime bosses had in Ivankov. "Yaponchik will impose order. He will be the center around which those who are organized and strong will unite, and he will strangle all this low-life, who engage in gunfights on the streets. And you will know precisely with whom you are dealing—with one strong boss."[18] Ivankov would likely have agreed with that assessment, later telling a Russian journalist, "Where I am, there is always order. Anybody will tell you this."[19]

Ivankov proved to be a hard man to find. As one New York crime investigator put it, "he was like a ghost."[20] For a while, all the FBI had on his whereabouts was a business called Slavic Inc. that Ivankov had set up as the base of what the bureau later concluded was his money-laundering operation in Brighton Beach. The FBI made startling discoveries when they investigated Slavic's paperwork. The listed company president was Vyacheslav "Slava" Fetisov, a Russian hockey star who was then playing in the NHL for the New Jersey Devils. This was no accident. It would later be discovered that Ivankov's grip extended all the way to Russian hockey players, many of whom sought to play in the NHL, but to "ensure their safety" had to provide kickbacks to the Mafiya.[21] Despite what law enforcement was turning up, Ivankov had cleverly concealed his whereabouts. "We had to go out and really beat the bushes," Moody said. Finally they received a tip. Ivankov had not only been right under their noses, but was living quite lavishly in one of Manhattan's most opulent pieces of real estate—Trump Tower.[22]

Exactly what Ivankov was doing in Trump Tower and how he got there has never been established, but Trump's Russian connections at this time were becoming increasingly bizarre. While investigators tracked Ivankov to Atlantic City and the Trump Taj Mahal, back in Russia, a film produced by a joint American-Russian company with uncanny allusions to Trump and his casino had just been released. *Good Weather on Deribasovskaya, or It Rains Again on Brighton Beach* was a satire about an American Taj Mahal–like casino that is secretly run by the KGB. It featured, among other scenes, scantily clad dancers in hammer-and-sickle undergarments performing for an enthusiastic audience. The credits acknowledge Donald Trump for scenes in the movie that were filmed at the Trump Taj Mahal.[23]

Ivankov also took over a minority share in the Rasputin restaurant, a well-known hangout for Russian mobsters in Brighton Beach. I spent a surreal night at the Rasputin once in the early 2000s. At our table, an already-opened vodka bottle waited for us. Milling about were beefy men in wool overcoats with generously proportioned blonds in furs. After a meal that involved surprisingly good potatoes with dill and lamb chops, the entertainment for the evening began. A female troupe danced around in revealing outfits that hinted at cultural stereotypes. Rasputin, it turned out, had been one of the sponsors of Alla Pugacheva and Philipp Kirkorov's 1994 performance at the Taj Mahal. The restaurant's name was inscribed on the trophy Trump presented to the duo.

When the FBI finally nabbed Ivankov at his girlfriend's apartment in Brighton Beach in June 1995, they found some disturbing clues linking him to the real estate mogul. Along with the spy gizmos seized during Ivankov's arrest, including a bug detector, an electronic voice changer, a lock pick set, two firearms, and a special passport kit similar to those found issued by the KGB to its spies, FBI agents also discovered a phone book that contained not just working phone and fax numbers for the Trump Organization, but also a number for the Trump Organization's Trump Tower residence.[24]

Ivankov's trial was held in the summer of 1996. The Russian vor was unrepentant. While awaiting trial, Ivankov tried to have Moody and two other agents killed. One of the FBI's sources warned them that a Russian hit man had arrived in the United States and was trying to find out where the agents lived. The suspected hit man was arrested on federal gun charges, but he refused to admit he was there on a contract killing and eventually was deported back to Russia. Asked if he took any precautions, Moody just laughed. Ivankov was convicted of extorting Russian émigrés who ran a successful Wall Street investment firm out of $3.5 million and was sentenced to nearly 10 years in prison. After serving out his sentence, Ivankov was deported to Russia in 2004; he was assassinated in 2009 outside a Thai restaurant.

Ivankov's arrest, conviction, and sentencing was a game changer for Russian organized crime in the United States. The flood of Russian criminals coming to America slowed to a trickle, and some returned to Russia, believing they could operate with more freedom back home. But with the FBI's new success came a consequence Moody had hoped to avoid—Russian law enforcement was growing shadowy. Every time the bureau found a helpful Russian law official, that person was quickly and quietly replaced. Ray Kerr, the head of the Russian Organized Crime

Task Force in New York, grew increasingly skeptical of any information the Russians did provide. It wasn't clear whether the information was simply an effort to use the FBI to settle scores or do their dirty work. At one Department of Justice meeting in Washington over a $7 billion money-laundering fraud at the Bank of New York, Kerr said it was obvious that the law enforcement officials Russia had sent over were trying to cover up for someone. Meanwhile, the FBI's Russian Organized Crime Task Force was tracing money flowing out of Russia right into the United States. In one early 1990s case in California, the bureau tracked a half-billion dollars' worth of diamonds and gold coins that were being systematically looted out of the Russian treasury and shipped to a San Francisco–based company called Golden ADA. Agents listening on wiretaps to suspects in the Golden ADA case heard phone calls being dialed directly into the Kremlin.

Not only was Russian law enforcement actively thwarting the FBI's organized-crime squad investigations into Russia, but Ray Kerr learned to his surprise that Russia had been spying on *him*. One day, he got a call from John O'Neill, who headed the FBI's counterintelligence investigations in New York. "Can you come up to my office?" O'Neill asked. The offices of the FBI's counterintelligence squad were on a different floor of the bureau's New York office. It was spook country, and criminal investigators like Kerr rarely had reason to venture there.

"Why was Robert Hanssen looking in your files?" O'Neill asked Kerr when he arrived. Kerr had no idea. Hanssen was the infamous FBI agent who spied for the Soviet Union and Russia for two decades until his arrest in 2001. He had compromised numerous intelligence sources, at least two of whom were killed. Kerr asked O'Neill to provide the reference numbers to the files Hanssen had examined so he could try and piece together what happened. After a review of the documents, Kerr realized that Hanssen had been trying to identify the Russian organized-crime squad's informants. For their own protection, informants weren't named in FBI criminal investigation files. Informant information, including their identities, was kept in a separate, secure file that Hanssen couldn't access without raising suspicion. However, the criminal investigation files do give clues that a skilled investigator could use to put two and two together and identify them. Hanssen didn't get far enough to identify any of the squad's sources, but the fact that he was even trying showed that the work Kerr's team was doing was making some powerful and well-connected people in Moscow very nervous.

Equally alarming was a brief news report that appeared in a Russian periodical that noted how Marina Salye, a St. Petersburg legislator heading a special investigative commission, was demanding that a former KGB colonel who had been appointed head of Saint Petersburg's Committee of External Relations step down. "Vladimir Putin has issued licenses, without government authority, for the overseas export of bartered oil, timber, and non-ferrous and rare-earth metals to questionable and little-known firms, often incorporated the previous day, with licenses issued in advance of being signed by Western Partners and without documentation of the goods' availability. And the prices assigned were for dumping—about two thousand times lower than the prevailing ones. The Commission is now sending documentation of its investigation to the Personnel Office, and Putin may have to answer before his hometown for having deprived municipal coffers of $122 million."[25]

Putin was never charged with any crime related to these accusations, even as Salye continued to be a thorn in his side until his ascendency to the presidency. Shortly after the election, in 2000, she met with opposition leader Sergei Yushenkov. Though the meeting was to be private, an FSB officer stood sentinel in the corner, with Yushenkov clearly nervous. Salye got the hint and soon after went into self-imposed exile, excommunicating herself from the world. Yushenkov, who stayed in Moscow, would be gunned down in his doorway only a few years later. When Putin reclaimed the presidency in 2010, a reporter for the *Los Angeles Times* flew out to interview Salye, then widely regarded as Putin's oldest foe still breathing, at her rural Russian home. When the reporter asked Salye what she thought of Putin's grip on power, her face turned hard. She gave an insightful reply: "Mafia is immortal."[26]

3.

A MILLIONAIRE
WITHOUT A DOLLAR

I N JANUARY 1997, A FORMER RUSSIAN general and presidential hopeful named Aleksandr Lebed made a trip to the United States for Bill Clinton's second inauguration. Lebed had just lost a bid to unseat Russian president Boris Yelstin in what would end up being Russia's only legitimate presidential race. He was planning to run again, and saw his visit as a chance to drum up American support for his prospects. While in the States, Lebed received another invitation, to come up to New York and meet with Donald Trump.[1]

Though *The New York Times*, who reported on Lebed's Trump Tower visit, were declined entry to the actual meeting, Trump allowed Mark Singer, a *New Yorker* staff writer then profiling him, to shadow him as he shook hands with Lebed.[2] As Trump showed off some of his personal artifacts—Mike Tyson's championship belt, Shaquille O'Neill's shoe, a photo of Madonna on the steps of Mar-a-Lago—the conversation turned to the fourth occupant in the room, Howard Lorber, one of Trump's self-professed "best friends." Lorber was then an executive with an American conglomerate with interests in tobacco and Russian real estate. He had accompanied Trump on a visit to Moscow only a few months earlier to consider sites for a Trump Tower that would have been the real estate tycoon's first overseas development. Lorber had already begun his own development projects in the Russian capital, but Lebed had not heard of any of them.

"See, they don't know you," Trump told Lorber. "With all that investment, they don't know you. Trump they know." When Lebed informed Trump that some "poisonous" reporters believed Trump would cram Moscow with casinos, Trump laughed it off and told him about his earlier trip. "We are actually looking at something in Moscow right now, and it would be skyscrapers and hotels, not casinos. I'll soon be going again to Moscow. We're looking at the Moskva Hotel. We're also looking at the Rossiya. That's a very big project; I think it's the largest hotel in the world. And we're working with the local government, the mayor of Moscow and the mayor's people. So far, they've been very responsive."

"You must be a very confident person." Lebed said. "You are building straight into the center." Trump took the compliment in stride. "I always go into the center," he said. To this, Lebed made a curious comment, citing Trump as a "litmus testing paper" for whether American investment in Moscow could be successful. "If Trump goes to Moscow, I think America will follow. You are a professional—a high-level professional—and if you invest, you invest in real stuff. Serious, high-quality projects. And you deal with serious people. And I deem you to be a very serious person. That's why I'm meeting you." Trump appeared to be flattered. "Thank you," he said, and offered him as a gift a copy of *The Art of the Deal.*[3]

Lebed's praise wasn't the kind Trump was hearing in the mid-1990s, when his empire was all but in ruins. The former "boy wonder," as he called himself, was now known as "a guy with nothing but fucking problems."[4] His Atlantic City casinos had collapsed under the weight of too much debt. His lenders had forced him to sell off parts of his real estate properties and business ventures, including his airline, Trump Shuttle. Things were bad enough financially for "The Donald" that during his trip to Moscow in November of 1996, he would experience a peculiar sort of humiliation. Although Trump had regained some financial stability, he was still pinching his pennies and had to suffer the indignity of flying commercial to get there. "We had to wait about an hour in London for a flight, right out there with all the other passengers," his paramour Marla Maples told *Playboy* magazine. "Well, you can imagine how that went over with Donald."[5]

This didn't stop Trump from staying at the Baltschug, one of the city's most venerated hotels, for his three-day visit. The accommodating and historical Baltschug, which dates back to the reign of Czar Nicholas II and sits on the Moskva River, with glorious views of St. Basil's Cathedral, Red Square, and the Kremlin, may have helped Trump lick his wounds. The Baltschug's neoclassical facade resembled the storied Plaza Hotel in New York, another prized possession Trump had reluctantly given up. During his ownership of the hotel, Trump made his famous *Home Alone 2* cameo.[6] But that was all in the past, back in a country that had ceased to be lucrative for a down-on-his-luck real estate mogul. At least in the Baltschug he was still treated like royalty, and it didn't hurt that some of the other guests offered glittering company. Singer Tina Turner, in town for a concert, was also staying at the Baltschug, as was supermodel Claudia Schiffer.

To make his announcement that he would be seeking to develop property in Moscow, Trump gathered the local press corps at the Baltschug. With the same bravado he would later show when he assumed the presidency of the United States, Trump promised to build not one but two Trump towers in Moscow. "[Moscow] is really a city with a great future, great potential," Trump said. "We're looking at building a super-luxury residential tower," he said, "which I think Moscow desperately wants and needs."[7] Trump already had a site picked out for one of his towers, the century-old Ducat tobacco factory only a stone's throw from the Kremlin, which churned out a billion cigarettes a year. But what Trump didn't know was that a battle for the site had taken place between developers and unionized workers of the factory.

Trump surveyed the site under a Moscow skyline dotted with construction cranes. A building boom was underway, thanks largely to the efforts of the city's imperious mayor, Yuri Luzhkov. One five-story building on the site, Ducat I, had already been built and leased to Citibank. A second, even bigger tower, Ducat II, was nearing completion, and had already been leased to Motorola, Conoco, and Morgan Stanley.[8] The third and biggest tower, Ducat III, was to be Trump's, who seemed to be making a move to get into the Moscow real estate market at the right time. A massive $350 million underground shopping mall was being built under Manezh Square, in the heart of the city, and a grand $250 million project was underway to rebuild the Cathedral of Christ Savior, the world's largest Orthodox church, which had been destroyed by Stalin. "Moscow is going to be huge! Take it from the Trumpster," he said at the time.[9]

But Moscow in the 1990s was anything but friendly to legitimate commerce—giant protection rackets led by the Mafiya and other organized criminal groups called the shots, leaving lower-tier gangs to wage bloody wars for whatever was left to claim. Bribes and kickbacks were the cost of doing business. Car bombings, a gunman in the stairwell, or a bullet-riddled car were how business was otherwise negotiated. The authorities, led by the shambolic Yeltsin, were not only powerless to stop it, but too often they were in on it, too. Only fools would dare do business in Moscow without a *krysha* to protect them. The closest thing Trump had to a krysha was Lorber, and Lorber's krysha was Vector Group's portly and puissant Bennett LeBow.

Trump hadn't been shown Ducat III at random; LeBow owned it, having purchased the former cigarette factory before the dust had even settled on the rubble of the former USSR. All he needed now was the right developer, and he found one in Donald Trump. "Donald is the preeminent marketer and developer in the world," *The Moscow Times* quoted LeBow as saying. "We want the best for Moscow—and Donald's it."[10] LeBow not only served up a site for Trump; he lined up financing and brought a wealth of experience and contacts in Russia that he had cultivated over the past few years, including businessmen suspected of having ties to Russian organized crime. LeBow brought Vadim Rabinovich—the Ukrainian representative of Nordex GmbH, a Vienna-based company that attracted interest from the CIA—to a Clinton-Gore fundraiser in September 1995 at the Sheraton Bal Harbour Hotel in Miami. Rabinovich even managed to pose for a photo with the president and likely would have cultivated these political ties further were he not in attendance under a revoked visa.[11]

LeBow had a divisive reputation. "Populist Hero or Bottom Feeder?" was the headline of a *Time* profile of the shrewd businessman who saw opportunity in flagging companies.[12] He had made a considerable profit buying and selling Western Union, but his prized possession, the Liggett Group cigarette company, teetered on the edge of bankruptcy. At one point, his reputation was so low that *Newsweek* described him as "a vaguely unsavory wheeler-dealer, just another of those arrogant raiders who tear up companies, kill off jobs and divvy up the booty over dinner at the 21 Club."[13] For a businessman like LeBow, Russia in the 1990s provided a plethora of bottom-feeding opportunities. After the fall of the Soviet Union, he moved aggressively into Russia, entering into a string of joint ventures with cash-strapped businesses. In the 1991 annual report of his holding company, Brooke Group, LeBow proudly told his shareholders that he had six separate subsidiaries operating in the former Soviet Union involved in everything from cigarettes, timber, and helicopters to real estate.[14]

Making money off these ventures was another matter. One of the profitable ones was Liggett-Ducat Ltd., a joint venture between LeBow's Liggett tobacco firm and the Russian Ducat cigarette factory. LeBow personally negotiated the deal, promising to build a new cigarette factory on the outskirts of Moscow. In exchange, he acquired rights to develop the site of the current Ducat factory.[15] Russia, however, was not like the United States, where a corporate raider like LeBow could swoop in, take over a company, and sell off the parts as he so chose. When he tried to do this in Moscow, he found that someone as entrenched in his position as Ducat's manager, Vladimir Tyumentsev, could easily out-maneuver him. Like many other people who actually got things done in Moscow, Tyumentsev had accumulated enormous power in the Soviet Union's complex and dubious planned economy. At its core, a web of demands, bargains, favors, and bartering helped union leaders like Tyu-mentsev stay in power and keep the Soviet economy rolling along like an oblong wheel. Even after Tyumentsev was discovered embezzling money from the factory profits, LeBow still couldn't get rid of him. The manager refused to accept his dismissal and called a strike. He com-plained to Moscow officials that LeBow was trying to swindle Ducat out of the valuable land beneath the factory by paying only $60,000 for property worth many times more. The buyer was Brookemil Ltd., a murky Brooke Group subsidiary incorporated in the Cayman Islands. It certainly looked fishy to the Mossoviet, Moscow's city council. They immediately ordered an investigation, and threatened to tear up the whole deal LeBow had negotiated for the Ducat factory site.[16]

This could not have come at a worse time for LeBow, whose Lig-gett tobacco company back in the United States was on the verge of bankruptcy. LeBow decided he had no choice but to yield. To retain a majority stake in the site and save his investors' money, LeBow ended up giving millions of dollars' worth of shares in the joint venture to Tyumentsev and his workers, and building his developments a couple miles north of the Kremlin. Slowly, over time, with the help of shady middlemen, LeBow bought the shares back, but by then he had lined up his star client.[17]

TRUMP'S APPETITE FOR A TOWER in Moscow had been whetted, but he would need approval from the mayor before he could satisfy his real estate craving. Luzhkov was a holdover strongman from the Soviet era and a close ally of President Yeltsin. Luzhkov kept a tight grip on Moscow; nothing got built without his say-so, and he and his staff usu-ally demanded their pound of flesh. The U.S. ambassador to Russia,

John Beyrle, wasn't shy about calling Luzhkov a crook. "Luzhkov used criminal money to support his rise to power and has been involved with bribes and deals regarding lucrative construction contracts throughout Moscow," he said in a cable later released by WikiLeaks. Corruption pervaded Moscow "with Mayor Luzhkov at the top of the pyramid," Beyrle wrote. "Luzhkov oversees a system in which it appears that almost everyone at every level is involved in some form of corruption or criminal behavior."[18]

Opportunities for "bonuses" were the real draw for a government job, and a businessman didn't need to climb very far up the mayoral pyramid to find corrupt city officials willing to let their palms be greased in exchange for a building permit. During his trip to Moscow, Trump met Deputy Mayor Vladimir Resin, a man who would later become infamous for being photographed wearing an extremely rare DeWitt Pressy Grande Complication watch, worth a cool million dollars.[19] Not the kind of luxury item a deputy mayor from a humble background and with no legitimately known business investments could afford. Still, Resin could throw weight around and was considered "one of the key people in charge of attracting foreign invest[ment] to the Moscow real estate market." According to Brookemil's president, David Geovanis, Resin was said to be "very receptive" to Trump's developments in Moscow.[20]

Except that wasn't true; Resin was too proud a Muscovite to take just any bribe. "We are not building any towers in the old part of Moscow," Resin declared. "We are not going to turn the ancient city into a Manhattan."[21] Resin and his staff were also privy to Trump's financial situation. "From what I hear, he's a millionaire without a dollar," one of his spokesmen sniffed.[22] Nonetheless, Resin offered him the chance to renovate a pair of rundown Moscow hotels located near the Kremlin, the Moskva and the Rossiya, which the city controlled through a joint-stock company.

On the surface, this seemed like a great deal. Moscow's hotel industry had a reputation for yielding high profits, and the demand for rooms exceeded supply. And while Trump was aware of the financial pitfalls of being a hotelier, Resin didn't inform him that in Moscow there were bigger risks to consider. Gangsters had taken over many Moscow hotels, and a few Western businessmen who got in their way had paid with their lives. An American hotelier named Paul Tatum was shot dead just a few days after Trump's visit, one murder in a string of four that had befallen hotel executives in Moscow during an 18-month period. Tatum's killer was never caught, but that was to be expected in a city more or less run by organized crime.[23] Trump appeared oblivious to the risk and began making plans to stamp his name across the city.

Of the two hotels Resin proposed Trump take on as renovation projects, the Moskva Hotel was the more iconic. It was a 180-room Soviet relic that dated back to the 1930s, and was particularly famous for the asymmetrical east and west wings. According to legend, its architect had shown two different plans to Stalin, who approved both. The hotel remained popular up until the end of the Soviet era, especially with expats who liked to congregate at the Spanish Bar, one of the only non-Soviet restaurants in town. But the Moskva fell out of popularity after the collapse of the USSR and its anachronistic accommodations were in dire need of an upgrade. It was certainly a prize catch for the right hotelier.[24]

The Rossiya was in even worse shape. This 3,000-room box was regarded as Europe's biggest hotel and had the reputation of being "Russia's hotel from hell." Though the Rossiya occupied prime real estate, sitting within spitting distance of the Kremlin, it had never quite recovered from a fire that had broken out in its halls several years earlier. It had become a joke to its staff, many of whom couldn't keep a straight face when claiming the hotel to be free of rats and cockroaches.[25] Bad as that was, an even more dangerous problem stalked the labyrinthine halls of the Rossiya. According to Paul Klebnikov, the founding editor of Russian *Forbes* who was later shot and killed for investigating corruption, the Rossiya Hotel was under the control of a Chechen gang lord named "Lechi the Bearded One."[26] In another report prepared by Russia's Interior Ministry that appeared in FBI files, the Rossiya was listed as one of several hotels in Moscow commandeered by a criminal group originating from the former Soviet Republic of Georgia. It seemed the only guests not booking rooms at the hotel were the five-star guests for whom it was intended.

Trump and LeBow submitted to Resin a $175 million proposal to renovate the Moskva, which would include expanding the 180 rooms of the hotel to 600, with the upper floors being converted into private condominiums. There were to be extensive amenities for residents, such as retail shops, a convention center, banquet halls, and public spaces. In exchange for giving the Trump Organization and LeBow majority ownership of the Moskva, Trump promised to turn the hotel around in 18 months.[27]

Trump and LeBow also met with government representatives in a conference room at the Moskva to discuss plans for the hotel. Trump was late to the meeting and a young expatriate businessman was sent downstairs to wait for him. When Trump arrived, two young Russian women accompanied him. The businessman told Jeffrey Toobin of the *New Yorker,* "I had never met Trump before, and I was nervous as hell. So I started panicking. I mean, this was a serious meeting. So I suggested to Trump that I wait downstairs at the bar with them. I'd keep them company until he was finished. He said no way. He thought it was hilarious. He wanted to go upstairs with them. So what could I do? The three of them went up to the meeting together."[28]

Resin later told the press that Trump's associates had presented "their vision and their conditions" to modernize these hotels and that an agreement was "practically reached."[29] Trump and LeBow's plan did not include the Rossiya, but that didn't stop Resin from announcing that Trump had won the contract to refurbish both hotels.

Just as was the case in Trump's 1987 trip to Moscow, however, nothing came of his 1996 visit either. Both times, Trump had made a big scene of flying in and out, and laying out grandiose plans that ended in very public failures, but his name would remain absent from Moscow's real estate boom. It's not entirely clear why these deals collapsed, but there is evidence that Trump may have realized he was headed for trouble. In an article about lawlessness in Moscow and the death of journalist

Paul Klebnikov, *The Washington Times* reported that Moscow was too dangerous for even the bumptious real estate developer Donald Trump. Trump was quoted as saying, "Do I have crazy written on my forehead?" after reportedly being asked about his investment in a "famous Moscow hotel."[30] Although this sounded exactly like Trump, he later denied it, not wishing to offend Mayor Luzhkov. "I wouldn't say anything like that," Trump said in a court deposition. "If I were—you know, I've never seen this article, but if I were in Moscow as a politician or something and Trump said this, I would be very insulted by it."[31] Far from insulting Mayor Luzhkov, Trump wanted to stay in his good graces, and his efforts to do so would mark one of the strangest chapters of his love affair with Russia.

■

IN JANUARY 1997, TRUMP RECEIVED a phone call from Michael Gordon, a reporter from *The New York Times* in Moscow, who had just interviewed a Russian sculptor named Zurab Tsereteli. Gordon wanted to know whether it was true that Trump and Tsereteli had discussed erecting a 311-foot-tall bronze statue of Christopher Columbus on the Hudson River. "Yes, it's already been made, from what I understand," said Trump, who had been introduced to the sculptor during his Moscow trip. According to Trump, the head of the statue was already in New York, while the body was still in St. Petersburg, waiting to be shipped. The whole thing was being gifted to America by the Russian government. "It's got $40 million worth of bronze in it, and Zurab would like it to be at my West Side Yards development," he said to Gordon, "and we are working toward that end . . . [T]he mayor of Moscow has written a letter to Rudy Giuliani stating that they would like to make a gift of this great work by Zurab. It would be my honor if we could work it out with the City of New York. I am absolutely favorably disposed toward it. Zurab is a very unusual guy. This man is major and legit." Trump hung up and spoke to Singer, the *New Yorker* reporter who then had unprecedented access to Trump's life. "See what

I do? All this bullshit. Know what? After shaking five thousand hands, I think I'll go wash mine."[32]

But Trump's hands never stayed clean for long. For years, Tsereteli had been trying to find a home in America for his gargantuan work *The Birth of the New World*, a sculpture of Christopher Columbus so massive that when erected, it would be the tallest statue in the Western hemisphere, craning over the Statue of Liberty by more than 100 feet. Tsereteli had finished *The Birth of the New World* in 1991, in time for the quincentennial of Columbus's famous 1492 voyage to the Americas. Though he had offered it for free to America as a gesture of goodwill, his creation languished for years in a St. Petersburg warehouse, largely because no American city wanted it. Aside from the prohibitive cost of erecting such a monstrosity, no one would confuse one of Tsereteli's sculptures with a work of art. One columnist called Tsereteli's Columbus "graceless as a herd of brontosaurus . . . configured in the shape of an exploded hydrant."[33] Historians argued that the steering wheel Tsereteli's Columbus was clutching did not exist in the explorer's lifetime. And Native Americans considered it an insult to honor a man who, to them, represented five centuries of genocide. Until Trump showed interest, the closest taker for the Columbus statue had been the namesake city of Columbus, Ohio, which pulled out its bid after the town erupted in protest against what had been dubbed "Chris Kong."[34]

It's odd to think that the same man who jackhammered Bonwit Teller's priceless facade would suddenly go to bat for a Russian artist's widely reviled work. Trump had once refused to buy a series of black, silver, and gold silkscreen paintings the artist Andy Warhol had made for the lobby of Trump Tower. ("I think Trump's sort of cheap," Warhol had written in his diary. "I get that feeling."[35]) In fact, Donald Trump's primary art purchases were paintings that depicted Donald Trump, one of which was purchased with $10,000 from his own charity. It stretched credulity to the breaking point to believe that Trump's interest in Tsereteli was purely aesthetic.

It turned out that, like other Russian celebrities, Tsereteli had strong relationships with crooked businessmen and corrupt politicians. The connection that likely interested Trump was Tsereteli's relationship with Mayor Luzhkov.[36] As the mayor's muse, Tsereteli was given several high-profile commissions, along with a Moscow mansion that once housed the German Embassy. Tsereteli's work began popping up all over Moscow, including a 15-story statue of Peter the Great, which was rumored to be a rejected early cast of *The Birth of the New World*, and was so excoriated by local Muscovites that someone once tried to blow it up. But Trump adored this "grandiose creation" and its creator, calling Tsereteli "the closest to me in spirit, the best sculptor of Russia."[37]

Trump may have also known that Mayor Luzhkov was chairman of the Columbus Committee of Russia, which actively sought to place Tsereteli's behemoth commemorations abroad. In 1993, Luzhkov appealed to President Yeltsin to waive export duties on crates destined for Seville, Spain, that contained yet another of Tsereteli's Columbus statues, *The Birth of a New Man*. While the shipping list included 600 tons of bronze for the statue, also listed were an additional 8,500 tons of copper that had no discernible purpose, an amount equal to 5 percent of Russia's annual copper exports at the time.[38] It would have been enough to build the Columbus statue many times over—had it been the right form of copper. The shipments actually contained a softer grade of copper used for electrical wiring. The whole thing appeared to be a scheme to avoid taxes on exports of Russia's natural resources.[39]

The copper export scam was linked to another backer of the Columbus project, Grigori Loutchansky, a man with the unusual distinction of being one of the most investigated men on Earth without ever having been convicted of a crime. Loutchansky was a founding partner of Nordex GmbH, the notorious Austrian trading firm that had been set up to help get Communist Party funds out of the collapsing Soviet Union.[40] However, this was not the only illicit activity uncovered by the CIA, which suspected Nordex GmbH of smuggling drugs, weapons, and even nuclear technology for the Russian Mafiya.[41] Loutchansky vigorously denied these accusations and has said, not without reason, that if even a fraction of the charges were true he would be behind bars. What is certain is that Loutchansky provided the seed capital to get Tsereteli's Columbus statue over to America. "I wanted to help Tsereteli because he is a friend of Yuri Luzhkov, and I did not want to spoil the relationship with the mayor of Moscow . . . He was asking me at the time to finance a beer brewery construction. So I gave Columbus $15,000 for its charter capital. And promptly forgot about it, until I read in the newspaper about some refined copper," Loutchansky told *Kommersant*.[42]

Bennett LeBow was also a big fan of Tsereteli the sculptor. LeBow had pushed hard to get the Columbus statue erected in Miami Beach. In August of 1992, he set up the New World Foundation Inc. to raise the estimated $20 million it would cost to erect the sculpture. He also offered to raise the $5 million needed to build a 130-foot island to house the statue in the waters off Miami Beach. "I've been doing some business in Russia and I know some of the people involved," LeBow said. "Miami is so close to where Columbus set foot, it's the perfect place."[43] Like Trump, LeBow was interested in Tsereteli for reasons other than his love of monumental sculpture. LeBow's PR spokesman described the sculptor as the "Russian Clark Clifford," referring to the former defense secretary and well-connected Washington lawyer.[44] Doing a favor for Tsereteli certainly didn't hurt LeBow's far-flung business interests in Russia.

Mayor Luzhkov and Tsereteli the sculptor joined LeBow in Miami for a celebration of the five-hundredth anniversary of Columbus's voyage to the United States. Tsereteli and his patron led a delegation of 10 Russians to present the people of the United States with pieces of the bronze robe from Tsereteli's Columbus. Despite all the fanfare, Miami Beach would be the first of many cities to say *nyet* to Tsereteli's Columbus. Fort Lauderdale, Cleveland, and Columbus all passed, as did Baltimore, which called the monstrosity "From Russia with Ugh."[45] Aides to Mayor Rudy Giuliani said that they would resist the "Tseretelization" of New York, Trump's lobbying notwithstanding.[46]

Tsereteli's statue did finally find a home, though it wouldn't be on the mainland United States. Puerto Rico agreed to accept the statue, spending $12 million to erect it, while the U.S. territory teetered on the brink of bankruptcy. It was inaugurated in 2016 in Arecibo, a beach town on the northern side of the island about 50 miles from San Juan. Hurricane Maria struck a year later, destroying the town. Only Tsereteli's Columbus remained standing to oversee the damage.

4.
POST-SOVIET PAYOUTS

TO UNDERSTAND THE NEXT PHASE OF Trump's business career, when he began to partner with criminals and accept criminal money from the former Soviet Union, we need to step back for a moment and take a look at the other side of the equation. While Trump sold apartments in Trump Tower to criminals in the 1980s and welcomed them into his casino in the 1990s, Russia was disintegrating into what Boris Yeltsin described as a "superpower of crime."[1] The world largely ignored Yeltsin's plea and allowed organized crime to have its way. A little-noticed academic paper published in the 1990s predicted the future. "The present passivity against the growing power and entrenchment of post-Soviet organized crime may usher in a new form of authoritarianism with very severe long-term consequences for the citizens of the [f]ormer Soviet Union—and indeed for the rest of the world," wrote Louise Shelley, a professor who studied Russian organized crime.[2]

Organized crime in the Soviet Union was an outgrowth of a peculiar paradox. Citizens were conditioned to believe that making a profit or owning property was a crime, even as Gorbachev's era of perestroika—which saw social and economic restructuring during the final days of the Soviet Union—was allowing greater leniency toward capitalism. At the same time, the state turned a blind eye to a flourishing black market, a sort of pre-digital Alibaba, where anything from boom boxes to bread could be bought.

In the last days of the Soviet Union, the ones who were keeping the lights on in Russia were members of organized crime. They had what no one else did: access to goods and services. Criminals had learned to exploit the shortages of consumer goods created by the lumbering Soviet planned economy. As a result, they were the only ones with an understanding of market capitalism, crude as it was, and they could deliver what the people needed. Russia couldn't get rid of organized crime. It needed it to survive. When the USSR fell, any controls on this black market economy vanished, and many post-Soviet states were built back up with help from criminals.

Trump's long-standing interest in building a tower in Russia reflected what was happening to nearly all the post-Soviet states, which were turning into the Wild East. After the fall of the Soviet Union, it was Boris Yeltsin who would bring Russia into a market-based economy, and his methods would leave an impact long after his presidency. Yeltsin had followed the advice of his minister of privatization, Anatoly Chubais, who believed that the cure for the economic cancer of 70 years of communism was a radical embrace of capitalism. Chubias's "shock therapy" abruptly shifted the economy from a planned to a market economy, delivering an enormous amount of shock but little therapy. Price controls were eliminated, which unleased hyperinflation. That was followed by a massive sale of formerly state-owned property to Russian citizens, who were given a book of vouchers that represented shares in companies formerly held by the Soviet Union.

Most Russians did not understand the value of owning shares in private corporations, and being desperately poor, quickly sold off their vouchers to more economically savvy people who had better knowledge of how this new system worked. Thousands of Soviet firms were privatized in this haphazard way, which left a select few insiders or speculators in control of the vast industrial might of the USSR. And it wasn't just newly privatized industries that were being hijacked. Billions of dollars embezzled from party funds and sales of natural resources were stashed by former KGB agents in private banks. In the span of Yeltsin's first five-year term, these insiders and speculators formed a powerful oligarchy of businessmen that enjoyed cozy relations with many entrenched crime lords and former party members turned independent politicians. Under this tripartite rule, there would be no middle class. These new rulers of Russia began stashing their wealth abroad and quietly bought up trophy properties in London, New York, and Florida.

Anti-Semites made much of the fact that seven of the early oligarchs, who controlled half of the Russian economy in the 1990s, were Jewish. So were many of the major crime lords in Russia. This was not some secret Jewish conspiracy, but rather a result of circumstances. Jews in the Soviet Union were systematically denied opportunities on the basis of their religion. As a result, many turned to the black market to make ends meet. When the Soviet Union fell, they had a head start on their fellow countrymen, who had been taught to hate and fear capitalism.[3]

With revenue in the new Russia trickling into private pockets rather than being reinvested in the interest of the people, oligarchs nearly gutted the economies of many post-Soviet nations. Russia went into a humiliating decline that left the average citizen hankering for a return to the days of the Soviet Union. Poverty, mortality, and crime rates actually increased among the general populace during this period. By the end of Yeltsin's first term, these oligarchs and the president they backed had become the most despised people in all the post–Soviet Union states.

With Russia leading the way for oligarchs to build their private businesses into conglomerate empires, many of them began eyeing other developing post-Soviet nations to divvy up. Among the most tantalizing was Ukraine. Out of all the newly independent nations that had formed after the collapse of the Soviet Union, Ukraine was barely staying on its feet and remained the most dependent on Russia for stability. Ukraine's GDP in 1994 was half of what it had been at the outset of its independence in 1991, while inflation during the same period had increased by 10,000 percent. With such a pitiful economy, Ukraine became a feeding ground for organized criminals and greedy tycoons who were quickly developing an international network to exploit once national industries and maintain dominance over them. Which is how one oligarch, proposing the novel idea of "sharing interests in Ukraine," came to host one of the most historic gatherings of organized criminals no one was ever to know about.

—

IN OCTOBER 1995, A BUSINESSMAN named Boris Birshtein held a meeting in an office in the Diamond Center, a large commercial jewelry space in downtown Tel Aviv. In attendance were several Russian and Ukrainian *vory*, a who's who of the Russian and Ukrainian crime world. If the former Soviet Union had had its own version of the 10 Most Wanted, eight of them were now sharing a room.

Over the course of nine days in Israel, the group traveled around the country, all while being monitored by the Israeli National Police (INP). Using wiretaps, the INP noticed that the group was making phone calls to Russia, Hungary, and Paris. According to a report later published by the FBI, two phone lines were identified as belonging to a couple of the biggest names in Russian organized crime. Sergei Mikhailov, or "Mihas," was the head of the Solntsevskaya organization, Russia's biggest and most powerful criminal gang. Semion Mogilevich, or "Seva," ran his own organization—one that laundered money for Solntsevskaya and was involved in virtually every criminal activity imaginable.

That Birshtein had been able to bring together such powerful and feared figures gives a clue to the importance of their meeting, and of Birshtein's influence. While any of these crime lords could have made their own deals in Ukraine, Birshtein had connections to make these deals even more lucrative. He had given as much as $5 million to the 1994 campaign of Leonid Kuchma, a pro-Russian politician running for his first term as the country's president. Another of Birshtein's underworld Ukrainian connections was a man named Olexander Volkov, an aide to President Kuchma.

Though the FBI report notes dryly, "The subject of the meeting was the sharing of interests in Ukraine," the country wasn't just an innocent pie, but a gangster's paradise.[4] In the years after independence, Ukraine was a country with virtually no law enforcement. As bad as things were in Russia, at least it had the state police agency, the MVD, to battle the gangs. Ukraine had nothing, and in the time it took the new nation to create its own rules and institutions, its criminals and corrupt officials built up enormous domestic and international influence. Kuchma warned that the country faced a "secret syndicate of Ukrainian gangsters . . . much more dangerous than the Sicilian mafia."[5] Even Kuchma's prime minister, Pavel Lazarenko, would later be discovered to have looted $114 million from the country's banks.

But Birshtein existed at the center of a vast Venn diagram of corruption, bribery, and deception. He was the primary manager of the KGB's offshore funds after the collapse of the Soviet Union. President Boris Yeltsin even recalled being introduced to Birshtein as a "KGB agent." The Russian newspaper *Izvestia* described Birshtein as a gangster who moonlighted as a double agent, working for the KGB and the Mossad, the Israeli spy service, all at the same time.[6] Born in Lithuania, Birshtein left the Soviet Union in the late 1970s for Israel, and later ended up in Toronto where he established the Seabeco Group, which partnered with the Russian government in a large state-owned fertilizer company and a steelmaking concern. Birshtein flew around the world in a private jet and was treated like a head of state. When he landed in Moscow, a police motorcade with flashing lights and sirens escorted his limousine to his villa in the Lenin Hills, which was patrolled by armed guards in Russian military uniforms, *The Toronto Star* reported.[7] In 1991, he was picked to serve as an economic advisor to newly independent Kyrgyzstan, one of the former Soviet republics. He met with Canada's then prime minister Brian Mulroney and other top officials, but two years later, Birshtein was caught up in a scandal—involving billions in laundered money, 7 million tons of missing oil, and key Russian politicians—that rocked the Yeltsin government and led to the resignation or dismissal of several senior cabinet ministers, and Birshtein was forced to flee Toronto, now persona non grata.

Birshtein left Canada and turned his attention to his underworld connections and Ukraine at the Tel Aviv meeting. Wherever Birshtein went, scandal seemed to follow and the opportunities would only multiply.[8]

ONLY ONE THING COULD HINDER the plan: a head of state who couldn't be counted on to play along. At the time of the Tel Aviv meeting, Russian politicians were gearing up for the country's second presidential election, an event that many nations in the world were eyeing closely. Among the most contentious points affecting the country was corruption, which ran rampant. The popularity of and trust in Boris Yeltsin, the incumbent president, had dipped to below 10 percent, following what was seen as a bungling of Russia's entrance to capitalism. Yeltsin was largely to blame for the initiative to privatize many of Russia's resources and commodities, which made fortunes for a few individuals (the oligarchy), while the rest of the populace suffered from a failing economy. Though Aleksandr Lebed, the presidential contender who had met with Donald Trump in New York, was popular among right-wing nationalists for his hardline military reputation, he was a distant third to Yeltsin's biggest challenger, Gennady Zyuganov, head of Russia's newly revamped Communist Party, who stumped on a platform of bringing stability back to the country and fighting the crime and corruption that was growing out of control. The Russian populace was listening and, in 1995, the Communist Party claimed a majority of seats in the State Duma, Russia's lower house of congress. For most of the election, Zyuganov was so far ahead of Yeltsin in the polls that when the Communist candidate attended the World Economic Forum at Davos, Switzerland, world leaders lined up to meet who they assumed would be the next president of Russia. Also in attendance and not at all oblivious to Zyuganov's popularity were three of Russia's most powerful oligarchs, Mikhail Khodorkovsky, Vladimir Gusinsky, and Boris Berezovsky, who would form what would later be infamously known as the "Davos Pact," a plan to get the extremely unpopular Yeltsin reelected.[9] They had indirect help from Yeltsin's chummy relationship with U.S. president Bill Clinton. The "Bill and Boris Show," as it has been dubbed, marked a period when Yeltsin came to be seen as Clinton's oafish but endearing Eastern European buddy, sharing chuckles on the White House lawn. It didn't help that even back home, Yeltsin was seen as an embarrassing drunkard who often had to be held in place as he teetered to and fro during speeches. But as Clinton supplied Yeltsin with American aid, the American president also launched NATO campaigns to democratize several former Soviet states, including Ukraine, Russia's longest-held territory. With Yeltsin being criticized on the left for bringing Russia to social instability, and on the right for being humbled by its former Cold War foe, a Yeltsin victory seemed highly unlikely. Yet, in an election widely considered to be fraudulent, Yeltsin was ushered back in for a second term in the summer of 1996. The oligarchs and vory had won.

With Yeltsin reelected, the oligarchy assured of its place, and Birshtein-funded candidate Kuchma installed in the Ukrainian presidency, the Ukraine plan only required getting the right people in the right positions. One of the most notorious of these would be one of Birshtein's former Seabeco employees, a man named Alexander Shnaider, who had left the firm to form Midland, a steel trade company with operations in Ukraine, where the steel industry accounted for 25 percent of the country's GDP. After the country's steel industry was privatized, Shnaider acquired 93 percent of shares of Zaporizhstal, Ukraine's fourth-largest steel mill. By the time of the Tel Aviv meeting, Shnaider had married Birshtein's daughter. But his new son-in-law was hardly Birshtein's only wily former employee; two other Seabeco alums, Alexander Mashkevitch and Patokh Chodiev, along with a Kazakh entrepreneur named Alijan Ibragimov, purchased many of Kazakhstan's natural resource companies and launched Eurasian Natural Resources Corp., a company that would end up with a revenue equal to nearly 5 percent of Kazakhstan's GDP. The "Kazakh Trio," as they would come to be known, would later expand their practices to include luxurious property and hotel ventures.

But while Birshtein was connected, Mogilevich, "the boss of bosses," was crafty. Unlike other vory, Mogilevich encouraged his people to use their heads before their fists and guns, and it was with his help that the Russian Mafiya evolved from petty criminals to a sophisticated inter-connected syndicate. While he wasn't immune to the dangers of the underworld (Mikhailov once accused Mogilevich of cheating him out of millions and tried to have him killed at a birthday party at his Prague Black & White club), Mogilevich tended to chase white-collar rather than blue-collar criminal pursuits. His lieutenants weren't street thugs, but often people with advanced degrees, which is how they were able to turn a Budapest-based magnet maker named Magnex, which Mogilevich had acquired to use as a front company for his criminal organization, into an international corporation.

In 1990, Mogilevich incorporated a company called Arigon Ltd. on the Channel Islands and used it to launder proceeds from extortion and trafficking, a service he extended to Mikhailov's Solntsevskaya organi-zation, while selling illicit oil to the Ukrainian railways on the side. In 1994, Mogilevich's Magnex company "acquired" Arigon, and renamed his growing company YBM Magnex (the initials apparently didn't mean anything). The reverse-takeover ballooned YBM Magnex's worth and it was publicly listed on the Toronto Stock Exchange only five months after Birshstein's Tel Aviv meeting.

———

IN 1995, BRITISH DETECTIVES ACTING on a tip that Arigon was run-ning a money-laundering operation raided the London law firm that represented it in a sting called Operation Sword. There they uncov-ered records that revealed Arigon was part of a network of companies owned by YBM Magnex International Inc., a corporation based in the quaint Philadelphia commuter village of Newtown. Also under the YBM umbrella was the Budapest-based manufacturer Magnex RA and the Alberta-based Pratecs Technologies. British authorities shut down Arigon but continued to track YBM Magnex, which was headed by none other than David Bogatin's brother, Jacob. While David served time in Attica, Mogilevich had provided Jacob Bogatin with $2.4 million in seed money to get YBM up and running in the United States. Bogatin later joined YBM's board along with such luminaries as David Peterson, a former premier of the Canadian province of Ontario. Soon after Arigon was shuttered, Pratecs became YBM Magnex, and YBM opened a new sales, finance, and distribution wing, United Trade, headquartering it in the Cayman Islands under the watch of a financier named Igor Fisherman.[10] YBM Magnex billed itself as a leading producer of permanent industrial magnets and high-tech bicycles that the company claimed were used by Russia's Olympic team. It boasted of its spacious Pennsylvania corporate office and warehouse and sent frequent press releases announcing significant deals and developments. Over four years, "net sales quadrupled, net income jumped nine fold, earnings rose by a factor of five, and the future looked just as promising," *The Philadelphia Inquirer* reported.[11] YBM Magnex was performing well enough that it was included in the Toronto Stock Exchange's index of 300 leading companies. When an accounting firm revealed to the FBI that YBM Magnex had tried to bribe one of its auditors to certify the accuracy of its financial statements, it seemed time to pay YBM Magnex a visit.

Charlie Murray, a veteran agent stationed at the Philadelphia bureau, had never heard of Mogilevich until British investigators informed him that YBM was in fact owned by one of the world's most ruthless gangsters. They described Mogilevich as a criminal involved with just about every illegal activity imaginable—an FBI report listed prostitution, weapons trafficking, smuggling of nuclear materials, drug trafficking, dealing in precious gems, and money laundering. Yet the only thing Murray could find on Semion Mogilevich was a 20-year-old currency-related conviction in Kiev. From decades of experience working La Cosa Nostra cases in New York and Philadelphia, Murray knew that mobsters usually left a trail, but Mogilevich had been able to conceal his steps. Murray knew this wasn't an easy thing to do, even for a powerful crime boss, and this fact didn't settle easy with him.[12]

Murray and his team didn't want to tip off the company or Mogilevich, and they kept the YBM investigation under wraps for more than a year as Murray built up a case to take down not just YBM Magnex but Mogilevich himself. The FBI got a judge's permission to wiretap YBM around Christmas 1997. For three months, agents listened to numerous incriminating conversations between Mogilevich associates, adding to the growing body of evidence of the YBM fraud. Murray declined to say what he overheard, but FBI reports note that Mogilevich's people had the habit of speaking openly on the phone, just as he had back in Tel Aviv. On May 13, 1998, the FBI descended on YBM's offices in Newtown armed with a search warrant. The company's site was so huge that officers had to be posted overnight so the search could continue the next day. During that time they discovered files containing bank statements, invoices, and purchase orders for millions of dollars in magnet sales, as well as thousands of pages of additional documents related to the profitable business. What they didn't find were magnets and bikes. The whole thing had been a carefully crafted illusion, a means of legitimizing the proceeds of Mogilevich's sprawling criminal enterprise. "It was a cash cow," Murray later told me.

When news broke, trading in YBM was halted, and a few months later, the company confirmed shareholders' worst fears. YBM's business was, as a class-action lawsuit put it, hopelessly mired in criminal conduct, its commercial activities impossible to audit and verify, and its common stock worthless. The sheer complexity of the YBM Magnex fraud, which involved tracing "magnet" sales and records to 25 countries, including the Republic of Nauru in the South Pacific, would take years to unravel. The company pleaded guilty to a charge of conspiracy to commit fraud in the United States and agreed to pay a fine of

$3 million. Investors ultimately lost $150 million, but Murray said that it could have been much worse. YBM had filed papers for a listing on the NASDAQ exchange, which would almost certainly have made the scale of the fraud exponentially larger.

Not long after the YBM Magnex investigation began, FBI agents were assigned to work hand-in-hand with the Hungarian National Police in Budapest on a joint organized-crime task force. Mogilevich relied on a network of former Hungarian police to keep him informed and word that the FBI was in town convinced him it was time to go. FBI Director Robert Mueller acknowledged the contributions of the task force during a visit to Budapest. "As soon as the task force began investigating his activities, Mogilevich realized he could no longer use Budapest as his base of operations," Mueller said. "He immediately fled the country, and is now hiding in Moscow." The hunt for Mogilevich was a top priority during Mueller's term as director.

Much of the evidence for the YBM case lay in Russia. "We just didn't have a warm and fuzzy feeling about working with the Russians at that time," Murray told me. It was clear to the FBI that Russian authorities were stalling for time. It took a year for Murray to get answers from Moscow. Russian law enforcement could make him wait, but Charlie Murray was a patient man. He had spent a decade investigating La Cosa Nostra concrete construction firms in a case that gave the FBI access to the leadership of the five New York Mafia families. So he would patiently wait for answers, make use of the scanty information that was provided, and then ask more questions. Still, he sometimes wondered about the outcome. With no extradition treaty between the two countries, there was no way to force Russia to hand over Mogilevich. "It was always in the back of my mind, if we indict this guy are we going to get them?" he said. As long as Mogilevich stayed in the good graces of the Kremlin, Russian law enforcement wasn't going to make Charlie Murray's job any easier. And Mogilevich's relationship with Vladimir Putin ran very deep.

AT THE TIME OF THE Tel Aviv meeting, Vladimir Putin was still a mid-level St. Petersburg bureaucrat. As an advisor to the mayor, Anatoly Sobchak, Putin's future was up in the air when Sobchak lost his reelection bid. Upon Yeltsin's reelection victory in the summer of 1996, however, Putin was tapped by the administration to be the deputy of its property management department, which managed the inventory of overseas property seized from the Communist Party.

Yeltsin noticed something of a leader in Putin and began preparing him for bigger responsibilities. Within three years, he was thrice promoted, first to deputy chief of Yeltsin's presidential staff, and then to the director of the Russian security service, the FSB, the successor to the KGB. But his ascendancy may have had something to do with the brutality he showed toward opponents. One revealing chapter in this story involves Putin's efforts to suppress an investigation by Yuri Skuratov, the Russian prosecutor general, into a kickback scandal that involved the head of the presidential property management department and members of Yeltsin's inner circle. Skuratov was told in no uncertain terms to drop the investigation, and, when he refused, he was shown what the Russians called *kompromat*: a tape of him, or someone who resembled him, having sex with prostitutes.

To his credit, Skuratov still held firm, and the tape aired on state television. It was a sensation, and a huge debate ensued over whether the tape was real or fake news. Putin personally led the inquiry and announced that the man in the video was indeed the prosecutor general. Skuratov finally resigned, and in a private moment, he said that Putin tried to cheer him up. "Alas, Yuri," Putin told him, "they say that there is a similar film about me."[13]

In August of 1999, Putin was named deputy prime minister, and at the same time, Yeltsin's designated successor. With Yeltsin's blessing, Putin announced his bid for the presidency. Three months later, on New Year's Eve, the last day of the twentieth century, Yeltsin abruptly resigned and Putin, still largely unknown to the Russian public, brought Russia into the twenty-first century as its acting president. Because of Yeltsin's resignation, the Russian presidential election of 2000, due to be held in June, was moved up to March. In the three intervening months, Putin used his temporary presidential powers to crack down on Chechen terrorism, then afflicting cities such as Moscow and St. Petersburg, an effort that made him not only much more recognized in Russia, but also boosted his popularity. When a formal election was held, Putin swept up the votes to victory. At the top of his agenda was making Russia great again.

A video posted to the Internet shows Putin's campaign office on election day. The future president is seen watching the results with a dozen friends and staff. The video seems innocuous enough, boring even, until one man turns his face to the camera. There has been intense speculation that the face may be that of Semion Mogilevich.

Alexander Litvinenko, a former KGB officer turned fierce critic of the Russian president, revealed the alleged ties between the Russian state and Mogilevich. According to Litvinenko, Russian intelligence used Mogilevich to carry out actions—including suspected weapons sales to al Qaida—that the state could not undertake on its own. "For this very reason the FSB is hiding Mogilevich from the FBI," Litvinenko wrote in a letter to Italian investigators.[14] Litvinenko also worked to transcribe and translate tapes of Ukrainian president Leonid Kuchma's conversations, which were secretly recorded by one of his bodyguards. In one conversation, Kuchma spoke with Leonid Derkach, the former head of the Ukrainian security services:

KUCHMA: Have you found Mogilevich?
DERKACH: I found him.
KUCHMA: So, are you two working now?
DERKACH: We're working. We have another meeting tomorrow. He arrives incognito.

Later in the discussion, Derkach revealed a few details about Mogilevich.

DERKACH: He's on good terms with Putin. He and Putin have been in contact since Putin was still in Leningrad.

KUCHMA: I hope we won't have any problems because of this.

DERKACH: They have their own affairs.[15]

In 2001, five years after Murray first heard Mogilevich's name, the U.S. Attorney's office in Philadelphia decided that the FBI had enough material to take to a grand jury. There was so much evidence that presenting it all to the grand jury took a year. Finally, on March 13, 2002, after six years of investigation, Murray's tenacity paid off. While he waited anxiously in federal court in Philadelphia, he learned that a grand jury had returned a 45-count indictment charging Mogilevich, Jacob Bogatin, and others with racketeering, securities fraud, and money laundering. Just as Murray had feared, however, all of the FBI's hard work failed to bring Mogilevich to justice. Mogilevich remained in Russia, possibly protected by the FSB. The FBI added him to its 10 Most Wanted list, but without a formal extradition treaty between the two countries, he was out of reach. Jacob Bogatin's defense attorney cleverly used Mogilevich's absence to get his client off. Bogatin refused to sever his case and argued he had to be tried alongside the Brainy Don. Unable to proceed, prosecutors had no choice but to let Bogatin go.

Litvinenko, the man who revealed Putin's ties to Mogilevich, sought and was granted asylum by the British government, where he continued to investigate the criminal dealings of the Putin administration. In 2006, he had a business meeting with two Russians at a bar in London. During his meeting, one of Litvinenko's contacts slipped radioactive polonium into his tea, killing him in what an inquest showed to be a Russian government plot. Disclosure of such highly sensitive and damaging information as Mogilevich's links to Putin, the British inquest concluded, may have been one of the reasons for Litvinenko's gruesome murder.[16]

Putin's rise from the KGB to the presidency of Russia revealed his deep connections, dating back years, to some of the same organized-crime figures who were in the shadows of Trump's business empire. These were connections that could be very useful to a man like Putin, who was intimately familiar with the Russian game of kompromat, the use of compromising sex videos to blackmail and gain leverage over political opponents. And Trump, a man of voracious appetites, was uniquely susceptible to blackmail.

PART II

THE COMEBACK KID

5.
LITTLE MOSCOW

IT WAS A LITTLE MORE THAN a year into the new millennium, and television producer Mark Burnett was on top of the world. The reality television series he had produced, *Survivor*, had become the most talked-about show in America after debuting in May 2000. By the finale of its first season, *Survivor* was reaching more than 50 million weekly viewers and it the most-watched summer show since *Sonny & Cher*. The show's second season was to air on January 28, 2001, right after Super Bowl XXXV. That morning, Burnett sat for an interview with CNN anchor Greta Van Susteren, who fired off questions about reality TV: "Where is it going? How long can this trend last? What does it say about our culture?"

Before answering, Burnett ticked off three more *Survivor*-esque shows he planned to produce. The third was the most outlandish. In *Destination Mir*, contestants in a made-for-TV astronaut-training competition would challenge each other for the opportunity to be "strapped inside a Soyuz rocket and blasted into outer space." Bill Carter, a media reporter for *The New York Times* who was shadowing Burnett, later wrote that soon after Van Susteren departed, Burnett, "half-crowing and half-cowed," admitted a rather juicy detail about *Destination Mir*.

"Putin is involved," he said.[1]

Burnett confessed that he had been negotiating with the Kremlin to have Putin on the show in some way, no matter the public response. "I think *Mir* is going to be hard only as a political thing," he told Carter. "The show will be easy. I really want to do a space show. And, typically, I'm quite good at making things happen." Nothing came of *Destination Mir*, but a few years later, Hollywood's darling reality-TV producer would have another hit series after he approached a notable real estate tycoon about a contest set in his signature building.

Like *Survivor*, *The Apprentice* was also set in a jungle, albeit one made of glass and concrete rather than flora and fauna. Its contestants competed for a high-level position within the Trump Organization rather than a $1 million cash prize, but *The Apprentice* was as seismic a television event as *Survivor*. Burnett had been right; his "dramality" model had struck a chord with America. Its host had initially waved off Burnett's pitch to lure him into the show. Reality TV "was for the bottom feeders of society," Trump believed.[2] It was the opportunity to revive his broken image before the entire country that won him over. While Trump had spent the 1990s desperately trying to recover the empire the 1980s Trump had built, the 2000s Trump was beginning once again to stand on his own loafered feet.

The Apprentice clinched that recovery by recasting Trump as America's CEO. "My name is Donald Trump," he says in *The Apprentice*'s opening monologue, "and I'm the largest real estate developer in New York. I own buildings all over the place, model agencies, the Miss Universe Pageant, jetliners, golf courses, casinos, and private resorts like Mar-a-Lago, one of the most spectacular estates anywhere in the world." Trump then adds a rags-to-riches story, "I was billions of dollars in debt. But I fought back and won—big league. I used my brain. I used my negotiating skills. And I worked it all out. Now my company is bigger than it ever was and stronger than it ever was and I'm having more fun than I ever had." Those words and images would be burned into the minds of millions of Americans for years to come.

In this opening monologue, which lasts over four minutes, Trump glossed over many facts. He was still emerging from bankruptcy, slapping his brand name on just about everything from steaks to a bicycle race to earn a few shekels. He was no longer the largest real estate developer in the city. His jetliners were gone and his casinos in shambles. He'd even made an abortive presidential run in 2000, announcing his bid for the Reform Party nomination on *Larry King Live* in October of 1999 and ending it a short time later.

It was a very different Trump who ran for president in the 2000 election. He stumped for universal healthcare and openly considered Oprah Winfrey as his running mate. After his withdrawal, Trump wrote in an op-ed that America wasn't ready yet for a "straight-talking businessman" president. Trump, then still Democrat-friendly, noted his discomfort with many of the Reform Party's supporters, including David Duke, a former grand wizard of the Ku Klux Klan, and conservative firebrand Pat Buchanan. Then there were the party's fringe voters, people who "wanted to repeal the federal income tax, believed that the country was being run by the Trilateral Commission." A presidential run paled in comparison to having built "one of the great skyscrapers of Manhattan," though he ended his piece by noting that he could not rule out another bid for the presidency.[3]

Trump toyed with the idea of another run in 2004, but by the time of *The Apprentice*'s debut that same year, he had happily set aside politics for entertainment. He had his own TV show filmed right in the comfort of his own home in his beloved Trump Tower, the other star of *The Apprentice*. Trump Tower featured prominently in the opening credits, soundtracked by the O'Jays song "For the Love of Money." It appeared imposing but desirous, the place where anyone with a wild dream of success would want to end up. Trump Tower appealed to millions of the "bottom feeders" who had now become his biggest fans. Trump's newfound nationwide TV popularity after *The Apprentice* would boost Trump Tower in New York as a brand. Throngs of tourists now flooded its galleries while its apartments remained a magnet for more affluent residents. It was the holy grail of business ambition, the closest thing to a castle one could own in America, and on its throne was Trump, America's greatest boss. At least that was the myth told to millions of viewers. Behind the scenes it would be other pieces of real estate—and the clients who were drawn to them—that would help Trump make a financial comeback.

—

AFTER THE FAILURE OF HIS earlier ventures in Russia, Donald Trump returned to the Baltschug Hotel in Moscow in the fall of 2002 with a new business model. He must have realized at some point that building in Moscow was not the only way to capture the vast flows of Russian money that were being looted out of the state. This time, he wasn't planning to build any Trump towers in Moscow or anywhere else in Russia. He was there to sell apartments nearly 5,000 miles away. Why build in Moscow when Trump could build in New York with Russian money?

Trump wanted to make it easy for well-heeled Russians to buy one of his luxury Manhattan apartments "without even leaving the country," *The Moscow Times* wrote. His real estate agent, Sotheby's International, had partnered with Moscow-based Kirsanova Realty to open an office in the Russian capital where Trump's apartments could be sold to Russians who were interested in buying abroad.[4]

Trump was offering apartments in two new buildings in Manhattan that bore his name. Trump World Tower stood right across the street from the United Nations headquarters on the East Side. At 72 stories, it would briefly hold the title of the tallest residential building in the world. On the West Side, two condominium towers known as Trump Place were being built on a tract of land overlooking the Hudson River known as the West Side Yards. Prices ranged from a minimum of $1 million to as much as $30 million for a penthouse. On top of that were astronomical property taxes reaching as high as $15,000 a month.

Trump was the star attraction at the Baltschug Hotel, but Moscow-based reporters noticed a curious thing about the event. No one in attendance would admit that they were there to buy an apartment. "Potential customers present at yesterday's presentation of New York real estate not only refused to identify themselves, but also did not admit they were interested in this real estate, insisting that they simply went for 'pies to eat,'" the Russian newspaper *Vedomosti* reported.[5]

The embarrassment could be explained by the fact that the few Russians who could afford a million-dollar apartment in New York didn't owe their wealth to business smarts. It was largely connections—who you knew, not what you knew—that determined who rose and who didn't in the new Russia of Vladimir Putin. The new class of Russian businessmen and criminals who would become Trump's customers didn't want to keep their money in Russia. The wealthiest of Russians weren't interested in a Trump Tower in Moscow. A tower in New York—now, that was something that interested them. As the 2003 arrest and imprisonment of Mikhail Khodorkovsky, the owner of the Russian oil giant Yukos and the country's richest man, made painfully clear, if you were wealthy in Russia, your money was never secure. Your money was only safe if and when it moved out of the country, beyond the reach of the Kremlin. Even if the owners never set foot in New York, an apartment in Trump World Tower was a secure way to store assets. It was a safety deposit box for wealthy Russians.

This was Trump's unspoken sales pitch: Come to New York. Come to Florida. You can enjoy your money, no questions asked. "Now, Russian connoisseurs of high-class housing will have the opportunity to become neighbors of well-known politicians, businessmen and Hollywood stars," said an executive with Sotheby's International Realty.[6]

Trump didn't deny that his condos were magnets for foreign money. He bragged about it in full-page ads in *New York* magazine. "The Trump Factor" was the headline over a personal letter signed by Trump. After noting seven of the top 10 most expensive condo sales were in buildings with his name on them, Trump wrote, "The world's most affluent buyers place a premium on the Trump name—and they're willing to pay a premium for it."[7]

—

LIKE TRUMP TOWER A MILE to the east, Trump World Tower lured several celebrity residents, including Derek Jeter, Sophia Loren, and Harrison Ford, along with future members of Trump's inner circle. Eastern European and Central Asian oligarchs, who carried the kind of pocketbooks Trump was hoping for, also leased several condos. An investigation by *Bloomberg BusinessWeek* found that one-third of the units sold on floors 76 through 83 by 2004 involved people or limited-liability companies connected to Russia and neighboring states. "We had big buyers from Russia and Ukraine and Kazakhstan," Debra Stotts, one of the World Tower's sales agents, told the magazine.[8]

The first wave of tenants was helped by a Ukrainian-born electronics store owner turned commodities trader named Sam Kislin, who later became a major donor to Rudolph Giuliani's 1994 and 1997 mayoral campaigns. Kislin began issuing condo mortgages to people like his longtime friend Vasily Salygin, a future official in the Ukrainian Party of Regions, the same party Paul Manafort would help return to power. Kislin and Trump's relationship stretched back as far as 1976, when the future president purchased 200 televisions on credit from Kislin's electronics store for his newly acquired Commodore Hotel. Exactly how Trump found the store isn't clear, for Joy-Lud Electronics was the only store in New York that catered exclusively to a Soviet clientele. Foreign Minister Andrei Gromyko paid a visit. So did Yevgeny Primakov, a future foreign intelligence chief. Ditto for Georgy Arbatov, who served as the Kremlin's American-based media spokesman. At the time, Kislin's business partner in Joy-Lud was Tamir Sapir, who would partner with Trump on a real estate development 40 years later and live in a massive Trump Tower condo of his own.

In 1989, Kislin opened a company in New York called Trans Commodities Inc. and began trading metals and raw materials from the Soviet Union. His Russian partner was Michael Cherney. Like Vyacheslav Ivankov, Semion Mogilevich, and others, Cherney's name surfaces repeatedly in this story. Cherney has long faced allegations— which he has denied—that he and his brother, Lev, are connected to Russian organized crime. Cherney handled the Russian end of the business using what he described to a London court as his "extensive connections in various governmental structures." When the partnership ended in 1992, Kislin and Cherney each received a $100 million profit.[9]

In addition to trading goods from the former Soviet Union, Trans Commodities Inc. sponsored more than 100 Russian nationals entering the United States. These included Joseph Kobzon, the "Frank Sinatra" of Russia, who was the "spiritual leader" of the Russian Mafiya, as well as another man described by the FBI as a contract killer. In addition, Kislin was a "close associate" of the late notorious arms smuggler Babeck Seroush, who later settled in Russia. A 1994 FBI report identified Kislin and his nephew as members of the organization of the *vor* Vyacheslav Ivankov. Kislin denied these allegations.[10]

Eduard Nektalov, a diamond dealer born in Uzbekistan, purchased a $1.6 million apartment in Trump World Tower in July 2003, a time when federal agents were investigating him for a money-laundering scheme. Nektalov sold his unit a month after he bought it for a $500,000 profit. He would be gunned down on Manhattan's Sixth Avenue in 2004.[11] Living one floor above Nektalov was Kellyanne Conway, who would become a familiar face to Americans as one of Trump's staunchest defenders and eventual counselor to the future president. An even bigger investor in Trump World Tower and other Trump properties was Michael D. Cohen, who joined the Trump Organization in 2006, as Trump's personal lawyer, a role once occupied by Roy Cohn, Senator Joseph McCarthy's heavy-lidded hatchet man during the Red Scare days, who advised Trump in the 1980s. Michael Cohen's bare-knuckled tactics had earned him the nickname of "Tom," a reference to Tom

Hagen, the consigliore to Mafia Don Vito Corleone in *The Godfather*.[12]

Like Tom Hagen, Cohen had grown up around organized crime, specifically the Russian Mafiya. Cohen's uncle, Morton Levine, was a wealthy Brooklyn doctor who owned the El Caribe Country Club, a Brooklyn catering hall and event space that was a well-known hangout for Russian gangsters. Cohen and his siblings all had ownership stakes in the club, which rented for years to Evsei Agron, the first Mafiya boss of Brighton Beach; his successor, Marat Balagula; and Boris Nayfeld.[13] Cohen's uncle said his nephew gave up his stake in the club after Trump's election.[14]

Cohen married into a Ukrainian family. I spoke to two former federal investigators who told me Cohen was introduced to Trump by Cohen's father-in-law, Fima Shusterman, a naturalized U.S. citizen from Ukraine with a 1993 conviction for a money-laundering-related crime. "Fima may have been a (possibly silent) business partner with Trump, perhaps even used as a conduit for Russian investors in Trump properties and other ventures," a former federal investigator told me. "Cohen, who married into the family, was given the job with the Trump Org as a favor to Shusterman." ("Untrue," Cohen told me. "Your source is creating fake news.") In addition, Shusterman, who owned at least four New York taxi companies, set his son-in-law up in the yellow cab business. Cohen once ran 260 yellow cabs with his Ukrainian-born partner, the "taxi king" Simon V. Garber, until their partnership ended acrimoniously.

Glenn Simpson, the private investigator who was independently hired to examine Trump's Russia connections during the real estate mogul's presidential run, testified before the House Intelligence Committee that Cohen "had a lot of connections to the former Soviet Union, and that he seemed to have associations with organized crime figures in New York and Florida, Russian organized crime figures," including Garber.[15]

Cohen wasn't the only member of his family who married a Ukrainian woman. His brother, Bryan, also had a Ukrainian father-in-law. Alex Oronov was a naturalized American citizen who raised his family in New York where he worked for many years as an art dealer specializing in Russian artists. Then, in 1994, Oronov left the art world behind and returned to Ukraine to help launch Grain Alliance, an agricultural venture to make Ukraine "the world's bread basket." It wouldn't be long before Oronov brought the Cohen brothers over to Ukraine to explore business deals in bioethanol.

Another curious episode in Cohen's life occurred in 1999 when he received a $350,000 check from the professional hockey player Vladimir Malakhov, who was then playing for the NHL's Montreal Canadiens. According to Malakhov, the check—made out to Cohen—was a loan to a friend. The friend, however, swore in an affidavit that she never received the money and never even knew the check had been written until it was discovered years later in a Florida lawsuit. So what happened to the money? Cohen was asked this question in a deposition and said he didn't know. He also didn't know Malakhov or anyone else in the case. One interesting lead was an incident involving Malakhov, who was approached in Brighton Beach and shaken down for money by a man who worked for the vor Vyacheslav Ivankov. "Malakhov spent the next months in fear, looking over his shoulder to see if he was being followed, avoiding restaurants and clubs where Russian criminals hang out," according to testimony an unnamed Russian criminal gave to the U.S. Senate in 1996. The problem went away when Malakhov was traded to Montreal.[16] Cohen offered his own theories as to the origin and fate of the check.

Q. You don't recall why this check was written to you for $350,000 in 1999 and how these funds left your trust account in any way, shape or form?
A: Clearly Vladimir Malakhov had to have known somebody who I was affiliated to and the only person I can—and I mentioned my partner's name, Simon Garber, who happens also to be Russian.[17]

Regardless of what he did or didn't know, Cohen was able to purchase a $1 million condo at Trump World Tower in 2001, persuading his
parents, his Ukrainian in-laws, and his partner in the New York City taxi
business to do the same in other Trump buildings. Cohen's in-laws Fima
and Ania Shusterman bought three units in Trump World Tower worth
a combined $7.66 million (one of which was rented to Jocelyn Wilden-
stein, the socialite known as "Catwoman" for undergoing extreme facial
plastic surgery to please her cat-loving husband).[18] Michael Cohen later
purchased a nearly $5 million unit in Trump Park Avenue. In a five-year
period, Cohen and people connected to him would purchase Trump
properties worth $17.3 million.

All the frenzied buying by Cohen and his family caught the attention of the *New York Post*, often described as Trump's favorite newspaper.
"Michael Cohen has a great insight into the real-estate market," Trump
told the newspaper in 2007. "He has invested in my buildings because
he likes to make money—and he does." Trump added, "In short, he's a
very smart person."[19]

During Trump's presidential run, reporters noticed a curious thing
about Michael Cohen. Questions about Trump's business or his taxes
went to his chief legal officer or another staffer, but Cohen handled questions about Russia. Cohen also took care of the many tabloid charges the
president faced. That included a $130,000 payment Cohen said came out
of his own pocket to silence porn star Stormy Daniels, who was about to
go public with a story of her affair with Trump. This was Cohen, doing
what he had always done. "I will always protect Mr. Trump," he said.[20]

A YEAR AFTER TRUMP WORLD Tower opened in 2002, another new development went on sale in Sunny Isles Beach, a seaside Florida town just
north of Miami. Trump had agreed to let Miami father-and-son developers Gil and Michael Dezer use his name on what ultimately became six
Sunny Isles Beach condominium towers, which drew in new moneyed
Russians all too eager to pay millions. "Russians love the Trump brand,"

said Gil Dezer, who added that Russians and Russian Americans had bought some 200 of the 2,000 or so units in Trump buildings he built.[21] A seventh Trump-branded hotel tower built up Sunny Isles into what ostensibly has become a South Florida Brighton Beach.

With direct flights from Moscow to Miami, Russian soon became the lingua franca of Trump Towers Sunny Isles Beach. "Thanks to its heavy Russian presence, Sunny Isles has acquired the nickname 'Little Moscow,'" journalist Ken Silverstein wrote. "Shops at a mall across the street from the Trump International Resort include a delicatessen offering blintzes and beef stroganoff, a furniture store with white leather sofas in the display window and restaurants serving an Eastern European clientele."[22] Nearby restaurants offered the same kitschy nightclub acts that I had once experienced myself at the Rasputin in Brighton Beach.

An investigation by Reuters found that at least 63 individuals with Russian passports or addresses have bought at least $98.4 million worth of property in the seven Trump-branded luxury towers. And that was a conservative estimate. At least 703—or about one-third—of the 2044 units were owned by limited-liability companies, or LLCs, which could conceal the property's true owner.[23] Executives from Gazprom and other Russian natural resources giants also owned units in Trump's Sunny Isles towers.

Numerous criminals were also drawn to Trump's towers in southern Florida. Residents included people like Vladimir Popovyan, who paid $1.17 million for a three-bedroom condo in 2013. *Forbes Russia* described Popovyan as a friend and associate of Rafael Samurgashev, a former championship wrestler who ran a criminal group in Rostov-on-Don in southeastern Russia.[24] Peter Kiritchenko, a Ukrainian businessman arrested on fraud charges in San Francisco in 1999, and his daughter owned two units at Trump Towers in Sunny Isles Beach worth $2.56 million.[25] (Kiritchenko testified against a corrupt former Ukrainian prime minister who was convicted in 2004 of money laundering.) Other owners of Trump condos in Sunny Isles include members of a Russian-American organized-crime group that ran a sports betting ring out of Trump Tower, that catered to wealthy oligarchs from the former Soviet Union. Michael Barukhin, who was convicted in a massive scheme to defraud auto insurers with phony claims, lived out of a Trump condo that was registered to a limited-liability corporation.

In an observation that several people I spoke with echoed, Kenneth McCallion, a former prosecutor who tracked the flows of Russian criminal money into Trump's properties, told me, "Trump's genius—or evil genius—was, instead of Russian criminal money being passive, incidental income, it became a central part of his business plan." McCallion continued, "It's not called 'Little Moscow' for nothing. The street signs are in Russian. But his towers there were built specifically for the Russian middle-class criminal."

Selling units from the lobby of the Trump International Beach Resort in Sunny Isles was Baronoff Realty. Elena Baronoff, who died of cancer in 2015, was the exclusive sales agent for three Trump-branded towers. Glenn Simpson, who spent a year investigating Trump's background during the campaign, testified before the House Intelligence Committee that Baronoff was a "suspected organized crime figure."[26]

An Uzbek immigrant who arrived in the United States as a cultural attaché in public diplomacy from the Soviet Union, Baronoff became such a well-known figure in Sunny Isles Beach that she was named the international ambassador for the community. Baronoff accompanied Trump's children on a trip to Russia in the winter of 2007–2008, posing for a photo in Moscow with Ivanka and Eric Trump and developer Michael Dezer. Also in the photo, curiously, was a man named Michael Babel, a former senior executive of a property firm owned by Russian metals tycoon Oleg Deripaska. Babel later fled Russia to evade fraud charges.

Baronoff had interesting connections to Sicily. She reportedly met her friend, the Russian foreign minister Sergey Lavrov, there. Baronoff was also close with Dino Papale, a local businessman, who described himself to *The New York Times* as "president of Trump's Sicilian fan club," while sporting a red "Make America Great Again" cap. Days after Trump's election in November, the local newspaper, *La Sicilia*, quoted Papale at length describing Trump's secret visit to the island in 2013. Papale hinted that he organized meetings between Trump and Russians.[27]

Michael Cohen's in-laws, the Shustermans, also bought real estate in Sunny Isles. In 2003, Cohen traveled down there to invest $1.5 million in a short-lived Miami-based casino-boat venture run by his two Ukrainian business partners, Arkady Vaygensberg and Leonid Tatarchuk. Only three months after its maiden voyage, it would become the subject of a large fraud investigation. But Cohen was saved from his bad investment by none other than Trump himself, who hired Cohen just before his casino ship sank.[28]

Meanwhile, Trump Towers Sunny Isles Beach was paying off. Trump's oldest son, Don Jr., would later note, "We see a lot of money pouring in from Russia." There is no question Trump owed his comeback in large part to wealthy Russian expatriates.

A Russian billionaire bought a mansion Trump was selling in Palm Beach that nobody else seemed to want. Dmitry Rybolovlev, a fertilizer tycoon, paid a record $95 million in 2008 for the sprawling oceanfront mansion called Maison de l'Amitié ("House of Friendship"). Trump had bought the home less than four years earlier for $41.35 million. The home was plagued by mold, and the fertilizer tycoon got permission to demolish Maison de l'Amitié and sell off the land beneath it. Rybolovlev said through a spokesman that he never met Trump, his family, or his advisors and has no connection to them whatsoever.

As was to be expected, given its history, as Trump rebuilt his real estate empire, criminal activity began to roost in the original Trump Tower. One case involved an eccentric U.S. Soccer Administration's vice president and FIFA executive committee member Chuck Blazer. Along with renting an $18,000-a-month Trump Tower apartment, Blazer reportedly also maintained a $6,000-a-month apartment just for his cats. Blazer would become a pal of Putin and a vocal supporter of Russia's winning bid to host the 2018 World Cup. He would later be one of the FIFA officials indicted on charges of bribery as part of a widespread corruption case.[29] But even Blazer's infractions cannot compare to the chicanery of two other tenants who would run a money-laundering operation only a few floors below Trump's penthouse. If Trump was unaware of the clandestine behavior occurring in his tower, it may have been because his attention was increasingly drawn outside of it.

6.

BUILDING TRUMP TOWERS AND HUNTING BIN LADEN

IN SEPTEMBER OF 2007, A LAVISH rooftop party was thrown in Manhattan's Tribeca neighborhood to celebrate the grand opening of Trump SoHo. It was the first Trump Tower to be built in years. Never mind that the property was only one quarter of the way completed. It already jutted into the New York skyline and bore the real estate tycoon's name and that was reason enough to celebrate. The inspiration for the party, held a short walk from the construction site, was the excesses of the French monarchy before the revolution. The doormen were liveried as eighteenth-century French footmen and coiffed with powdered wigs. An elevator draped in blood-red velvet curtains with gothic mirrors brought people to the penthouse. Waiters dressed in black tuxedos with black-and-red masks roamed the floor. Red glass candelabras and vases full of red ostrich feathers stood on a 90-foot table adorned with 5,000 red roses. Chefs served 1,000 guests racks of lamb chops, fillets of beef, crab claws, shrimp cocktails, sushi, and oysters, while five open bars poured out a never-ending stream of Grey Goose vodka. Warming up the evening were routines performed by Cirque du Soleil, followed by a two-hour set by Louis Vega's 14-piece salsa band. The whole affair was rumored to have cost a quarter of a million dollars.

Trump SoHo was the building Donald Trump had unveiled in 2006 on the season finale of *The Apprentice*, promising that "this brilliant, $370 million work of art" would be "an awe-inspiring masterpiece." He just needed everyone else to see his new piece of real estate that way. Despite the newfound popularity of his TV show, Trump's efforts to rebuild his empire had not gone smoothly. His publicly traded company, Trump Hotels & Casino Resorts, was forced into bankruptcy in 2004. Trump had drained the company cash for his own purposes, and investors lost money every single year under his leadership. At a dinner with British billionaire Richard Branson, he brooded over how bankers and people he had thought were his friends had shunned him when he was nearly bankrupt. Trump told Branson that he had drawn up a list of five people who he would devote the rest of his life to destroying.[1] With the launch of Trump SoHo, Trump could show everyone that he was back on top.

After Vega's set wrapped up at the Trump SoHo launch party, the din of conversation quieted down as Trump grabbed a microphone and took the opportunity to thank his partners in Trump SoHo. As the cameras flashed, two men joined Trump in front of the crowd: Tevfik Arif, a native of Kazakhstan who founded the New York–based real estate development company Bayrock Group, and Felix Sater, Bayrock's managing director. Bayrock had partnered with the Trump Organization in developing Trump SoHo, and on that night, they couldn't be happier, having helped spearhead Trump's comeback. The fact that Sater was standing on the stage with Trump was astonishing to anyone who knew his background. But Arif would've been completely unknown to most guests. The three of them standing together made for one of the unlikeliest teams in Manhattan real estate history.

Tevfik Arif was a former deputy director of the Soviet Ministry of

Trade's hotel division who turned to the rare-metals sector after the fall of the Soviet Union. With his brother, Refik, Arif acquired a Kazakh-based chromium plant, developing close ties to the infamous "Kazakh Trio," some of whom had worked for Boris Birshtein.

With his newly acquired wealth, Arif caught the luxury real estate development bug. He worked on several hotels and condominiums before deciding to venture boldly into the American real estate market in 1999, purchasing a condo project and strip mall, both in Brooklyn's Little Odessa neighborhood. After testing the waters, Arif established what became Bayrock Group LLC, renting spaces on the twenty-fourth floor of Trump Tower, one floor below Trump's own offices.[2] Although Arif had an impressive address, it was the only thing that set him apart from being just another foreign businessman whose English was reme-dial at best. He needed someone who could navigate the New York real estate market on its own terms and in its native language. He found that person in a former investment banker named Felix Sater.

Of all the characters in this story, Felix Sater is one of the most fas-cinating and enigmatic, and there is some strong competition for that honor. Sater has managed to live several lives in the space of one. Born in the Soviet Union in 1966 with the word Jew stamped in his pass-port, he immigrated with his family to Brighton Beach at age seven. As a young stockbroker, he climbed up the Wall Street ladder until a vicious bar fight sent him to prison in 1994. Upon his release, he joined up with a Mafia-linked "pump-and-dump" stock fraud that swindled investors out of $40 million. To avoid prison a second time, he became a government informant, putting himself at tremendous risk by traveling to the Middle East to hunt terrorists. While he was doing that, he started developing Trump SoHo and other projects in Fort Lauderdale, Phoe-nix, and Moscow for Donald Trump.

Sater's father, Michael, had brought his family over from Russia during the great Jewish flight in the 1970s. In Brighton Beach, he was known by his Russian patronymic, Sheferofsky, and the inexplicable nickname of "Tile." Sater's father ran protection rackets on local Rus-sian businesses with help from a gangster in the Genovese family, the biggest and most powerful of New York's five Mafia families. Vladimir Kozlovsky, a veteran crime reporter for *Novoye Russkoye Slovo*, a now-defunct Russian-language newspaper published in New York, got to know Sheferofsky well. He learned the family name was Satarov. He never met Sheferofsky face to face, but they spoke together on the phone on occasion. "He needed to talk to somebody who knows the subject," Kozlovsky told me. "I was one of the few who knew Russian crime in the United States." Kozlovsky described Sheferofsky as "one of maybe a dozen main Russian mobsters in America."

Many have claimed that Sheferofsky was no petty extortionist, but a Russian Mafiya underboss tied to Semion Mogilevich, the Brainy Don. Over the course of reporting this book, I have come to the conclusion that this is probably not true. Experts on the Russian Mafiya and sources in the intelligence community have told me that they doubt the Mogilevich connection to the father or son.

Growing up in Brighton Beach, Sater came to know Michael Cohen, Trump's personal lawyer. A mutual acquaintance was Laura Shusterman, Cohen's future wife. Sater briefly attended Pace University before dropping out to pursue a career on Wall Street. He spent his days with a phone glued to his ear, cold calling potential clients while simultaneously working toward obtaining his brokerage license. Sater worked at venerable firms like Lehman Brothers and Ladenburg Thalmann and for some operators from the shadier side of the street like Rooney Pace and Gruntal & Co.

The pressure to get the voice on the other end of the phone to invest was intense, but Sater could be persuasive. One day, he called up a businessman in Scranton, Pennsylvania, and got him to invest $30,000 in a computer reseller. A few days later, Sater got the businessman to invest more than $30,000 in TriStar Pictures. By the end of July, Sater had persuaded him to invest $150,000 with Sater's firm. In the end, those investments turned out to be worth almost nothing, but that was part of the Wall Street game.[3]

On the evening of October 1, 1991, Sater's life took the first of a dramatic series of turns. He had joined some of his buddies at El Rio

Grande, a Midtown bar close to Gruntal & Co. that was famous for its margaritas. While the evening began in celebration, by the end of it, another patron, a commodities broker, would be rushed into surgery, his face horribly slashed with the jagged end of a smashed margarita glass. Sater had stabbed the commodities broker over a perceived slight involving a female patron that both men hardly knew. The brutal fight cost Sater his job, his brokerage license, and a year behind bars. He was then newly wed and due to be a father.

Sater emerged from prison in 1995 to find a different opportunity lying in wait for him. Though felons are not allowed to trade stocks, he could legally work at a brokerage firm if his duties were clerical. His old friends Gennady "Gene" Klotsman and Sal Lauria had a job for him at a new brokerage operation called White Rock Partners & Co. Sal Lauria was a native of Sicily who had grown up in New York around his friends in the Mob. Klotsman, like Sater, was a Russian-born Jew from Brighton Beach with a father mixed up in Russian organized crime. A tall, stocky man who always wore a bowtie, his motto was "Dress British, think Yiddish."[4]

White Rock rented office space a few blocks from Wall Street with a view of the Statue of Liberty. The regular brokerage operation was on the ninth floor. Since a convicted felon like Sater couldn't be seen on the brokerage floor, his offices were out of sight, five floors below. White Rock operated brokerage for "microcap" companies that were too small to be listed on the New York Stock Exchange or the NASDAQ markets. This was a world of grifters, scam artists, and mobsters, who relied on the aggressive, high-pressure sales tactics of "boiler rooms" to find easy marks willing to hand over their savings.

In its three years of existence from 1993 to 1996, White Rock ran a classic pump-and-dump stock scheme, buying large blocks of shares to artificially inflate the price of low-value stocks. White Rock made markets for tiny companies with little market value. Working with brokers in notorious boiler rooms like J. W. Barclay & Co., A. R. Baron & Co., and D. H. Blair, White Rock drummed up sales. Then came the "dump." As the stock price rose, Sater and Klotsman would unload large blocks of shares secretly held by companies they had set up in tax havens out-side the country. Sater and his partners cashed out millions of dollars in profits while their investors, many of them Holocaust survivors, were left with nothing. The money was skillfully laundered with help from a jeweler in New York's Diamond District. Since there was so much money to be made illegally, the Mob got involved and soon came knock-ing on the door of White Rock demanding a piece of the action. As a result, members of several different New York families became familiar presences in the offices of White Rock.

—

THIS MIGHT HAVE GONE ON indefinitely had the police not received a phone call from the manager of a Manhattan Mini-Storage one night. A "Marina Shap" had failed to pay her storage bill for several months in row. When the manager broke the lock and opened the door, he found a 12-gauge shotgun and two Tec-9 assault pistols, the kind of weapons carried by the bad guys in gangster films. Also in the storage locker was an ordinary looking box and a gym bag both filled with documents that appeared to be bank statements or financial records. Some were written in Russian. The manager called the police.[5]

Police called up the FBI's Russian organized-crime squad in New York. Raymond Kerr, the head of the FBI's organized-crime squad, answered the phone. The NYPD told him they had seized some docu-ments in Russian from the storage locker. Was the FBI interested? "We'll come out and take a look at it," Kerr told them. He told one of his agents, Leo Taddeo, to go check it out. A week later, the police called again. "Are you going to come and take a look at this stuff?" This time, Agent Taddeo went to go take a look.

Marina Shap, it would turn out, was really Felix Sater. And the documents he had left behind showed he had set up more than 30 for-eign shell companies and corresponding bank accounts in Switzerland, Luxembourg, the Netherlands, Ireland, the Channel Islands, and the

Netherland Antilles, all of which involved White Rock's $40 million Wall Street scam as well as both the Russian Mafiya and La Cosa Nostra. New York City Police Commissioner Howard Safir described White Rock in Hollywood terms: "It could just have well been called *Goodfellas* meet the *Boiler Room*."[6]

Within a few weeks of the discovery at Manhattan Mini-Storage, an arrest warrant was out for Sater, and the FBI, concerned about the Mob's growing influence on Wall Street, came looking for him. The only problem was that by that time Sater and his partners were no longer in the country, but in Russia. They had watched the FBI take down other shady brokerages and realized it was only a matter of time before the FBI came back with handcuffs. So they headed for Russia to run one last Hail Mary play to avoid prison.

One evening in Moscow, Sater's life took yet another dramatic twist. At a business dinner, he was introduced to an American arms dealer named Milton Blane, who took down Sater's number. They met the next day at an Irish pub. Sater says Blane told him he worked for the Defense Intelligence Agency and he wanted Sater to work as an asset or informant. U.S. intelligence wanted "a peek" at a high-tech KH anti-radar missile system that could be used to knock out U.S. missile and aircraft defense systems. He told Sater to go get it. "The country needs you," Blane told Sater. And that marked the beginning of Sater's lengthy career as an undercover government informant for both the FBI and U.S. intelligence.[7]

Whatever you might say about him, and plenty of bad things have been said, Felix Sater did try to make amends by putting himself at personal risk to gather critical intelligence for the U.S. government. According to prosecutors, Sater traveled to the Middle East to collect intelligence on Osama bin Laden and other terrorists in the late 1990s. After the September 11 attacks, the FBI sent this Yiddish-speaking Jewish guy from Brighton Beach, Brooklyn *back* to the Middle East to collect more intelligence on al Qaida and related groups. Sater delivered information on American companies acting as al Qaida fronts, the names and passports of al Qaida operative worldwide, and much more. He also alerted U.S. authorities to potential assassination plots against President George W. Bush and Secretary of State Colin Powell.[8]

Prosecutors say Sater worked as an informant for over a decade, providing information involving Russian organized crime and information crucial to the conviction of more than 20 people, including financial scam artists, members of La Cosa Nostra, and suspects in a multiyear FBI investigation that resulted in two cybercrime cases brought against predominantly Russian hackers.

In a statement to the House intelligence committee, Sater said he provided the government with information on the location of hidden al Qaida training camps, including information about the location of terrorist leader Osama bin Laden. He also said he organized a team of mercenaries composed of Russian ex–special forces and Afghanistan Northern Alliance fighters in an effort to kill bin Laden.

"Information I provided, including the personal satellite telephone numbers of Osama bin Laden, was relevant to the bombing of al Qaida training camps in 1998 by President Clinton," Sater told the House intelligence committee.[9] Sater had hinted at this in a little-noticed interview with a Russian publication, *Snob*. (In the same interview, Sater said Trump knew about his intelligence work and was very proud of it.)[10]

If you wanted to talk to Osama bin Laden in Afghanistan back in the 1990s, you dialed 00-873-682505331.[11] That connected you to a satellite phone that had been acquired from a Long Island firm by al Qaida operative. The phone was Osama bin Laden's sole means of communication with the outside world from late 1996 through the fall of 1998, when a newspaper revealed that U.S. officials were eavesdropping on the calls, according to the September 11 Commission.

This was a critical piece of intelligence that Sater provided, for it allowed U.S. officials to track and monitor calls made to and from the satellite phone and trace more than 1,000 numbers. It provided a virtual road map to al Qaida's global network, exposing callers in Britain, Yemen, Sudan, Iran and many other countries. (The CIA declined comment.) The satellite phone became a central piece of evidence at the trial in New York of the al Qaida operatives responsible for the 1998 bombings of the U.S. Embassies in Kenya and Tanzania.[12]

Prosecutors also confirmed a long-rumored story, writing in court documents that Sater "passed on information regarding a willingness by leaders in Afghanistan to sell Stinger missiles."

Ray Kerr, who headed the FBI's Russian organized-crime squad in New York at the time, told me he was taken aback when one of his agents, Leo Taddeo, told him in the fall of 1998 that Sater could get access to Stinger missiles.

"Are you kidding me?" Kerr said.

"He's got connections in that part of the world," Taddeo told him.

The CIA wanted the Stingers back. Badly. The spy agency had supplied these devastatingly accurate, shoulder-fired weapons to the Afghan rebels, the mujahideen, to destroy hundreds of Soviet aircraft in the 1980s. The missiles were a factor in the Soviet Army's humiliating withdrawal from Afghanistan, but when the war ended, they became a huge liability. Hundreds of unfired Stingers remained behind, and the CIA soon grew very worried that Stingers might fall into the wrong hands. A Stinger that could bring down a Soviet Hind gunship could easily bring down a defenseless civilian airliner. Their removal was a big priority for the Clinton administration.

Kerr could hardly believe that this "wise guy wanna-be," as he put it, could deliver, so he told his agent, Leo Taddeo, to get corroboration. The FBI instructed Sater to go back and get five serial numbers off the Stingers. Sure enough, that's what Sater did. The FBI sent the numbers to the Defense Intelligence Agency. Word got back to the FBI that Sater's information checked out. "What the rest of the story is, I don't know what the rest of the story is," Kerr said. That wasn't unusual in the FBI's relationship with the CIA.

Unbeknownst to Kerr, Sater's attorney began lengthy negotiations with the CIA general counsel's office. (David Kendall, President Clinton's personal lawyer, made the introduction.) According to *The Scorpion and the Frog*, a tell-all book about the White Rock fraud by Sal Lauria, Sater's friend, the CIA agreed to use Sater and his friends to buy the missiles back for $300,000 each. According to Lauria, another Sater codefendant in the Wall Street fraud, Gene Klotsman, got greedy and raised the price to $3 million. The CIA called off the deal.[13]

The information Sater provided was so valuable that, after years of cooperating, he walked out of court on the day of his sentencing in 2009 without having to serve a day in prison. Although Sater could have been ordered to pay up to $120 million in restitution to the victims of his fraud, the judge imposed a $25,000 fine, which Sater later called "symbolic." Loretta Lynch, who oversaw Sater's case as U.S. attorney in Brooklyn, was asked why his sentence was so lenient during her confirmation hearing to become President Obama's attorney general. Lynch noted his involvement in exposing La Cosa Nostra activity and providing "information crucial to national security." Sater said he provided the names and photos of North Korean military operatives purchasing equipment worldwide to build the rogue nation's nuclear weapons program.

Prosecutor Todd Kaminsky said Sater's cooperation was of a breadth and depth that is seldom seen. "It involves violent organizations such as al Qaida, it involves foreign governments, it involves Russian organized crime," Kaminsky said in a court hearing. So extraordinary were Sater's contributions that a special ceremony was held in the federal building in New York City honoring him.

BOTH TEVFIK ARIF AND FELIX Sater had houses in the affluent Long Island seaside village of Sands Point, just outside New York City, that was home to many newly wealthy ex-Soviet expats. While it's not known how the two men met, what is known is that soon after being hired by Bayrock, Sater was already making moves within Trump Tower.

A chance encounter led to a meeting with Nathan Nelson, then the executive vice president of real estate management at the Trump Organization. An impressed Nelson soon introduced Sater to two other executive vice presidents, Russell Flicker and Charley Reese. All three Trump Organization executives agreed that Sater ought to meet their boss, and within a few months of starting with Bayrock, Sater had his first meeting with Donald Trump.

It was the first of many coups for Bayrock Group that were arranged by Sater, who seemed to be the right man at the right place at the right time. In 2002, Trump was still clawing his way back from his bruising casino bankruptcy in the 1990s and was hungry for deals to get him back on top. "It's not very hard to get connected to Donald if you make it known that you have a lot of money and you want to do deals and you want to put his name on them," Abe Wallach, who was the future president's right-hand man at the Trump Organization from 1990 to about 2002, told *Bloomberg*. "Donald doesn't do due diligence. He relies on his gut and whether he thinks you have good genes."[14]

Trump must have sensed that Sater had good genes. Sater pitched the Trump Organization on deals in Arizona and Florida—sites where Bayrock had acquired an interest and wanted to build luxury hotels and stamp them with the Trump brand name. Trump and his representatives liked what they heard. "I would say we discussed and in principle had an agreement," Sater later said, "a verbal understanding that they were in."[15]

The relationship with Trump gave little-known Bayrock Group a huge leg up in the competitive global real estate market, and their partnership engendered an aggressive pursuit of real estate deals around the globe: from Arizona, Florida, and Colorado in the United States to Turkey, Poland, Russia, and Ukraine, until it culminated in the construction of Trump SoHo.[16]

For over half a decade, Sater would call his proximity to Donald Trump his "Trump card," and even had a business card bearing the Trump Organization logo, on which was printed "Felix Sater: Senior Adviser to Donald Trump," which he used whenever and wherever he could. "My competitive advantage is, anybody can come in and build a tower," Sater said. "I can build a Trump tower, because of my relationship with Trump."[17]

This period also marked a remarkable turnaround for Felix Sater, who just a few years earlier had been facing years if not decades in prison and the end of his business career. By working as an undercover government informant, he had avoided doing time in prison. Now he was a driving force behind a growing firm making some of the biggest deals the Trump Organization had made in years. As a measure of just how important Sater was to Bayrock, Arif soon promoted him to managing director, and rewarded him with nearly half of all of Bayrock Group's profits beginning in 2003.[18] Sater moved his family into a $1.75 million mansion in Port Washington, New York, the following year. In his last year at Bayrock, he bought a $4.8 million condo on exclusive Fisher Island in Miami.

Arif, however, remained in charge of Bayrock. "He was the boss," Sater said in a deposition. He then continued, using a phrase reserved for Mafia chiefs: "He was the boss of all bosses." With Sater's background, it wasn't the kind of offhand remark one took lightly. There were numerous reports in the Russian press that traced Arif back to the Soviet criminal underworld in Tashkent, Uzbekistan, involving two local hoods who would go on to bigger things, Michael Cherney and Alimzhan Tokhtakhounov. In a memo obtained by the *Wall Street Journal*, Sater's attorney warned of a possible lawsuit that would include details of Arif's wrongdoing in the post-Soviet metals business in Kazakhstan. Sater was blunt. He told his former boss: "The headlines will be, 'The Kazakh Gangster and President Trump.'"[19]

Even as his real estate career took off, Sater continued his undercover missions for the federal government, working all the while without compensation. "I was building Trump Towers by day and hunting Bin Laden by night," he later said.[20] Of all the buildings Sater wanted to erect with his new partner, none pulled harder at Sater's attention than a Trump tower in Moscow.

He got his first chance in 2005, when Donald Trump signed a letter granting Bayrock exclusive rights to negotiate a deal on behalf of the Trump Organization in Russia: "I am delighted at having the opportunity to partner with Bayrock Group LLC on yet another world-class development. Moscow is one of the fastest growing cities in the world and offers the best location for a Signature Donald J. Trump development," the letter read. Trump had signed off on it after Sater had told him excitedly about a possible deal in Russia. It was a "mega-financial home run," Sater explained, an excellent site for a Trump tower right in the center of Moscow. "I came to Mr. Trump and said that I have a very good opportunity in Moscow that I'd like to negotiate with the owner of the property there and I think there's a good opportunity to turn . . . that into a Trump Tower," Sater said.[21]

The site for the Trump Tower Moscow was to be an industrial area located on Kutuzovsky Prospekt, a major Moscow thoroughfare. It was the former location of the Sacco & Vanzetti pencil factory, named in honor of a pair of American anarchists who became socialist martyrs when they were executed—wrongly, many believed—for murder. Sater made several trips to Russia to negotiate with a banker named Ilya Haykin, a representative of the site's owners. According to later testimony by Sater, the negotiations progressed very far. A $75 million price for the property was agreed upon.[22]

Back in New York, Sater said he would pop his head into Trump's office to deliver updates in person.[23] Arif also brought two men from Russia who had the rights to the proposed Moscow site up to see Trump. The deal Trump was negotiating called for him to invest nothing and take an ownership stake of around 20 to 25 percent. "Bayrock knew the people, knew the investors, and in some cases I believe they were friends of Mr. Arif," Trump said.[24] Sensing the beginning of an expanding partnership with the Trump Organization, Arif sketched out a grand vision for a series of Trump towers across Eastern Europe, including in Ukraine, Poland, and Turkey.

In the end, not one of those deals got off the ground. Trump blamed the collapse of the deals on author Tim O'Brien, a former business reporter for *The New York Times*, whose book *TrumpNation* asserted that Trump was not a billionaire as he repeatedly claimed, but worth a paltry $150 to $250 million.[25] After O'Brien's claims about Trump's wealth were excerpted in *The New York Times*, according to Trump, Arif had called him with some bad news: "I think all those deals are dead."[26] Arif declined to testify in the O'Brien lawsuit and sent Sater on his behalf, who showed the flag for Trump. "After the publication of the book, the developers mysteriously went radio silent," Sater said. "Me personally, I just don't believe in coincidences."[27] Trump filed a $5 billion defamation lawsuit, claiming that the book had cost him several deals, including Sater's tower in Moscow and Arif's Eastern European proposal. The lawsuit was ultimately dismissed.

An article in the Russian edition of *Forbes* posits other reasons for the deal's failure. The site's owners blamed the notoriously corrupt Moscow city bureaucracy for dragging its heels. Another problem: Ilya Haykin, a friend of Arif's and the man with whom Sater was negotiating, fled Moscow for London after his name surfaced in connection with a series of land scams.[28]

During his time at Bayrock, Sater earned Trump's trust. Trump even asked him to look after his children, Ivanka and Don Jr., on a visit to Moscow. "Donald asked me if I wouldn't mind joining them there," Sater said. "They were on their way there, and he was all concerned. They were there by themselves, and he knew I traveled there and knew my way around. He asked me if I wouldn't mind joining them and looking after them while they were in Moscow."[29] Sater, already in Europe, agreed and joined the Trump children in February 2006.[30] It was during the Moscow trip that Sater used his Kremlin connections to impress Trump's daughter, Ivanka. Sater would later boast: "I arranged for Ivanka to sit in Putin's private chair at his desk and office in the Kremlin."[31]

IN MANHATTAN, TRUMP ASSEMBLED A sales force in Russia to push Trump SoHo and his other properties. One was a Belarusian-American businessman named Sergei Millian. "You could say I was their exclusive broker," Millian said. "Then, in 2007–2008, Russians bought dozens of apartments in Trump houses in the United States. But I would not want to disclose specific amounts and names."[32] (Interestingly, Millian was also a source, apparently unwittingly, for the salacious material in former MI6 officer Christopher Steele's Trump Dossier.)[33]

Roger Khafif, a Miami developer, also hosted sales meetings in Russia for Trump. "Russians like brands," he said, "and Trump was famous in Russia" during the 2000s real estate boom. "These were good days for Trump. He was the only man in town for real estate."[34] Khafif would go on to develop Trump Ocean Club in Panama, another project that attracted Russian money. Alexandre Ventura Nogueira, who handled advance sales for the Trump project in Panama, told Reuters that he learned some of his partners and investors in the Trump project were criminals, including some with what he described as connections to the Russian Mafiya.[35] (One Manhattan attorney told me, "Look, I'm a drug lawyer. I stayed on four occasions at the Trump hotel in Panama to meet clients. The only customers seem to be criminals.")

Trump even peddled sales of Trump SoHo to Russian buyers himself, inviting Russian journalists to breakfast at Trump Tower. "Donald Trump invited us to report on a new project, which is largely designed for Russians," reported *Seagull* magazine.[36] Bayrock helped bring in investors as well, including the Icelandic holdings firm FL Group, which invested $50 million in Trump SoHo and other Trump projects. Jody Kriss, a former Bayrock employee who later sued Sater and Arif, claims that Arif's backing included "hidden interests in Russia and Kazakhstan." Kriss says Sater and Arif told him the money in FL Group was from Russians "in favor with Putin."[37]

Trump SoHo gave Trump a taste of what Russian money could do for him and his status, and he found that he liked it. He broke ground in October 2007 on a new 65-story hotel and condominium with his name on it in downtown Toronto. The Trump International Hotel and Tower in Toronto was built by Canadian investor Alexander Shnaider, the son-in-law of none other than Boris Birshtein, who had coordinated the Russian's Mafiya's Tel Aviv meeting nearly 20 years earlier.

Up to $310 million in construction finance credit for Trump's Toronto tower was provided by an Austrian bank, Raiffeisen Zentralbank Österreich. Raiffeisen was a newcomer to the North American market but had financed several of Shnaider's previous projects. A secret 2006 State Department cable released by WikiLeaks stated that U.S. officials believed that Raiffeisen served as a front for Semion Mogilevich. To maintain that facade, Mogilevich's front company paid two Raiffeisen executives $360,000 a year each, which the State Department cable described as "bribes."[38] Andrey Kozlov, a deputy chairman of the Russian central bank, was gunned down in 2006 after he blew the whistle on large amounts of rubles that were being laundered through Raiffeisen.

In addition, Shnaider put his own money into the Trump Toronto project after receiving hundreds of millions of dollars from a separate asset sale that involved VEB, a Russian state-run bank. Shnaider sold his stake in a Ukrainian steel mill, Zaporizhstal, for about $850 million. His lawyer told the *Wall Street Journal* that about $15 million from the asset sale went into the Trump Toronto project, before changing his statement a day later.[39] Vladimir Putin was then chairman of VEB's supervisory board and the deal would likely have required his approval. VEB, whose full name is Vnesheconombank, was placed on the U.S. sanctions list in 2014, along with other businesses and individuals close to Putin. The truth about Trump's real estate comeback was that the money used to finance many of his projects appeared increasingly dirty.

▬

THE LAUNCH OF TRUMP SOHO in September of 2007 proved to be the high point for Bayrock. A few months later in December, the firm started its downward slide that began when Sater's criminal past—the secret the government had been so carefully guarding for him—spilled out into public view. Someone had tipped off *The New York Times*, which managed to confirm details of Sater's sealed indictment in the White Rock fraud, his pump-and-dump scheme, and his subsequent secret guilty plea. "I'm not proud of some of the things that happened in my 20s," Sater said. "I am proud of the things I'm doing now."[40]

A month after the *Times* article came out, Sater was forced to leave Bayrock. "The company that I had built with my own two hands," as he described it, was taken away from him. "Otherwise the banks would say there's a criminal involved," Sater said during his sentencing. "I had to get out. At that moment I thought my life was over. Here I am trying to rehabilitate myself and keep getting the rug pulled out from under me. I thought that was the case until a week later my daughter came home and said, 'The kids at school say my dad is a terrorist.'"[41]

Trump, probably realizing that he could face lawsuits from angry lenders and business partners, claimed to be surprised to learn of Sater's past. "We never knew that," Trump told *The New York Times*. "We do as much of a background check as we can on the principals. I didn't really know him very well." Most of his dealings with Bayrock were with Arif, Trump said.[42] This was the first of what would be years of denials and evasions by Trump about his relationship with Felix Sater.

In a deposition a week after the *Times* article came out, Trump distanced himself even further. "I would say that my interaction with Felix Sater was, you know, not—very little." Hoping to head off litigation for his business dealings with a convicted felon, Trump insisted that Sater was an employee, not a principal, at Bayrock.[43]

Far from laying the matter to rest, however, Trump's relationship with Felix Sater periodically bubbled up over the years, to Trump's obvious annoyance. If Mr. Sater "were sitting in the room right now," Mr. Trump said in a 2013 deposition, "I really wouldn't know what he looked like."[44] He ended an interview that same year with John Sweeney of the BBC when the British journalist continued to press the real estate developer with questions about Felix Sater. In a 2015 interview with the Associated Press, Trump, despite laying claim to "one of the great memories of all time," seemed to be having trouble recollecting who Sater was. "Felix Sater, boy, I have to even think about it," Trump said, referring questions about Sater to his staff. "I'm not that familiar with him."[45]

Trump's attempts to downplay his relationship with Sater strained credulity, and worse, raised suspicion. He appeared in photos with Felix

Sater, who was a frequent visitor to his office. They traveled on business together. And most significantly, he asked Sater to chaperone his children in Moscow. Looking at the totality of his evasions and denials about his relationship with Felix Sater, Trump definitely appeared like a man with something to hide.

Sater flatly contradicted Trump's version of their relationship. In a little-noticed interview with the Russian publication *Snob*, Sater was asked if his criminal past was a problem for Trump. "No, it was not," he said. "He makes his own decision regarding each and every individual."[46] Sater was shopping a deal to build a Trump World Tower Moscow in the midst of Trump's presidential run. Between September 2015 and January 2016, Sater tried to broker a deal for a Moscow company called IC Expert Investment Company. (Sater worked for IC Expert's owner, Andrei Rozov, after he left Bayrock.)

Trump signed a letter of intent in October with IC Expert Investment for a Moscow hotel-condo with the option for a "Spa by Ivanka Trump." Providing financing was VTB, a Russian bank subject to U.S. sanctions. Sater's contact at the Trump Organization was his old friend, Trump's lawyer Michael Cohen. In mid-January, Sater urged Cohen to send an email to Dmitry Peskov, Vladimir Putin's press secretary, "since the proposal would require approvals within the Russian government that had not been issued." Cohen sent the email, got no reply, and said he abandoned the proposal two weeks later.[47]

What Cohen called his old friend's "colorful language" attracted attention from congressional investigators and Special Counsel Robert Mueller's office:

> Michael I arranged for Ivanka to sit in Putins private chair at his desk and office in the Kremlin. I will get Putin on this program and we will get Donald elected. We both know no one else knows how to pull this off without stupidity or greed getting in the way. I know how to play it and we will get this done. Buddy our boy can become President of the USA and we can engineer. I will get all of Putins team to buy in on this.[48]

Sater gave an unsatisfactory answer to *BuzzFeed* about why he wrote this email. "If a deal can get done and I could make money and he could look like a statesman, what the fuck is the downside, right?"[49]

Shortly after Trump took office, Sater teamed up with Cohen to submit a Ukrainian peace plan to then national security advisor Michael Flynn that would have opened the door to lifting sanctions on Russia.[50] In the end, it wouldn't be Sater, but his former Bayrock boss, Tevfik Arif, whom Trump wanted to get as far away from as possible.

ON THE NIGHT OF SEPTEMBER 28, 2010, a large yacht bobbed in the waters off of Bodrum, Turkey. Suddenly, a police helicopter swooped in and hovered over the yacht. Ropes were thrown down and Turkish police officers descended onto the deck. On board the yacht, police detained nine young women, including three teens, and found numerous contraceptives in the cabins. According to a charging document filed by prosecutors, all three members of the "Kazakh Trio" were found on board: Alexander Mashkevitch, the Kazakh-Israeli billionaire whose name appeared in a list of strategic partners for Bayrock Group, and his partners Patokh Chodiev and Alijan Ibragimov.[51] The raid was the culmination of a months-long investigation by Turkish authorities into a prostitution ring. According to a prosecution document, the ring trafficked in underage girls brought in to pleasure wealthy businessmen at luxury hotels in Turkey. It was financed and run by Tevfik Arif, who would be charged with trade in human beings, prostitution, traffic in juveniles under 18, and the creation of criminal organizations with the purpose of the commission of crime.

Questioned by police, Arif told them: "I spend my spare time with other businessmen . . . The rule is that businessmen take their beloved to such meetings. And I ensure transfer for them. And that is all. Two or three months ago I rented that yacht. Together with other businessmen from Russia and other countries we negotiated about investments. We were having rest," he said.[52]

The raid created a media firestorm in Turkey that reached back to Trump Tower. The yacht raided by police was the *Savarona*, one of the largest in the world, which had a special place in Turkish history. Built in 1931, the yacht had been purchased by the Turkish government a few years later from its original owner, Emily Roebling Cadwallader, the granddaughter of engineer John Roebling, who designed the Brooklyn Bridge. The yacht came to Istanbul in the final days of the life of Mustafa Kemal Atatürk, the revered founder of modern Turkey. Shortly before his death in 1938, Atatürk spent six weeks on the *Savarona*, where he welcomed foreign heads of state and held cabinet meetings. His stateroom on the yacht is preserved as a historical monument.

The *Savarona* had been rented for a week at Arif's request. The $300,000 fee was paid by his friend, Alexander Mashkevitch. Through a spokesman, Mashkevitch denied his involvement in the event. "He was on board," said the spokesman, Roman Spektor. "From our perspective, he wasn't involved in any immoral or criminal actions. It's a real provocation. It's a real dirty lie in order to discredit him, because he's a well-known member of the worldwide Jewish community."[53] Mashkevitch resigned as president of the Euro-Asian Jewish Congress the following year; his spokesman said it was not connected to the raid on the yacht.

Police had been eavesdropping on Arif's phone calls for several months, listening in on conversations that described the trafficking of young women and children as young as 13 for prostitution. The girls were brought in from Russia and Ukraine, and were hired from modeling agencies. One member of the ring corresponded with a woman in Russia who procured girls from a modeling agency.

"Do you want all models for sex? I should know it because many don't agree for sex," the woman asked in one message intercepted by the police.

"Client wants sex," replied one of the alleged members of the ring.

Other conversations, including those involving Arif, were more discreet. Arif is referred to as the "boss," the girls or young women are "models," and clients are "guests." The age of minor girls was described by days of the month, as in this conversation between Arif and his majordomo, Gunduz Akdeniz, about a procurer of women named Igor:

AKDENIZ: All guests will also go there.
ARIF: Where from?
AKDENIZ: Those who are from Igor.
ARIF: There was only the 16th.
AKDENIZ: . . . There is the 16th but she said she can't go alone, she will go together with the 19th contract.
ARIF: Ok, let her go.

In a conversation from March 2010, Arif and Akdeniz discussed the arrival of five girls—including two 16-year-olds—to meet "guests" such as billionaire Alexander Mashkevitch at a luxury hotel owned by a friend of Arif's. Police surveillance confirmed that the women were indeed delivered to the hotel.

Arif was acquitted of all charges in 2011. The prosecution's case was hurt when the ring instructed the girls not to testify. "Keep the girls as silent as the grave," read one text. The damage to his reputation, however, was severe. When news of the *Savarona* bust spilled out, Arif's friends couldn't get away from him fast enough. Donald Trump had toasted Arif in Turkey and at the opening of Trump SoHo. Now, he turned his back on him. "I really don't know him very well, Mr. Arif," Trump said, adding that he had only met him "a couple of times."[54]

Bayrock was soon forced to vacate their Trump Tower offices, around the same time that a private buyer was purchasing a condo just below Trump's own penthouse.

7.

THE CONDO CASINO

ONE FEBRUARY EVENING IN 2002, SPECIAL agent Ray Kerr was sitting at home with his wife watching the pairs figure skating competition taking place at the Winter Olympics in Salt Lake City. Kerr had headed the FBI's special squad for Russian organized crime since its inception in 1994, having tackled dozens, if not hundreds, of cases concerning illicit Russian activity in the United States. As he watched the Russian duo Elena Berezhnaya and Anton Sikharulidze skate onto the ice, however, he settled in to enjoy an intense competition. While figure skating was a competitive sport that Russia had long dominated with breathtaking flair, the Canadian team, Jamie Salé and David Pelletier, had made a spectacular challenge for the gold during the first of two routines. During the closing round, the Russian team went first, but it seemed like this would not be their night. During a key side-by-side jump, Sikharulidze stumbled while attempting to land a double axel and spun out of control for a moment. Off the ice, as he watched the replay, Sikharulidze seemed to realize that his mistake had cost him a gold medal. He hung his head and banged his fist on his leg.

The Canadian pair took the ice. Scott Hamilton, an NBC announcer and former Olympic ice-skating champion, announced that all the Canadians had do was "skate clean"—avoid falls or touching the ground—and the gold medal was theirs. Their performance was unmistakably flawless, and they knew it. They cheered on the ice, while several commentators declared the execution of their routine to be "perfect." However, when the final scores flashed up on the screens, the crowd in Salt Lake made an audible gasp and began to boo. One person can clearly be heard screaming "No!" at the top of their lungs while Hamilton commented on the ignominy of what was transpiring before him. "They won that program," he declared. "There's not a doubt of anyone in the place, except maybe a few judges. That will be debated forever."[1]

On his couch at home, Kerr also felt puzzled. "I know nothing about ice dancing," he said. "But I think if you almost fall down, you're probably not going to [t]ake the gold medal." His sentiment was felt by millions of people the world over, resulting in a firestorm that within hours had found a prime suspect. While judges from the United States, Canada, Germany, and Japan gave higher scores to the Canadian team, judges from Russia, the People's Republic of China, Poland, and Ukraine voted for the Russian duo. The tie-breaking judge was France's Marie-Reine Le Gougne. At the hotel lobby that night, Le Gougne was approached by an official with the international skating union, and evidently collapsed into tears after being asked a few questions, creating a scene witnessed by many other officials. She then admitted to being pressured by the president of the French Ice Sports Federation, Didier Gailhaguet, to make the Russian pair the winners. Securing her vote was part of a wider plot that involved an equal gesture from a Russian judge to vote for a French duo set to compete for the ice dance medal a few days later. The Canadian team were later awarded the gold, but surprisingly, the Russian pair were allowed to keep their gold medals, as there had been no evidence of the pair, or the Russian team, being in on the cheat. So who had paid off Gailhaguet?

A few days later, Kerr learned of an interesting message from the bureau's legal attaché in Rome: investigators from the Venice bureau of the Guardia di Finanza (GF), Italy's treasury police force responsible for investigating financial crime and smuggling, had wiretapped an incredible conversation concerning the figure skating controversy. For two years, the GF had been investigating Alimzhan Tursunovich Tokhtakhounov—known as "Taiwanchik" (Little Taiwanese) due to the Asian features of his Uzbek heritage—an Uzbek-Russian gangster living in northern Italy, who was the ringleader of the "Sun Brigade," a Russian organized-crime group operating in Italy connected to the powerful Izmailovskaya Bratva. While listening in on Tokhtakhounov's calls for evidence of money laundering, they overheard what sounded like damning evidence that he had been responsible for coordinating the bribe. A member of Russia's Olympic delegation in Salt Lake City can be heard saying, "Our Sikharulidze fell, the Canadians were ten times better, and in spite of that, the French with their vote gave us first place." And in another, Tokhtakhounov could be heard speaking to the mother of Russian-born Marina Anissina, who was skating for France in the ice dance competition, promising that her daughter would win gold no matter what. "Even if she falls," Tokhtakhounov said, "we will make sure she is number one."[2]

TOKHTAKHOUNOV WAS A ZELIG-LIKE FIGURE in the post-Soviet crime world, seemingly able to become simpatico with a wide array of people, including many Russian and Uzbek entertainers, politicians, business-men, gangsters, and athletes (he once played for an Uzbek soccer club). His mafia connections extended to Russian Bratvas, the Uzbek Mafia, and even the *vor* Vyacheslav Ivankov's American affairs. "He is a key facilitator for everyone," Louise Shelley, a professor at George Mason

University and an expert on the Russian Mafiya told me. "People parked their money with him." Like his friend Ivankov, Tokhtakhounov, too, was a vor, a title he'd earned after being sentenced to prison twice—first for passport violations and again for "parasitism," the uniquely Soviet crime of not working.

After the fall of the Soviet Union, Tokhtakhounov moved to Germany, where he played a role in trading military hardware. In one case mentioned in FBI documents, he helped move a shipment of machine guns and anti-aircraft defense systems worth around $20 million from Germany to an "Arab entity" via Africa. One of Tokhtakhounov's contacts notified him that this operation had caught the attention of the German authorities, forcing the Uzbek gangster to flee. Incredibly, he had made it only as far as Paris when he decided to take up a different kind of career: overseeing the Paris offices of a Russian modeling agency. His fashion world career was apparently successful enough that he later wrote a novel loosely based on his experience called *Angel from Couture: A Novel from High Fashion*. Writing of Tokhtakhounov's criminal past, *The New York Times* described the work as "a semi-autobiographical story that focuses on the love affair of a young model and an older man."[3]

Tokhtakhounov's esteem in the French city reached a high point when, at a lavish ceremony in 1999 at the Prince de Galles Hotel in Paris, he was knighted by the Order of Constantine the Great and St. Helen for "selfless, chivalrous spirit and philanthropy."[4] A crystal goose filled with black caviar beckoned the guests mostly from the former Soviet Union, including fellow Uzbek Michael Cherney, Tokhtakhounov's childhood friend, who after his partnership with Sam Kislin joined the aluminum and metals corporation Trans-World Group. Also in attendance were the singer Joseph Kobzon; NHL star Pavel Bure; and the French-Russian ice dancer Marina Anissina, who, with Tokhtakhounov's help, would win gold at the 2002 Winter Olympics. Not long after the ceremony, Tokhtakhounov's Mafia ties were discovered. He was stripped of his rank and forced to leave France. This was how he ended up in Italy, and it wouldn't be long before he would be forced out of that country as well.

The discovery of Tokhtakhounov's involvement in the skating scandal had as much to do with the work of the Guardia as it did with Tokhtakhounov himself. By his own admission, Tokhtakhounov had a habit of being loose-lipped during phone calls. In a later interview, he said his unvarnished manner of speaking was inspired by advice he'd been given early on by a friend: "Alik, if you are an honest man, the more openly you speak over the phone then the better those who are listening will understand that you are honest," Tokhtakhounov recalled. "When I lived abroad I always spoke openly over the phone, and people on the other line would say to me, 'Why are you talking so much?' and I would [think], 'Since I'm honest, they are going to understand that I'm honest.' But it turns out that things aren't like that abroad." Tokhtakhounov cited his honesty as being at the root of the accusations that he moonlighted as a drug and weapons dealer. To thrust this point home, he gave an example of a call he'd once had with a friend who lived in Tashkent, who wanted to send him some "pomegranates." According to Tokhtakhounov, the Italians translated pomegranates as bombs. *Kishmish* ("raisins") was translated as hashish. "And so they tell me I'm trading in weapons and drugs," he said.[5]

A federal grand jury in Manhattan found Tokhtakhounov utterly devoid of honesty and voted to indict him on charges of conspiracy to commit wire fraud, sports bribery, and a violation of the Travel Act. Speaking to reporters, the U.S. attorney in Manhattan, James Comey, described the scheme as a "classic quid pro quo: 'You'll line up support for the Russian pair; we'll line up support for the French pair and everybody will go away with the gold, and perhaps there'll be a little gold for me.'"[6]

An international warrant was issued for Tokhtakhounov's arrest, and on a summer day in 2002, officers with the Italian Guardia arrived at Tokhtakhounov's home and took him into custody. Home for the Russian vor was a two-story villa in the Tuscan seaside village of Forte dei Marmi in northern Italy, where he was known as a somewhat reserved but extremely polite man. Neighbors could not help but notice the chains of limousines that regularly arrived at his villa bearing Russian visitors accompanied by attractive young women. Italian authorities asked Tokhtakhounov what he did for a living. *"Bees*-ness," he replied. What kind of business? *"Bees*-ness."

An Italian court granted Comey's extradition request, and Tokhtakhounov seemed destined to live out the rest of his days in an American prison. But his extradition never happened. Tokhtakhounov sat in the Santa Maria Maggiore prison in Venice for only a year, after which his ruling was overturned in July 2003 by Italy's highest court, and he was released from prison and returned to Russia, where he has remained ever since, outside the long reach of U.S. law enforcement. Kerr learned that the Russian Mafiya had worked behind the scenes to free Tokhtakhounov. "Later on, we got some information that the wiseguys over there put a lot of money on the streets," Kerr said. "They were trying to get this guy out of Italy and back in Russia." Tokhtakhounov would not be heard from again until many years later, not until he became affiliated with one of the most significant criminal activities to occur at Trump Tower.

—

IN 2009, VADIM TRINCHER, A professional gambler, won the Foxwoods Poker Classic, one of the world's biggest poker tournaments. With his prize money, Trincher purchased an apartment in Trump Tower just a few floors below Trump's gilded penthouse. The seller was Oleg Boyko, a Russian tycoon who was close to President Boris Yeltsin and became one of the first oligarchs. (Boyko had bought the apartment in 1994 from Donald Trump himself.) Trincher's new pad was a lavish $5 million condo and the capstone to his unexpected career as a professional poker player.

Trincher gambled out of necessity. Born in Kiev, he was a math prodigy who could beat adult chess players by age eight. Because he was Jewish, however, he was sent to a university in a regional backwater and was expelled when his parents expressed a desire to emigrate to Israel. He played chess and backgammon for money to support his family.

In 1989, at the age of 28, Trincher arrived in the United States seeking political asylum from the Soviet Union, with $350 in his pocket, the maximum he was allowed to take out of the country. As he had in Ukraine, Trincher made a living in America by playing backgammon before deciding, at the age of 45, to make a career change from board games to card games. He taught himself competitive poker, which was more popular in America, and more lucrative. He won Foxwoods in a mere four years.

Trincher's win at Foxwoods brought him a level of international fame, and many people in the poker world expected him to continue competing. Instead, just as he had given up backgammon for poker, Trincher retreated from the competitive poker circuit to partner up with Taiwanchik, now living in Russia, for even higher-stakes gambling—international racketeering. The "Taiwanchik-Trincher Organization," as the Feds later referred to it, conducted both online and telephonic sports betting with several (and often shadowy) international figures, many of them Russian and Ukrainian oligarchs who could afford to bet nearly $2 million on a soccer match and not flinch if they lost it all. Salim Abduvaliyev, described in a State Department cable as an Uzbek "Mafia chieftain" who facilitates bribery at the highest levels, was a frequent caller. Another regular, Gennady "Roman" Manashirov, a native of Azerbaijan, had once boasted of buying a $720,000 Mercedes-Maybach sedan just to ferry his eight-year-old son to school. (He was later charged with bribing officials in Russia's Interior Ministry.)[7]

Though his son Illya Trincher briefly took over his father's cards, even appearing on Season 3 of *High Stakes Poker*, Illya eventually branched out like his father, partnering with Helly Nahmad, the young scion of one of the world's largest art-dealing empires, and owner of the entire fifty-first floor of Trump Tower, to form a high-stakes gambling club of their own. Seven-figure card games attracted several notable professional players and a well-heeled clientele of businessmen, celebrities, and athletes such as Alex Rodriguez, Leonardo DiCaprio, and Tobey Maguire.[8] Over the course of the club's six-year existence, these gambling dens brought in roughly $100 million in proceeds that were later laundered through shell accounts in Cyprus, before heading back to the United States, where it was invested in real estate or hedge funds. Not one cent was legitimately acquired.

Eventually the FBI became privy to the Trump Tower gambling operations. For two years, they listened in on Vadim Trincher's phone conversations in his apartment below Trump's residence. What they learned was that although Trincher ran the operation out of a Trump Tower apartment, it was really Tokhtakhounov who was behind the scenes. In one phone conversation in 2012, Tokhtakhounov explained that a client grumbling over his debts would pay up because Tokhta- khounov, a vor, was standing behind the organization. "Why would he be complaining?" he could be heard saying. "He knows that I'm there. I'm not nobody to fuck me up." The FBI also discovered just how much money was being pooled in, with Tokhtakhounov collecting $12 mil- lion from the ring's gambling proceeds in little more than a year. When Trump accused Obama of wiretapping him at Trump Tower, he was half-right. Trump Tower had been wiretapped, not to eavesdrop on his dealings, but to investigate one of the world's biggest illegal high-stakes gambling rings, operating just below his own penthouse.

Tokhtakhounov's mobster status was the key to the whole gam- bling operation. He knew the kings of the underworld, but he also had contacts in the highest levels of Russian political and business circles. According to prosecutors, Tokhtakhounov used those connections to recruit millionaires and billionaires to place their bets with his friend Vadim Trincher in Trump Tower. His stature as a vor also allowed him to resolve disputes with gambling clients and ensured they paid their debts, sometimes with threats of violence and economic ruin.

WITH THE MONEY HE WAS earning from running his gambling den, Trincher and his wife, Elena, sought to make powerful friends outside of it. The Trinchers became enthusiastic supporters of Republican can- didates, including Donald Trump during his extremely brief appearance in the 2012 presidential campaign. The effort consisted largely of a website called ShouldTrumpRun.com, formed by Trump's attorney, Michael Cohen, to gauge interest. The Trinchers donated thousands of dollars to GOP institutions and presidential hopefuls, including the Republican National Committee, the National Republican Senatorial Committee, George W. Bush, John McCain, and Lindsey Graham. A 2011 lawsuit filed by the couple revealed that a fundraiser they had planned to host for Newt Gingrich was canceled due to a leak from an upstairs apartment.[9]

But there were clear signs that Trincher didn't care about party affiliation as much as he wanted to be a political insider. In one wiretapped conversation, Trincher told a friend in Kiev that he had attended a charity poker tournament along with former president Bill Clinton. The tournament's entrance fee was $10,000 per person, which benefitted the William J. Clinton Foundation, and about 100 people attended. Among the guests were Chelsea Clinton and her friend Ivanka Trump. Records show that Trincher gave between $5,000 and $10,000 to the Clinton Foundation in 2012, as did Ivanka.

Unlike the other political friends Trincher was hoping to make, his connection to the Clintons was through Illya, who mingled with politically connected figures in the world of poker. Illya had made friends with Marc Lasry, a poker fanatic who ran a $12 billion New York investment fund. Lasry was close to the Clintons, and he had employed Chelsea Clinton and Clinton confidant Doug Band at his fund, Avenue Capital Group. Illya had made Lasry's acquaintance after attending a Clinton Foundation fundraiser held at Lasry's home. Hedging his bets with politicians seemed to be Trincher's next gambling game, but just as influence seemed to be cashing in, Trincher's luck abruptly folded.[10]

One predawn morning in April 2013, the FBI arrived at Trump Tower. Agents knocked on Trincher's door and showed the apartment's beleaguered owner a warrant to search his home. In the four years since he had taken ownership of the luxurious 3,000-square-foot apartment, Trincher had spared no expense in decorating it. So lavish was one of the lavatories—with walls lined with handcrafted alabaster, a faucet with 24-karat gold overlay, and a $350,000 floor made of amethyst imported from Tanzania—that it earned a spot on a TV show called *Extreme Bathrooms*.

Inside the apartment, agents found millions of dollars in jewelry and gold and more than $2 million in casino chips, which a prosecutor described as an underground form of currency, far easier to move around than bundles of cash. Agents also found eight phones, four of which were "burner phones" that the FBI often saw in drug cases. Trincher was led away in handcuffs as SWAT members stood sentinel at the entrance to Trump Tower.[11] A total of 34 people would eventually be indicted as part of the ring, and many more would feel its impact. When then ambassador to France Charles Rivkin departed the position to become assistant secretary of state, the Obama administration considered Illya Trincher's friend Marc Lasry as Rivkin's replacement. A week after Illya Trincher was indicted, Lasry pulled his name from consideration, reportedly over his ties to the Trincher poker ring.[12]

As part of a plea deal that resulted in a five-year prison sentence, Vadim Trincher agreed to forfeit cash and property worth more than $20 million. He gave up a Patek Philippe watch, poker chips, cash, gold, and two companies he had acquired as payment from clients, but in the end, for reasons that remain unclear, he was allowed to keep his Trump Tower apartment. (The prosecutor, Harris Fischman, declined comment.)

The person the FBI wanted most, however, was Tokhtakhounov, who emerged as the power behind the entire operation. And it was Tokhtakhounov who would continue to elude the FBI by remaining in Russia, although prosecutors said there were signs that he had traveled outside the country under an assumed name. The luxurious life Tokhtakhounov once led in Europe continued to tempt him out of Russia. But when he was spotted again, it was back in Moscow, on the red carpet of the 2013 Miss Universe contest hosted by Donald Trump himself.

8.

MISTER UNIVERSE

L**ATE IN THE EVENING OF NOVEMBER** 9, 2013, a cadre of Moscovian elites poured into Crocus City Hall, a concert hall near one of Moscow's biggest shopping malls, to attend the sixty-second Miss Universe pageant. The night was abuzz with celebrities—among them Aerosmith's Steven Tyler, who was to be one of the pageant's judges, and Mel B, the Spice Girl known as Scary Spice, who would co-present—along with some interesting characters nonchalantly joining in. One such attendee caught the attention of photographers. He looked like he had stepped out of a music video, clad in a black jacket with a chain-link fence design over a garish blue suit. It was none other than Alimzhan Tokhtakhounov, the gambling-ring leader and gold-medal fixer who was still wanted by the FBI, flashing a big grin as he strolled carefree into the pageant.

To any enthusiast of the Miss Universe pageant, the fact that this would be the first time the bathing suit competition was held in a city with a climate ill-suited for such apparel may have seemed strange. But while warm weather and beaches may have been alien to Moscow, money was not, and it was money that had lured its co-owner Donald Trump back to his mistress city. In June 2013, when Moscow had been announced as that year's host locale, Trump, by then an active Twitter user (he had been on the platform since 2011), tweeted up a publicity storm on its behalf. "The Miss Universe Pageant will be broadcast live from MOSCOW, RUSSIA on November 9th. A big deal that will bring our countries together!" he wrote in one tweet.[1] "Do you think Putin will be going to The Miss Universe Pageant in November in Moscow—if so, will he become my new best friend?" he pondered in another tweet in June.[2] That same month, Trump sent a personal letter to Putin inviting him to the pageant. At the bottom of the typed letter, he handwrote a postscript, noting that he looked forward to seeing "beautiful" women during his trip.[3] While the Russian president never confirmed his attendance, Trump may have been intrigued by the fact that Putin hadn't confirmed his absence, either.

While in Moscow, Trump was asked by Thomas Roberts, the MSNBC reporter hosting the pageant, whether he had a relationship with Putin. Trump confirmed it and expressed his admiration for the Russian president: "I do have a relationship with him," he replied, and noted that as president, Putin "had done an amazing job. A lot of people would say he's put himself at the forefront of the world as a leader." It was as if he were speaking directly to Putin himself, for Trump added that the Russian president was "probably very interested" in both the pageant and what he was saying at that very moment. Trump was reportedly in great spirits as he sat in the front row right next to the man who had paid $20 million to bring this extravagance to Russian soil, the Azerbaijani real estate mogul Aras Agalarov.

The two tycoons chuckled over jokes while they ogled the 86 women who waltzed by in swimsuits and cocktail dresses. But that wasn't to be the evening's only entertainment. Midway through the show, pop singer Emin took to the stage. Flanked by the Miss Universe contestants, Emin belted out a 10-minute repertoire of clubby pop songs while a team of dancers performed a rather jejune choreography of twirls and kicks. When it was over, the audience cheered its appreciation, especially Emin's father, Aras Agalarov. In fact, not only was the handsome and charismatic Emin Agalarov one of Russia's most popular pop singers, but it was he who had brokered the introduction between the elder Agalarov and Donald Trump.

Emin and Trump's relationship owed itself to the music video for his song "Amor." The singer had attended high school and college in America, and the influence of Western culture was apparent in his music. Emin sang many songs in a crooning, perfect English. It didn't hurt his massive popularity in Russia, but it failed to attract Western fans. With "Amor," the title song on his forthcoming album, Emin sought to change that. He hired a British publicist named Rob Goldstone, and the two of them came up with an idea for making a high-quality music video. Emin wanted to find "the most beautiful woman—model—in the world that we could." He continued, "We figured we should reach out to the Miss Universe organization and contact the current Miss Universe."[4] That happened to be Olivia Culpo, who played the role of his sweetheart in the video while Emin crooned for her in the darkness of Los Angeles, where most of the video was shot.[5]

But the video was only part of the plan Emin and Goldstone pitched to the Miss Universe Organization. What if the Miss Universe pageant were to be held in Moscow, where Emin could perform "Amor" and another single, "In Another Life," alongside other models to a viewership of millions? Not only that, but what if the Agalarovs paid for the whole thing? The idea sounded like music to Trump's ears. After convincing NBC, the other owner of the Miss Universe Organization, Emin flew that June to meet Trump in person at his gilded Vegas International Hotel where the deal was confirmed, only five months before the show. At Emin's invitation, Trump would later make a cameo in the video for "In Another Life." At the end of the song, the lovestruck Emin closes his eyes and reopens them to find himself in a boardroom meeting with Trump. (The scene was filmed in the Moscow Ritz). Trump chastises Emin and then delivers the line that had made him famous across America: "You're fired."

Emin had gotten his wish to perform before a global audience, but his hopes of gaining Western fans never took off. As Olivia Wells, who competed as Miss Australia, noted, this was likely due to Emin's lack of talent. "Us girls all knew he had zero talent," Wells said. "We were all laughing about how easy life would be if you had a dad who could just buy you a TV event to try and make you famous. That was the joke, that Miss Universe was in Russia because Agalarov wanted to buy his son a big break even though he was shockingly bad."[6] Trump was more complimentary. "Emin was WOW," he wrote on Twitter.

␣

REGARDLESS OF AGALAROV'S INTENT IN bringing the pageant to Moscow, Trump's brief stay in the city would haunt the future president long after the winner was crowned. Trump had arrived on the eve of the pageant, departing from Asheville, North Carolina, where he had attended the Rev. Billy Graham's ninety-fifth birthday party. Trump flew to Moscow on a private jet owned by his friend Phil Ruffin, who was married to a former Miss Ukraine who had competed in the 2004 pageant and judged the one the following year.

Not long after his arrival in Moscow, Trump was escorted to a dinner at Nobu, the famed sushi restaurant of chef Nobu Matsuhisa, who was a friend of the Agalarovs and would be among the panel of judges for the pageant. Agalarov owned both the rooftop Moscow franchise of Nobu as well as the building it crowned. Joining the dinner party was Herman Gref, chief executive of Sberbank, Russia's largest state bank and Agalarov's biggest creditor. Over plates of sushi served beneath sea urchin–inspired chandeliers, Trump and his hosts discussed interest rates and the prospect of a breakup of the European Union, which Trump said was unlikely. "We talked about business," Agalarov said, "but not his business."[7]

Though it wouldn't happen over gourmet Japanese, Trump and

Agalarov did make time to talk about Trump's business. Agalarov was developing a property he was calling "The Manhattan," a 57-acre site within the Crocus complex where the pageant was to be held. "We began to discuss joint work in the area of real estate a few days ago," Agalarov said on the day of the pageant.[8] According to a brochure produced by his American architecture firm, the project had been inspired by his son's experience living in New York City and was designed to emulate the feel of a Madison Avenue condo. The plan called for 13 towers totaling more than 10 million square feet of space. But Trump had another idea.

During the pageant, two of the partners involved in Trump SoHo, Alex Sapir and Rotem Rosen, flew to Moscow to discuss with Agalarov the idea of replicating the building for Agalarov's proposed development. "The Trump SoHo has a lot of very high-profile Russian visitors and they have been telling us they wish there was something modern and hip like it in Moscow," Alex Sapir told *Real Estate Weekly*. "Over the last ten years, there have been no big new hotels built in Moscow. A lot of people from the oil and gas businesses have come to us asking to be partners in building a product like Trump SoHo there."[9]

Because Trump only had two days in Moscow, he kept his focus on two things: Putin and the pageant. Putin's spokesman, Dmitry Peskov, called Trump upon his arrival in Moscow. Earlier, Peskov had conveyed the president's interest in a meeting but Trump's last-minute change of travel plans had made it impossible for the two men to meet. In the end, Putin was unable to accommodate him in his schedule. Instead, the Russian president sent his regards in a note accompanied by a traditional Russian gift, a decorative lacquered box, hand-delivered to the Miss Universe offices in New York by Aras Agalarov's daughter, Sheila. Trump would make much of this gift, commenting during the Conservative Political Action Conference, apropos of nothing, that "Putin even sent me a present, beautiful present, with a beautiful note. I spoke to all of his people."[10] The note's message has never been made public.

For Trump, the pageant had been a hit, which he attributed to his popularity there. "The Russian market is attracted to me," Trump told

Real Estate Weekly. "I have a great relationship with many Russians, and almost all of the oligarchs were in the room."[11] His ebullient mood during that time may have been noticeable to those around him, including people who may have wanted to take advantage of Trump's desire to have a good time in Moscow.

According to a dossier compiled by Christopher Steele, a former spy with MI6, Britain's equivalent of the CIA, Russian intelligence managed to gather *kompromat,* or compromising material, that displayed Trump's "personal obsessions and sexual perversions." This took place in the luxury suite Trump had rented in the Ritz Carlton, the same $13,000-a-night suite that Barack and Michelle Obama had stayed in during the president's first visit in July 2009. Steele, the ex-spy, noted, not incorrectly, that Trump despised the Obamas. At the time, he was leading a "birther" campaign against the president, based on the racist lie that Obama was born not in Hawaii, but in Africa, and therefore had no right to be president.

According to the report, Trump had a particularly perverted idea to defile the bed the Obamas had slept in while getting a fetishistic thrill. He employed a number of prostitutes to perform a "'golden showers' (urination) show in front of him." Steele's source was a "a close associate of Trump who organized and managed his recent trips to Moscow." Two other of Steele's sources, including a female staffer at the Ritz, confirmed the story. Steele noted that the hotel was known to be under the control of Russian intelligence, with cameras and microphones in all the main rooms, a possibility that Trump later publicly indicated he was well aware of.

The allegation remains unconfirmed. Trump has emphatically denied it as fake news produced by a "failed spy" and no witnesses have publicly confirmed it. Keith Schiller, Trump's longtime bodyguard, told congressional investigators that he was approached by a Russian who offered to send five women up to Trump's suite at the Ritz. "We don't do that type of stuff," Schiller told the Russian, and later laughed about it with Trump.[12] (On the other hand, Schiller acted as the go-between for porn star Stormy Daniels's trysts with Trump. "That's how I got in touch with him," Daniels told *In Touch Weekly* in 2011. "I never had Donald's cellphone number. I always used Keith's."[13])

According to Steele's report, which he submitted months before the 2016 election, this was not the first time that Trump had behaved inappropriately in Russia. His report quoted a high-level intelligence officer as saying that "TRUMP's unorthodox behavior over the years had provided the authorities there with enough embarrassing material on the now Republican candidate to be able to blackmail him if they so wished."[14] In a subsequent report, Steele's sources told him that Trump had taken part in sex parties in St. Petersburg, Russia, and made use of "extensive sexual services there from local prostitutes." However, all witnesses had been "silenced"—bribed or coerced to disappear. Trump also paid bribes in St. Petersburg for deals involving real estate.[15] One person who would know what hijinks Trump had been up to in St. Petersburg was Aras Agalarov.

ARAS AGALAROV HAD GROWN UP in Baku, the capital of the former Soviet republic of Azerbaijan. His father died when he was 13, so young Aras sold goods on the black market to help support his family. He hawked videocassettes of *The Godfather* and other American movies, a practice he continued until he left Baku for Moscow in 1983. He moved his family, including three-year-old Emin, to enroll as a graduate student at the N. M. Shvernik Higher School of Trade Unions in Moscow. After defending a thesis in economics, he worked as a junior research associate at one of the USSR's institutional dinosaurs, the All-Union Central Council of Trade Unions, a body dominated by the Communist Party that oversaw all unions in the country. Agalarov was well on his way to an unremarkable career as a Soviet functionary.

He changed course when premier Mikhail Gorbachev unleashed the pent-up capitalist initiatives of the Russian people during perestroika, the restructuring of the collapsing Soviet economy. A new law permitted small businesses called "cooperatives"—partnerships of three or more individuals in which profits were shared. Agalarov in 1987 formed a cooperative called Saffron, and began importing scarce printers and copiers into the Soviet Union. When computers emerged on the market, he began importing them as well. He exported *matryoshka*, the hand-painted Russian wooden nesting dolls. Agalarov's dolls were forerunners of the globalized economy: they were fashioned out of Mexican lumber, hand-painted in Russia, and sold all over the world.

Agalarov staged a computer show, COMTEK '90, a Soviet-American joint venture, at the Russian World Trade Center, a huge complex not far from the Kremlin. At the trade show, he met an American named Mark LoGiurato, a 25-year-old speech pathologist turned entrepreneur. LoGiurato was so impressed by the potential he saw in Moscow that he took a job running the American side of the joint venture out of the offices of Comtek Expositions Inc., in Wilton, Connecticut.

Within a few years, LoGiurato was putting together nine different trade shows in the former Soviet Union, the biggest of which was the computer exhibition. Young employees, many of whom spoke Russian, filled Comtek's freewheeling office in Wilton, Connecticut, which was decorated with Agalarov's ubiquitous matryoshka. Through Crocus, Comtek helped produce Ted Turner's Goodwill Games in St. Petersburg, Russia, in the summer of 1994.

In the winter of that year, an unusual visitor arrived at Comtek's offices. "There's a woman here from the CIA," a receptionist told LoGiurato. He was sure one of his friends was pulling his leg, but in walked a beautiful brunette who looked something like the actress Natalie Wood. The woman pulled out a badge and introduced herself as a CIA officer. She explained that she was there as a gesture of goodwill from the U.S. government. She pulled out a picture of Alexandr Rutskoi, the former vice president of Russia who had launched an unsuccessful attempt to seize power from Boris Yeltsin the previous year.

"How do you know him?" the woman asked.

"I don't know him," LoGiurato replied.

Next, she pulled out a picture of LoGiurato shaking hands with

Rutskoi at a Comtek trade show in Moscow. LoGiurato explained that this was just one of hundreds of hands he had shaken as part of his job. He had shaken Gorbachev's and Boris Yeltsin's hands as well. The politicians would all show up for the opening day of the trade show for press pictures. In fact, LoGiurato was on TV so much that Russians started to recognize him as a celebrity.

The CIA officer then explained the purpose of her visit. "We're not allowed in that country, but we'd like you to tell us what's going on during your visits. You don't have to do anything, just tell us what you see and report back to us," LoGiurato said she told him. He replied that he had no interest and no time. He was trying to build a business and he didn't want interference from the government. She returned a second time, and LoGiurato turned her down again. "I was adamantly against it," he said. "It just didn't feel right." (The CIA declined to comment.)

The failed CIA effort to recruit LoGiurato was an interesting twist in an old spy game played at trade shows. The Soviet Union had long used trade organizations and trade shows for spying. Expocentre, the large Soviet trade show hall on the Moskva River, was staffed with KGB agents. Western trade shows were targeted for intelligence collection.

A few months after the CIA visit, the FBI stopped by Comtek. Large inflows of money from Russia into Comtek's bank accounts at Chase Manhattan via the First Republic Bank of New York had attracted the bureau's attention. (Gross receipts of the joint venture in 1995 and 1996 were running at around $20 million a year.) The way LoGiurato saw it, the FBI seemed to have a hard time accepting that any company that operated in Russia in the 1990s was a legitimate operation. "We showed them all the contracts," he said. The FBI left after a few hours.

The government didn't lose interest in Comtek, however, for the FBI investigation was followed by a criminal investigation by the Internal Revenue Service (IRS). The focus of the IRS investigation was an Irish shell company called ECI Management Services Ltd. that Crocus and Comtek set up to take over payment of royalties from the Russian trade shows. ECI was a way of distributing overseas profits before they reached America. "From where I sat everything was up and up," Lo-Giurato said. The government didn't see it that way. To the IRS, it looked like tax evasion.

Agalarov and his fellow shareholders at Comtek denied that they were cheating on taxes, but the government wasn't reassured when they asserted their Fifth Amendment rights against self-incrimination in response to requests for information from the IRS about ECI. Comtek was sold in 2000, but the tax investigation dragged on for years. In 2003, a tax court judge found no evidence that Comtek or Crocus were formed to evade taxes, but he did deliver a stinging denunciation of Agalarov's business practices. Crocus, like ECI, was a financial "black hole," Tax Court Judge Renato Beghe wrote in his ruling on the case. "The stipulated facts in this case present a mysterious world where real-life agreements are disregarded, financial records are nowhere to be found, and a myriad of other relevant information is absent."[16]

WHATEVER HAPPENED THAT NIGHT AT the Moscow Ritz, Trump returned to New York drunk with excitement from his time in Russia and took to Twitter to say so. "I just got back from Russia—learned lots & lots. Moscow is a very interesting and amazing place! U.S. MUST BE VERY SMART AND VERY STRATEGIC."[17] Then he composed a tweet to Agalarov. "I had a great weekend with you and your family. You have done a FANTASTIC job. TRUMP TOWER–MOSCOW is next. EMIN was WOW!"[18] Aras responded by retweeting his son's response: "Mr. Trump thank you for bringing #missuniverse to us we had an awesome time TRUMP tower Moscow—lets make it happen!"[19]

A year later, Trump and the Agalarovs were still talking about building a tower in Moscow, and Agalarov delivered regular updates on the project to the Russian press. But the ship had sailed on an Agalarov-backed Trump Tower in Moscow; a complex of apartment buildings of 40 to 50 stories each had been scheduled for construction in the same area Agalarov had shown Trump's SoHo partners. Even after Trump announced he was running for president in June 2015, the Agalarovs remained bullish on the building project. "Donald Trump, despite the difficult international political situation, is still interested in this project," Emin Agalarov said.[20] Trump's election, however, did finally put the project to rest, but Agalarov insisted that the bonds of loyalty they had built were strong. "Now that he ran and was elected, he does not forget his friends," he told *Forbes*.[21]

It was a friendship based on shared interests. Agalarov's company Crocus Group was a conglomerate that executed massive construction projects such as convention centers that hosted world-class trade fairs, including the Moscow Millionaire Fair, an annual display of conspicuous consumption by Russia's ultra-wealthy elite. Not surprisingly, Trump debuted his Trump Vodka there in 2007. The press called Agalarov "the Donald Trump of Russia."[22] *Forbes* estimated Agalarov's fortune in 2013 at $1.8 billion, but Agalarov, like Trump, liked to inflate the estimates of his wealth. In an interview with the British journalist Luke Harding, Agalarov brushed off the *Forbes* report and insisted that he was far richer, perhaps on the order of $10 billion, with his land holdings worth $6 billion alone. And like Trump, much of Agalarov's business catered exclusively to the wealthy. When Agalarov branched out into luxury condominiums, many Russian oligarchs would move in. When Agalarov moved into restaurants, he made sure only the best chefs like Nobu would be represented.

In other ways, the two men could not be more different. Mark LoGiurato, Agalarov's American business associate, told me that he never could make sense of Agalarov's business ventures with Donald Trump. They seemed out of character for Agalarov. "He's a businessperson, not a snob, not egotistical like our current president. I never understood them together, but business is business," LoGiurato said. Agalarov was an Azeri Muslim, whose wife was from a Jewish family. And even in business, comparing Agalarov to Trump somewhat understates the scale of Agalarov's business empire and his connections to the highest reaches of the Kremlin. Like his fellow oligarchs, Agalarov used money to gain political power and then used his political power to make even more money.

The public sector in Russia is notoriously rife with corruption, according to the "Russia Corruption Report" produced by the respected Business Anti-Corruption Portal. "Bribes, kickbacks and other irregular payments are often exchanged to obtain public contracts and licenses. Companies report favoritism in decisions of government officials, and public funds are frequently diverted due to corruption," the site stated.[23] Although there is no evidence that Algalarov's Crocus Group obtained infrastructure contracts through underhanded means, in the years leading up to Miss Universe, Crocus started winning major state contracts, even if the final products turned out to be less than stellar.

In 2012, when Crocus was picked to construct new campus buildings for a state-funded university located in the Russian Pacific-coast city of Vladivostok, the work was so shoddy that brand-new buildings leaked in the autumn rains. Poor performance, however, did not stop Crocus from receiving even more lucrative state contacts. It was Crocus that would be tapped to build stadiums for the 2018 World Cup and reconstruct the battered Moscow Automobile Ring Road that encircles the city. Agalarov portrayed himself as doing the bidding of the Kremlin, describing the state contracts as a "status project" that didn't actually make him any money.[24] Yet, according to *The New York Times*, Crocus was written into a 2014 treaty between Russia and Kyrgyzstan for the express purpose of excluding any competitors in a $127 million job.[25]

Agalarov clearly enjoyed his political connections, with the Kremlin viewing the oligarch with rare admiration. Just days before the Miss Universe ceremony, Russian President Vladimir Putin had awarded Agalarov the Order of Honor, given to Russian citizens for extraordinary achievements. Agalarov also wrote an open letter defending Yury Chaika, the general prosecutor of the Russian Federation, and his family from allegations of widespread corruption levied by Alexei Navalny, the anti-corruption campaigner and opposition politician. "The first impression is shock," Agalarov wrote in an open letter published in

Kommersant after watching the popular video Navalny produced on Chaika. The video attempted to "cover a person and his family with mud to try and manipulate public opinion." He concluded his letter by comparing Navalny to Hitler's propaganda minster, Joseph Goebbels.[26] Agalarov's friendship with Chaika would later have major consequences for Trump's presidential campaign.

DONALD TRUMP WOULD DECLARE HIS presidential run in June 2015, descending the escalator at Trump Tower to give an inflammatory speech that blamed Mexico for sending its most problematic people to the United States: "They're bringing drugs. They're bringing crime. They're rapists," he said.[27] Several networks cut ties with him as a result of the speech, including NBC, which owned half of the Miss Universe Organization. Trump bought NBC out, and sold the beauty pageant to William Morris Endeavor/IMG only three days later.

Emin Agalarov kept up his relationship with the Trumps, even giving a private performance for Trump at his National Golf Course in Doral, Florida, in March 2014. A year later, when the singer performed at Highline Ballroom, a concert venue in New York City, his publicist invited Trump's son Don Jr. to attend. The two became chummy enough that just over a year later, when Emin needed to set up a meeting with the Trump campaign to provide dirt on Hillary Clinton, it would be to Don Jr. that he turned.

On June 3, 2016, on behalf of his client, Emin's publicist Rob Goldstone emailed Don Jr. the following message:

Good morning
Emin just called and asked me to contact you with something
very interesting.
The Crown prosecutor of Russia met with his father Aras
this morning and in their meeting offered to provide the Trump
campaign with some official documents and information that

would incriminate Hillary and her dealings with Russia and
would be very useful to your father.

This is obviously very high level and sensitive information but
is part of Russia and its government's support for Mr. Trump—
helped along by Aras and Emin.

What do you think is the best way to handle this information
and would you be able to speak to Emin about it directly?

I can also send this info to your father via Rhona, but it is
ultra sensitive so wanted to send to you first.

Best

Rob Goldstone

THERE IS NO CROWN PROSECUTOR in Russia. This is most likely a reference to Yury Chaika, the prosecutor general Agalarov had publicly
defended. All signs point to Chaika as the one who orchestrated the plan
to deliver the dirt on Hillary Clinton to the Trump campaign. The news
was enticing enough that within minutes Don Jr. had replied:

Thanks Rob I appreciate that. I am on the road at the moment
but perhaps I just speak to Emin first. Seems we have some time
and if it's what you say I love it especially later in the summer.
Could we do a call first thing next week when I am back?

Best,

Don

Over the course of a week, Goldstone and Don Jr. worked out a
meeting for 4 PM on June 9, 2016. Don Jr. invited along his brother-
in-law, Jared Kushner, who was a top campaign official, along with
Trump's newly appointed campaign chairman Paul Manafort. Don Jr.
was informed that two people would be in the meeting, one of whom
was described to him as a "Russian Government Attorney," later identified as Natalia Veselnitskaya, an in-house counsel for the Chaika family.

The main subject of the meeting was the Magnitsky Act. This law,
pushed by investor Bill Browder and signed by President Obama in

2012, sanctioned Russian officials for the death of Sergei Magnitsky, an accountant who was beaten and left to die in a prison cell after uncovering a $230 million Russian tax fraud. The law was particularly vexing to the Kremlin and Chaika had dispatched Veselnitskaya to organize a campaign to undermine the law.

In an interview with *Bloomberg*, Veselnitskaya said that Don Jr. had promised to review the Magnitsky Act. "Looking ahead, if we come to power, we can return to this issue and think what to do about it," Veselnitskaya quoted Don Jr. as saying. "I understand our side may have messed up, but it'll take a long time to get to the bottom of it."[28] Manafort typed notes on his cellphone, which were later turned over to congressional investigators. His notes included cryptic statements such as "Value in Cyprus as inter," "Ilici," "133 million," "Active sponsors of RNC"—a possible reference to the Republican National Committee—"Russian adoption by American families," and "Browder hired Joanna Glover," a mistaken reference to Juleanna Glover, Browder's DC lobbyist who was a former press secretary to Vice President Dick Cheney.

Veselnitskaya then brought up the Ziff brothers, a wealthy American magazine family who had invested with Browder, quoting an elaborate theory that involved Browder, tax evasion, and Clinton contributions. When Don Jr. asked for documentation, Veselnitskaya replied that she had no proof to offer. The 20-minute meeting quickly fell apart, with Kushner leaving early. Both Kushner and Don Jr. said they viewed the meeting as a waste of time. In his carefully worded testimony to the Senate Judiciary Committee, Don Jr. said the meeting at Trump Tower provided "no meaningful information" on Hillary Clinton.

Steve Bannon, the former White House strategist who told author Michael Wolff that he thought the meeting was "treasonous," referred to the president's son as Fredo. That was yet another *Godfather* reference, this time to the gullible and weak-minded son of Mob boss Vito Corleone who craved, but never received, his father's approval.[29] ("Fredo has a good heart, but he is weak and stupid, and this is life and death," says his younger brother, Michael, who supersedes him as head of the family business.) With his Fredo-like gullibility, Don Jr. could not understand the forces arrayed before him and what consequences his actions might have.

What Don Jr. couldn't see was that the meeting bore some familiar fingerprints. James Clapper, the former director of national intelligence under President Obama, said the Trump Tower meeting was "classic, textbook Soviet and now Russian tradecraft." Russian intelligence was notorious for using intermediaries, and may have been testing the waters to see whether the Trump campaign would accept dirt from them. If it was an intelligence operation, it was not a waste of time at all for the Russian side. The message that the Kremlin got back was twofold. First, the Trump campaign would play ball. Rather than call the FBI immediately, the president's son and two top campaign officials accepted the meeting. If it wasn't criminal, it was quite possibly "felony stupid," as one DC attorney put it to me. Secondly, the message the Kremlin got back from the Trump meeting was that the dirt on the Ziff brothers *wasn't good enough*. Don't you have something better? And, as if by magic, three days later WikiLeaks founder Julian Assange revealed to *ITV* that his organization had obtained hacked emails stolen from the Clinton campaign.

ALONG WITH THE PUBLICIST ROB Goldstone, who had sat in on the meeting, Veselnitskaya was joined by Rinat Akhmetshin, a former Soviet army officer turned rambunctious Washington lobbyist working on behalf of Russian (and oligarch) interests. After news of the meeting blew up, a *Financial Times* journalist named Katrina Manson interviewed Akhmetshin at a Washington restaurant near the capital. At what became a five-hour lunch, the colorful Akhmetshin described himself as a hired gun who would do anything for money and brushed off claims by members of Congress and the media of being a Russian spy. "I have zero interest in working for Russian government," he told Manson. "I don't want to complicate things and quite frankly they will never trust me because I hang out with too many Agency"—

CIA—"people." Akhmetshin said he had been asked to join the meeting because of his work lobbying against the Magnitsky Act, which he claimed was hastily signed without being thoroughly understood. Over wine and rabbit pâté, Akhmetshin reported how Veselnitskaya's papers showed "how bad money ended up in Manhattan and that money was put into supporting political campaigns," adding that he thought Veselnitskaya was giving Don Jr. "low-hanging fruit" by tossing the Trump campaign a lead he believed could devastate Clinton's campaign.[30]

While Akhmetshin's reason for being at the meeting made sense, what another participant named Irakly Kaveladze was doing there has never been made clear. Kaveladze has held various positions in Crocus, including his current title of vice president. LoGiurato, who had met Kaveladze as a young man, considered him to be Agalarov's "eyes and ears" in America, further describing him as smart, well educated, and fluent in English. "Somehow he's related to Aras, I'm not sure how, or maybe Aras is his godfather—something like that," LoGiurato said, adding that on a personal level, he found Kaveladze to be "a really good guy."

Kaveladze studied at the Moscow Finance Institute, a prestigious business school where his classmates included Mikhail Prokhorov, the future owner of the New Jersey Nets and head of Nornickel, one of the world's biggest metals producers. Admission to the institute was granted to those who could call on high-level influence and favors known as *blat*. By the time he graduated in 1990, Kaveladze spoke English fluently. "They didn't teach English to just anyone," said an FBI source. Kaveladze left Russia soon after, opening up Crocus's first U.S. office in New York in 1991. He adopted an American variation of his name: Ike. While it appeared he was trying to help Agalarov establish a presence in the United States, Kaveladze's primary occupation soon became helping Russians move their money out of the country in the midst of post-Soviet turmoil. His fluency in English and his suspected money laundering led some to suspect that Kaveladze was somehow involved with Russian intelligence.

If Kaveladze was a Russian spy, Agalarov and Crocus afforded him a convenient cover. Shortly before the fall of the Soviet Union, in 1990, the administration of Soviet premier Mikhail Gorbachev called for the creation of "an invisible economic structure" to conceal Soviet state funds and wealth. Richard L. Palmer, a former CIA chief of station in the former Soviet Union who focused on Russian organized crime, said that part of this plan involved the creation of shell companies in Delaware.[31] Corporate disclosure laws in Delaware allowed companies to conceal information about the people involved, the principal place of business, or even the specific business activity of the corporation.

In fact, shortly after his arrival, Kaveladze had established two corporations in Delaware: International Business Creations Inc., and later the Euro-American Corporate Services, which helped Russian brokers register thousands of Delaware corporations and set up hundreds of U.S. bank accounts. What Kaveladze's Russian clients did with their accounts isn't known, but according to Palmer, these types of corporations would assume loans from offshore banks, which were then used to invest in Russia under the protection of American laws.

From 1991 through January 2000, Kaveladze's clients wired more than $1.4 billion into hundreds of accounts that he or his company opened at two U.S. banks, Citibank and Commercial Bank of San Francisco, with much of that money coming from overseas. His business eventually became the subject of an investigation by Congress. "These transfers raise concerns that the U.S. banking system may have been used to launder money," the Government Accountability Office, the investigative arm of Congress, concluded in a report on its investigation into Kaveladze's businesses.[32]

At Citibank, where some $725 million passed through 136 accounts that Kaveladze opened for himself and his clients, Kaveladze identified his primary client as Crocus International, "a legitimate shoe distributor in Russia that formerly employed Mr. Kaveladze," the bank's general counsel, Michael Ross, wrote in a letter to the Senate.[33] (While working on the computer trade show business, in 1991 Agalarov launched what became a chain of stores selling high-end shoes and fashion.) The bank noted that it found no illegal activity in the Kaveladze-related accounts. But no one at the bank had bothered to ask the obvious question: Why did a Russian shoe seller need to move millions of dollars through U.S. banks?

Incredibly, Citibank opened the accounts without requiring that the account holder even set foot in the bank, something that would be unimaginable today. Kaveladze explained that he was seeking to aid other Russians in securing a safe place to park their money while Russia underwent wrenching political and economic upheaval. Just as he had impressed LoGiurato, Kaveladze struck both the branch manager and the sales manager as a likeable, well-educated Russian businessman.

Citibank allowed most of the money to pass through the Kaveladze-linked accounts unmolested, but one instance did raise suspicions. In July 1994, the branch manager noted a $1 million wire into one of Kaveladze's business accounts and an $850,000 wire transfer out three days later. Asked for an explanation, Kaveladze said the funds were earmarked for a business in Brazil and the receiving party could accept only $150,000. A Citibank loss-control manager reviewed the confusing transaction and determined, somewhat remarkably, that it was not cause for concern.

More than $600 million was wired into the second bank involved in Kaveladze's operation. Commercial Bank of San Francisco was a small, privately held bank, formed in the mid-1970s. Kaveladze partnered with a Commercial Bank director and owner named Boris Goldstein, who had made a fortune in software in Latvia and used it to invest in banks. The Government Accountability Office reported that Goldstein had "a close relationship with companies associated with members of the former Soviet Union's intelligence agency."[34] Goldstein invested in a Latvian bank called Sakaru, which had the last chairman of the Latvian KGB as its business manager. Findings from this part of the investigation were referred to the U.S. attorney in San Francisco, Robert Mueller, the future special counsel, but no charges were ever filed.

When Congress started poking around in his activities, Kaveladze protested that he was being scapegoated. He said he had done nothing wrong, but he was nevertheless liquidating his company "due in part to concerns about money-laundering issues that were raised in 1999 when the media reported allegations that Russian organized crime had laundered billions of dollars through the Bank of New York." Kaveladze blasted the Bank of New York scandal as an "ethnic witch hunt" in an op-ed written at the time. "The Russian businessman and the Russian-American have become stock villains from Central Casting," he wrote.[35]

As for Kaveladze's boss, Aras Agalarov was part of a "Russian Central Asian crime nexus," said Glenn Simpson, who spent a year investigating Trump's organized-crime connections, in testimony before the House Intelligence Committee.[36] According to numerous press reports and the website of a respected Russian billionaire, Agalarov's main source of capital in the 1990s was not his shoe stores or his trade shows but his share in Cherkizovsky market. This huge market in northeastern Moscow was dominated by criminal gangs. It was a crossroads of sorts for people from Asia and the former Soviet republics who were engaged in all manner of shady dealings, selling everything from drugs to counterfeit Asian products to counterfeit clothes made locally by illegal aliens. Among the original owners of the Cherkizovsky market were Zarakh Iliev and God Nisanov, two members of Moscow's rapidly growing community of "Mountain" Jews—the Tats—who hailed mostly from Azerbaijan. Agalarov later went into business with both men in the Grand furniture hypermarket and Food City, a wholesale market on the western outskirts of Moscow.[37]

In 2006, the Agalarov family joined with the ruling family of Azerbaijan when Emin married Leyla Aliyeva, daughter of Azerbaijan's despotic ruler, Ilham Aliyev. A cable from the U.S. Embassy in Baku released by WikiLeaks compared the Aliyevs to the Corleone family in *The Godfather*, which appears to be a popular pop culture reference among politicos.

The same year of the Agalarov wedding, an Azerbaijani vor, a top-level Russian gangster named Ikmet Mukhtarov, was gunned down in Moscow. Mukhtarov was killed instantly when assassins unleashed a torrent of bullets as he sat in a Mercedes 500 on Leningradsky Prospekt. The respected Russian daily *Kommersant* reported that Mukhtarov's killing was part of a string of slayings connected to a Mafiya war for control over incomes from several large markets and shopping complexes in Moscow. The car in which Mukhtarov was killed belonged to one of the co-founders of Crocus International.[38]

PART III
THE RED HOUSE

9.

BLOOD MONEY

C AN THEY REALLY STEAL THIS THING from me?" Donald Trump asked.

It was early spring of 2016, and Trump had called Roger Stone at his home in Florida. Stone was Trump's longtime friend and his off-again, on-again political consultant who had been urging him to run for president for years. Even though he had a commanding lead in the race for the Republican nomination, Trump was worried. A committed core of GOP "never Trump" stalwarts were upset that the party was on the verge of nominating a man whom they felt was deeply unqualified to be president. Trump was becoming obsessed with the idea that he could win the primaries and still lose the nomination. Stone stoked his fear.

"Yes, they can steal it, and they will try," Stone told Trump.

"Even though I won all the primaries?"

"Yes, they're going to play games with the rules," Stone said.

Trump wanted to know what to do about it.

Call Paul Manafort, Stone told him.[1]

Stone had introduced Trump to Manafort, his old friend and business partner, at the 1988 GOP convention in New Orleans. (Another version of this story says it was Roy Cohn who had introduced them.) In 1980, Stone and Manafort had co-founded Black, Manafort and Stone, a Washington lobbying firm that had a reputation for taking on controversial but high-paying clients. The firm had even helped Trump resolve a dispute with the Federal Aviation Administration over the height of a few of his buildings. It didn't hurt that Manafort owned an expensive condominium in Trump Tower and occasionally bumped into Trump in the building.

Another of Trump's longtime friends, the real estate investor Thomas J. Barrack Jr., also championed Manafort. Barrack had been urging the real estate tycoon to hire Manafort as a "delegate wrangler." Barrack had known Trump for 30 years, but he had known Manafort even longer. The two men had met in the 1970s when they were both young lawyers working in Saudi Arabia.[2]

Trump had his campaign manger, Corey Lewandowski, set up a meeting. The loyal Lewandowski invited the man who would replace him to a dinner on March 28 at Mar-a-Lago. When Manafort arrived, Trump's first remark was, "Wow, you're a good looking guy."[3] The 66-year-old political operative had the carefully coiffed look of a network news anchor, exactly the sort of establishment figure whose approval Trump so desperately craved. Normally, Trump liked to dine outside and mingle with guests at his resort, but when Manafort arrived, he and Trump dined alone, inside, by the fireplace.

Manafort had drawn up a two-page list of talking points in his pitch to work for the Trump campaign. Manafort promised that the GOP convention in Cleveland would be a worry-free "Trump-controlled convention." Roger Stone said he told Trump that Manafort knew more about convention politics "than anyone in America." That was an exaggeration, putting it mildly. Manafort's last convention job had been an informal one at the 1996 GOP convention in San Diego, and it had been even longer, some 40 years, since Manafort last helped fend off a convention challenge.

"I am not looking for a paid job," read the item at the top of Manafort's list of bullet points. This was highly unusual to say the least, and what made it even more worrisome was that, at the time, Manafort was deeply in debt. When he appeared before Trump, Manafort's life was in shambles. He owed millions of dollars to a powerful Russian oligarch who was hounding him for money. His daughters had caught him having an affair with an expensive mistress. He had entered a clinic in Arizona.

Lower down on his list of talking points, Manafort described himself as a Washington outsider in a section headed "Not a part of the political establishment." Only a complete outsider like Trump, and possibly not even Trump himself, believed that. Paul Manafort wasn't about to drain the Washington swamp. He had helped make the nation's capital into what it is today, and a drained swamp would mean Manafort would have to give up his many homes, cars, and fine clothes. Manafort also promised not to bring "Washington baggage." Paul Manafort *was* Washington baggage, as Trump would soon learn.

MANAFORT HAD BEEN AROUND WASHINGTON since his early days on the Nixon campaign. "Influence peddler" was how Manafort described himself. In the lobbying practice he set up with Roger Stone, Manafort had gone around the world and, as Stone put it, "lined up most of the dictators in the world that we could find—pro-Western dictators, of course." A big early client was Ferdinand Marcos, the corrupt ruler of the Philippines. Marcos was said to have handed $10 million in cash to Manafort, who promised to deliver it to President Reagan's reelection campaign. Other clients included Jonas Savimbi, who stoked Angola's civil war for decades; Kenya's Daniel arap Moi; and the leopard-skin-hatted Mobutu Sese Seko of Zaire. In 1992, the brutality of Manafort's clients earned his firm a prominent spot in "The Torturers' Lobby," a report by a Washington, DC, nonprofit, as well as a top "blood-on-the-hands" rating of four in *Spy* magazine, which pronounced Black, Manafort and Stone the "sleaziest of all in the Beltway."[4] Hacked text messages that were posted online revealed that even his daughters were troubled by what one called their father's lack of a "moral or legal compass."

"Don't fool yourself," Manafort's daughter Andrea wrote her sister. "That money we have is blood money."

Then again, Trump may also have been intrigued by another part of Manafort's background: his deep connections to post-Soviet Russia. Manafort's most recent work was in Ukraine, where he had helped elect pro-Russia strongman Viktor Yanukovych president in 2010. He had transformed President Yanukovych's Party of Regions from what was viewed as a band of mobsters and oligarchs into a legitimate democratic force. Manafort also had a connection to a powerful Russian oligarch named Oleg Deripaska who was said to have the ear of Vladimir Putin. Emails showed that Manafort had offered to conduct private briefings for Deripaska, during the campaign. As he dined with Trump at Mar-a-Lago, some wondered, did Manafort offer to act as an intermediary between the Trump campaign and the Kremlin?

Whatever Manafort said during that fireplace interview, it got him the job. He moved quickly to professionalize the Trump campaign's delegate outreach and calmed Trump's fears about losing the convention. At the same time, he began angling for a bigger job. While Lewandowski was out working himself sick on the campaign trail, Manafort was meeting regularly in Trump Tower with Trump's children. Within a month, Trump had promoted Manafort to campaign chairman and chief strategist.

And then the stories came tumbling out. *The New York Times* disclosed that a secret cash ledger found in President Yanukovych's party headquarters listed $12.7 million in cash payments earmarked for Manafort. Trump was furious. "I've got a crook running my campaign," he said.[5]

—

MANAFORT'S RELATIONSHIP WITH OLEG DERIPASKA, the Russian oligarch who would become his patron, began in 2004. Manafort's partner, Rick Davis, was invited to the Moscow offices of Basic Element, Deripaska's holding company, where he was introduced to the Russian with the cold, pale eyes. Then 36, Deripaska had emerged from the bloody post-Soviet "aluminum wars" as director general of Rusal, the world's largest producer of aluminum. At the meeting, Davis was given a difficult assignment. It involved resurrecting the career of a man named Igor Giorgadze, an exiled ex-minister of state security in the former Soviet republic of Georgia who was also a former KGB officer. Georgia had embraced the West, and Deripaska wanted to pull it back into Russia's orbit, with help from Davis's firm Davis Manafort Partners.[6]

The firm did what it could, but it was a tall order to rehabilitate a man who had years earlier plotted to kill the country's then president, Eduard Shevardnadze. The Georgian assignment wasn't for naught, however, because the introduction to Deripaska would bear rich fruit for Davis and Manafort. Deripaska had a problem that he hoped Davis Manafort Partners might be able to help him resolve: he was not allowed in the United States. For years, the State Department had denied the oligarch a visa, reportedly over concerns of his ties to organized crime.

Russian aluminum has long been ruled by organized crime, which likely played a role in Deripaska's stunning rise. For a time, he was a protégé of sorts to Michael Cherney, the post-Soviet aluminum king linked to organized crime. Testimony by one of Deripaska's former business partners in Stuttgart, Germany, revealed that the oligarch had close connections to the FSB, the Russian intelligence service, and those contacts were of strategic importance to Cherney and others.[7] In court proceedings across Europe and the United States, Deripaska has been accused of involvement in laundering €8 million, extortion, and threatening the lives of his competitors—charges he forcefully denied.[8]

One FBI agent who spent his career chasing terrorists and spies said the oligarch was one of the few people who ever scared him.[9]

As part of the campaign to help Deripaska get his U.S. visa, Davis arranged a meeting with a group of U.S. senators, including John McCain, one of Putin's fiercest critics in Congress. The meeting was held in Klosters, a village just outside Davos, Switzerland, where McCain was attending the World Economic Forum. Though nothing came of the meeting (the Kremlin later issued Deripaska a diplomatic passport), the oligarch was grateful for Manafort and Davis's efforts. "Thank you so much for setting up everything in Klosters so spectacularly," Deripaska wrote in a note. "It was very interesting to meet Senators McCain, [Saxby] Chambliss and [John] Sununu in such an intimate setting." The letter then went on to mention a business deal that Manafort had proposed. "Please will you send me the information on the metals trading company we discussed," the tycoon wrote, adding that he "would be happy to see if I can do anything to help."[10]

Deripaska wasn't just any oligarch, but one very close to Putin. He enjoyed what the U.S. ambassador to Russia, William Burns, described as a "favorable relationship" with the Russian president. "He is a more or less permanent fixture on Putin's trips abroad, and he is widely acknowledged by our contacts to be among the 2–3 oligarchs Putin turns to on a regular basis," Ambassador Burns wrote in a 2006 State Department cable released by WikiLeaks.[11] Deripaska boasted to an American analyst that he wanted to make himself "indispensable to Putin and the Kremlin."[12]

Sensing a monumental opportunity to align himself with the biggest fish in the post-Soviet pond, in 2005 Manafort drafted a proposal for Deripaska. In it, Manafort said he would seek to "bolster the legitimacy of governments friendly to Putin and undercut anti-Russian figures through political campaigns, nonprofit front groups, and media operations." In a confidential memo later obtained by the Associated Press, Manafort laid out a play-by-play strategy that would "refocus, both internally and externally, the policies of the Putin government." He surmised that "this model can greatly benefit the Putin Govern-

ment if employed at the correct levels with the appropriate commitment to success."[13]

When the memo leaked, Manafort and Deripaska were quick to
insist that nothing had come of it. Deripaska went so far as to sue the
Associated Press for defamation for daring to even imply that he had
anything to do with this memo. Lawyers for the Russian oligarch stated
emphatically, "Mr. Deripaska never had any arrangement, whether
contractual or otherwise, with Mr. Manafort to advance the interests
of the Russian government or to implement the purported proposal in
the 2005 Manafort Memo."[14]

Deripaska put Davis Manafort on retainer the following year,
offering them a $10 million annual consulting contract.[15] Deripaska
dispatched Davis to Montenegro to manage a referendum campaign
that ended with the country declaring its independence. Deripaska
had recently acquired Montenegro's biggest aluminum plant, which
then accounted for two-fifths of the country's GDP. According to
information received by *The Nation*, Deripaska had told one of his
closest associates that he had bought the plant "because Putin encouraged him to do it" and that "the Kremlin wanted an area of influence
in the Mediterranean."[16]

Thanks to Deripaska, doors were opening up for Davis Manafort
Partners all over the former Soviet Union. Deripaska recommended
Manafort to Rinat Akhmetov, a Ukrainian coal-and-steel tycoon and
a political kingmaker in Ukraine's Russian-speaking Donbas region.
Akhmetov paid Manafort $12 million to "Westernize" the image of his
holding company, System Capital Management. Akhmetov, apparently
pleased with Manafort's work, introduced him to another would-be
client whose reputation was in desperate need of an overhaul: Viktor
Yanukovych.[17]

—

UKRAINE WAS IN THE MIDST of a revolution, and oligarchs like Rinat
Akhmetov were unsure which way the political winds were blowing.

For over a decade, Ukraine had been governed by its inept and corrupt president Leonid Kuchma. In line to succeed Kuchma were two men who sought to take the country in opposing directions. One was the Ukrainian prime minister and Party of Regions leader Viktor Yanukovych, a candidate widely seen as friendly to oligarchs and to Russia. Opposing him was Viktor Yushchenko, a former prime minister who had lost his position when he took a stand against corruption.

The election became a major battle between Putin and the West. Yushchenko had formed a popular opposition party, Our Ukraine, and openly spoke of his desire to strengthen ties with the European Union. Putin himself stumped for Yanukovych—including making two high-profile trips to Kiev during the campaign. The Russian president had staked considerable resources on his victory by dispatching Russian spin doctors to Kiev, and bombarding Ukrainian viewers with pro-Yanukovych coverage via Russian state TV. U.S. officials have said there were credible reports that Russia funneled large amounts of money into the Yanukovych campaign.

It would end up being an exhausting and nasty election, Yushchenko's popularity versus Yanukovych's moneyed connections. The first round of voting on October 31, 2004, showed Yushchenko slightly ahead but with less than 50 percent of the vote required for outright victory. In the revote on November 21, Yanukovych outpolled Yushchenko. Voter fraud was immediately suspected, with reports coming in of ballot stuffing, voter intimidation, and new registrants swelling the electoral rolls.

A massive protest dubbed the "Orange Revolution" (the color a reference to Yushchenko's campaign banner) broke out on the streets the next day. It brought Ukraine to a standstill and stalled Yanukovych's claim to the presidency, much to the consternation of his supporters. Galvanizing the movement was Yushchenko himself, who had nearly died during the campaign. It was later discovered that his food had been spiked with dioxin, a poison found in the Vietnam-era herbicide Agent Orange. Yushchenko emerged disfigured by the poison, but determined to lead his country.

Charges of corruption, dioxin poisoning, and Russian meddling heightened the drama of the Orange Revolution. Politicians began to speak openly about splitting Ukraine into two countries. The supreme court ordered a revote and on December 26, Yushchenko won by a landslide.

Down but not out, Yanukovych retreated to the sidelines and plotted his next move. In the summer of 2005, Yanukovych and his political patron, the coal tycoon Rinat Akhmetov, traveled to the Baltschug Hotel in Moscow. There, they met Paul Manafort. Akhmetov wanted Manafort's help with the upcoming Ukrainian parliamentary elections. Manafort agreed and hired more than 40 consultants, many from Washington, and provided the Party of Regions with polling, advice on advertising, and help crafting an overall strategy. According to the *Wall Street Journal*, Davis Manafort Partners was paid $20 million for its initial work in Ukraine.[18]

Manafort set up a base of operations in Ukraine in a nondescript office at 4 Sofia Street near Kiev's Independence Square. There was no sign on the door, and a passerby might easily have missed it. Managing the office was a former Russian army linguist named Konstantin Kilimnik who was "assessed to have ties to a Russian intelligence service."[19] Manafort had worked with Kilimnik on Rinat Akhmetov's campaign. At the time, Kilimnik had been working as a translator in Moscow for the International Republican Institute, a U.S. not-for-profit group that promoted democracy around the world. Kilimnik was dismissed around that time, and he left Moscow and his family for Kiev and Manafort.[20]

Rick Davis took leave from the partnership to run Senator John McCain's unsuccessful presidential campaign against Barack Obama, and Manafort took the reins in Ukraine. He promoted Rick Gates to be his right-hand man and set out to transform the Ukraine Party of Regions from a "haven for mobsters and oligarchs," as a cable from the U.S. ambassador John Herbst had described it, into a legitimate political party.[21] Manafort set up a meeting with Ambassador Herbst, and sought the counsel of a Swedish economic counselor to the Ukrainian government named Anders Åslund, who recalled Manafort as coming off as "highly intelligent and absolutely ruthless." When Manafort told Herbst he would be working with Yanukovych, the ambassador gave him his blessings: "That was something that I thought was a fine idea," Herbst said. "As I said to him, 'If you can help Yanukovych win an election fair and square, good.'" Herbst added, "They would just update me on things they were doing and it all seemed pretty straightforward and nothing problematic."[22]

Manafort began by helping Yanukovych appeal outside of his base, suggesting he give speeches in Ukrainian while in the western half of the country, and in Russian in the pro-Russian eastern half. Manafort then convinced Yanukovych to open up about his past delinquencies, certain assault and robbery convictions that had landed him in jail as a young man. Under Manafort's grooming, Yanukovych shed his rough, pro-Russia image. "He got Yanukovych to wear the same suits as he did and to comb the hair backwards as he does," said Åslund. "Manafort taught him how to smile and how to do small talk." And he did it "from a back seat. He did it very elegantly."[23] Even Herbst was impressed. In a cable, he reported how Yanukovych was undergoing an "extreme make-over," with Manafort doing all of the "nipping and tucking."[24]

Manafort spoke of Yanukovych in Nixonian terms. "His vision is to have a relationship with Ukraine's historic neighbors, while integrating with the West over the longer term. Like Nixon to China, he's the only national leader who can do that."[25] In the meantime, Manafort had inserted himself into a role that Herbst described as "maybe *the* political adviser to Yanukovych."[26] The campaign worked. The Party of Regions won a landslide victory in Ukraine's parliamentary election in 2006, with the repackaged Yanukovych 2.0 reelected as the country's prime minister.

———

ALTHOUGH HE WAS EARNING MILLIONS for his political consulting work in Ukraine, Paul Manafort began using his connections to make even more money. He met Dmitry Firtash, a wealthy Ukrainian businessman involved in the natural gas trade who had friends in top posts in Yanukovych's administration, and pitched him on his grand vision for Bulgari Tower, a $1.5 billion skyscraper project in midtown Manhattan on the corner of Park Avenue and Fifty-Sixth Street. It was said to be one of the most valuable development sites in North America.

The Ukrainian natural gas tycoon had millions to invest because Gazprom, the natural gas giant controlled by the Kremlin, had given his unpronounceable company, RosUkrEnergo, a monopoly on all gas trades between Russia and Ukraine. This incredibly lucrative deal was widely viewed as a partnership with organized crime. Firtash was believed to be a front man for Semion Mogilevich. In court papers in Chicago, where Firtash was indicted in a separate international racketeering conspiracy, prosecutors described him as an "upper-echelon" associate of Russian organized crime.[27] In 2008 Firtash agreed to commit $112 million to Manafort's Bulgari Tower project and wired in a $25 million deposit. The deposit came from Raiffeisen Zentralbank, the Austrian bank that U.S. officials believed served as a Mogilevich front. The tower deal later collapsed.[28]

While he was lining up investments from Firtash, Manafort proposed to Oleg Deripaska that they go into business together. The resulting company was Pericles Emerging Market Partners LP, a private equity fund in the Cayman Islands. Manafort described it to Deripaska as a vehicle to pursue investments that "leverage [our] business and political relationships" in Ukraine. Pericles sought to achieve an impressive compound annual return rate of 30 percent by investing in Ukraine, as well as other areas of interest to Deripaska—Russia, the former Soviet republics, Montenegro, and eastern and southern Europe. The offering memorandum touted Davis and Manafort's experience with political campaigns "at the highest level." The Russian oligarch gave Manafort a tentative commitment to invest $200 million in the fund.[29]

Manafort tasked the management of Pericles to Rick Gates, who visited Deripaska's representatives in Moscow and provided a "fund plan" that described various investment opportunities. Of the many ideas Gates pitched, Deripaska's team felt only one had merit: the acquisition of Chorne More ("Black Sea"), a Ukrainian telecommunications firm.

In April of 2008, Deripaska paid nearly $19 million to fund the acquisition of Chorne More, then paid Manafort an additional $7.35 million in fees.[30] Years later, Deripaska learned that the purchase price of Chorne More was $1.1 million *less* than Manafort and Gates had led him to believe. Gates and Manafort had simply pocketed the difference, laundering it through accounts in Cyprus that the two men used as "their personal piggy banks," the oligarch said in a lawsuit.[31]

What Gates and Manafort also withheld was the fact that Chorne More wasn't worth nearly what Deripaska paid for it. Chorne More was valued at only $4.5 million and took in only $1.5 million in revenue. To top it off, the company was run not in a proper office, but in "a dingy, Soviet-style apartment building about six miles (10 kilometers) from the city center."[32]

Around the time of the Chorne More purchase in early 2008, *Forbes* ranked Deripaska as the ninth-wealthiest man on the planet, with a net worth estimated at $28 billion. The telecommunications company investment was a trifling fraction of his wealth, and it would hardly ruin him if the venture sank. With the advent of the global financial crisis in the fall of 2008, however, Deripaska's businesses were hit particularly hard. Much of his wealth was wiped out and the struggling tycoon went hat in hand to the Kremlin for a $4.5 billion bailout. Putin put Deripaska in his place the following year in Pikalevo, a town that was struggling following the closure of one of Deripaska's aluminum refineries. In a televised broadcast, Putin compared factory owners who didn't pay workers' wages to cockroaches, and then forced Deripaska to sign a document restarting the plant. As the oligarch walked away, Putin snapped, "Give me back my pen."[33]

A humbled Deripaska went looking for pennies wherever he could find them, and he instructed Manafort and Gates to liquidate Pericles and sell off Chorne More. Manafort and Gates agreed, but for the next two years, Pericles neither shuttered its doors nor sold off Chorne More. In fact, investigators later discovered that Chorne More was not owned by Pericles, but by a mysterious British company. The last Deripaska heard from Manafort was in June 2011. After that, Manafort and Gates stopped responding to Deripaska's team. "It appears that Paul Manafort and Rick Gates have simply disappeared," Deripaska's lawyers wrote in a Cayman Islands petition.[34]

Manafort hadn't disappeared; he remained in Kiev with Yanukovych, who was still cutting his checks. As Deripaska worked to keep his empire intact, Manafort worked his sorcery on Yanukovych's presidential campaign in Ukraine's 2010 election. Once again it became a battle of Western and Eastern ideologies, with no clear favorite among the candidates. The administration of President Yushchenko, the man who had defeated Yanukovych in the days of the Orange Revolution, was widely seen as chaotic, with infighting taking precedence over policymaking. Yanukovych had been dismissed as prime minister after a year. His replacement was the co-leader of the Orange Revolution, Yulia Tymoshenko, a steely, blond-bunned politician dubbed "the gas princess" for the enormous fortune she amassed in the 1990s with sweetheart deals in the natural gas business.

In the first round of voting in the 2010 Ukrainian presidential election, Prime Minister Tymoshenko and Manafort's man Viktor Yanukovych emerged as the front-runners. To prep for the second round, Tymoshenko hired AKPD, a consulting firm run by David Axelrod, Obama's former chief strategist, to help bolster her campaign. But AKPD couldn't navigate the complex world of Ukrainian politics like Manafort, and after the dust settled from the second round, his years of steering Yanukovych toward his goal paid off. On February 7, 2010, Yanukovych emerged as the winner and was declared Ukraine's fourth president. Manafort was exalted in the Ukrainian press as a "mythical figure."

Almost as soon as he was sworn in, Yanukovych embarked on a platform to rebuild Ukraine's political alliance with Russia and counter his predecessor's pro-Western initiatives. He bluntly quashed the long-running NATO membership debate among Ukrainian politicians. And while he publicly called for a free and democratic Ukraine, reports of press censorship proliferated, and his political opponents, including the defeated Tymoshenko, landed in jail on trumped-up charges.

Tymoshenko's imprisonment triggered a fierce international outcry, among them a call to boycott Ukraine's bid to host the 2012 European soccer championship. Yanukovych stressed that Tymoshenko "broke the rules" and wagged his finger at her champions. "I am disappointed by the premature conclusions of some European politicians who do not understand the depth of these issues and rush to make political pronouncements. This practice pushes me away from Europe. It pushes me away."[35]

The one Westerner he didn't alienate was Paul Manafort, who continued working behind the scenes for President Yanukovych. Manafort had "walk-in" privileges that allowed him to enter the president's office unannounced. Yanukovych placed such faith in his American advisor that his staff started using Manafort to deliver messages they really wanted the president to hear. "Paul has a whole separate shadow government structure," Rick Gates, his right-hand man, told a group of Washington lobbyists. "In every ministry, he has a guy."[36]

Manafort arranged political cover in the United States for President Yanukovych. He hired two firms in Washington—Mercury Public Affairs and the Podesta Group—to lobby members of Congress on behalf of Ukraine and President Yanukovych's interests, paying both firms $1.1 million each.[37] When Tymoshenko was put on trial, Manafort directed his Washington lobbyists to assure Congress that it was all perfectly legal and appropriate. Manafort secretly paid $4 million to the prominent New York law firm of Skadden, Arps, Slate, Meagher & Flom for a supposedly independent report on Tymoshenko's trial.[38] The report found no political motivation in Tymoshenko's prosecution. Skadden Arps' work was led by Gregory B. Craig, a former White House counsel under President Obama. Later, a Skadden Arps attorney named Alex van der Zwaan would plead guilty to lying to prosecutors about a conversation he had with Rick Gates over the Tymoshenko report. He also admitted to deleting records of email exchanges sought by prosecutors.

Manafort was making good money with Yanukovych, very good money. The only problem was that it was dirty. It was hard to miss how deep Yanukovych's corruption and cronyism went. Much of the funding allocated for Ukraine's economic development went to Donbas, Yanukovych's home region, and a majority of key governmental and economic posts were given to friends of his from that region, many of whom were clearly unqualified for their positions. That was icing on the cake compared to the staggering $70 billion taken from the Ukrainian treasury and secreted away in foreign accounts, including those of Yanukovych's son Oleksandr, who during his father's presidency became one of the wealthiest people in the country. The cherry on top was the presidential palace Yanukovych had built—a giant monument to corruption, complete with a private zoo and a faux galleon moored on a private lake.

Manafort had been stashing away his paychecks from Ukraine in banks registered to shell companies in Cyprus, the tiny European nation that has long served as an offshore financial center for Russian oligarchs. Manafort used his Cyprus accounts to pay for $5.4 million worth of home improvements at his house in the Hamptons, an exclusive community at the tip of New York's Long Island. Another $1.3 million from Cyprus went to a "home automation, lighting and home entertainment company" in Florida, where Manafort had another home. Money from Cyprus also bought a $3 million brownstone in Brooklyn, a $2.85 million condo in SoHo that he rented on Airbnb, and a property in Arlington, Virginia. Special Counsel Robert Mueller would later follow this money trail to return an indictment charging Manafort in a conspiracy to launder money and evade taxes.[39]

The beginning of the end of Manafort's sojourn in Ukraine came in the winter of 2013, when Yanukovych broke with his American advisor and rejected a major trade deal with the European Union, opting instead for closer ties with Russia. For the second time in his career, a major protest broke out, this time in Kiev's Euromaidan Square. Protestors amassed to demand his impeachment for plundering the country's wealth and turning Ukraine into a police state. Tension mounted as the demonstrations, which began peacefully, went on for months. Violence broke out on February 18, 2014, in clashes between protesters and police that lasted several days. At least 82 people were killed over the next few days, including 13 policemen; more than 1,100 people were injured. In the pandemonium, President Yanukovych boarded a helicopter and, with help from Vladimir Putin, fled to Russia where he remained.

Now effectively unemployed, Manafort and Gates shuttered their Ukraine operation. Manafort faded from the scene as he dealt with his mounting personal problems back home, but his wealth and his Ukrainian connections became something of an inside joke back in Washington. Roger Stone, Manafort's old friend and business partner, sent out an email in 2014 to a group of friends asking "Where is Paul Manafort?" The choices were:

- "Was seen chauffeuring Yanukovych around Moscow."
- "Was seen loading gold bullion on an Army transport plane from a remote airstrip outside Kiev and taking off seconds before a mob arrived at the site."
- "Is playing golf in Palm Beach."[40]

10.

THE DOSSIER

TUCKED AWAY IN THE VISITOR'S CENTER for the U.S. House of Representatives is a specially constructed, classified space known in military acronymic jargon as a SCIF, a Sensitive Compartmented Information Facility. To enter a SCIF, one must leave all electronic devices outside of the room and submit to a search before going in. On a crisp fall afternoon in 2017, a private researcher named Glenn Simpson was screened to enter this secure space for a closed-door session with the House Intelligence Committee. The 53-year-old ex-reporter, his Van Dyke beard gray with age, took his seat before the panel, raised his right hand, and swore an oath to tell the truth. After some preliminary introductions, Representative Trey Gowdy, a lanky former federal prosecutor from South Carolina, asked Simpson about the nature of his business. "It's a commercial research firm," Simpson said, "sometimes also does strategy, public affairs. The primary line of work we're in is research.

Generally, it specializes in public records research, other sorts of journalistic style information gathering."[1]

The events Simpson had been called to Congress to explain, however, weren't found in any public documents buried in some musty archive. He had commissioned a former British spy to produce what turned out to be an explosive dossier of intelligence on Donald Trump. The dossier, paid for by the Democratic National Committee (DNC), had caused shock waves that were still reverberating in Washington nearly a year after its publication. This kind of work, which Washington euphemistically called political opposition research, was not what Simpson's company, Fusion GPS, usually did. Most of the firm's work was related to fraud, corruption, policy disputes, and high-dollar litigation, he said, and typical clients were banks, corporations, and big law firms. But every few years, Fusion GPS was called on to do opposition research, and this time, Simpson had uncovered what was by far the biggest story of his career, in or out of journalism. It was a story that had the potential to rival or surpass Watergate: the president of the United States had engaged in compromising sexual behavior in Russia and authorities there had been cultivating him for years and had enough material on him to blackmail him. The question was whether it was true, and the jury was still out on that, but if it was, then it was the biggest story of his generation.

Simpson had given up a career as an investigative reporter at *The Wall Street Journal* to do private investigations. The investigative reporting in which he specialized was becoming too costly even for a successful newspaper like the *Journal*, even more so since its acquisition by Rupert Murdoch. A self-described "document hound," Simpson would show up at a lawyer's office with a giant pile of papers and ask to go over them. He produced high-profile and, yes, expensive stories on terrorism financing, tax evasion, political corruption, and Russian organized crime. His subjects were powerful and wealthy people with the resources to defend themselves. He had been sued more than once for libel. In the end, he had been vindicated, he noted with some pride. "I'm 4-and-0," he said.

Over at the *Journal*, a Saudi businessman named in a story as a suspected terrorism financier sued Simpson for libel in London. The case offered a revealing look at the inside-the-Beltway world of what Simpson called the "elaborate rituals" that had developed in Washington between sources and journalists. These correspondences were conducted with such complexity that a London jury was confused about whether Simpson's source at the Treasury Department had actually confirmed the Saudi's links to terror finance. Simpson explained that sensitive sources within federal departments confirmed facts for journalism in a paradoxical way—by not denying them. This practice skirted secrecy laws and, more importantly, allowed a source to insist that they had said nothing. This was true only in a superficial sense, but in the through-the-looking-glass world of Washington journalism, saying nothing really meant saying something. "We are all gravely serious about what we do," Simpson told the jury.[2]

However Glenn Simpson defined his specialty, he not only had the résumé of a veteran reporter, but also the firsthand experience of being reported. As a young teen growing up in suburban Philadelphia in the early 1980s, Simpson fell into a hard-partying crowd, swigging alcohol as early as ninth grade, especially a concoction he called "jungle juice" made from spirits he'd swiped from his parents' liquor cabinet. During his senior year, Simpson threw a party at his house that ended abruptly when an 18-year-old friend was killed after staggering outside and into the path of an oncoming vehicle. Authorities had taken the unusual step of arresting Simpson's mother on charges of corrupting minors and conspiracy to aid underage drinking. While the most serious charges were later dropped, the humiliating and tragic episode had ended up on the front page of The Philadelphia Inquirer.[3]

Simpson got serious about journalism at George Washington University. He was hired as a reporter for Roll Call, Capitol Hill's foremost newspaper. Early on in his career there, Simpson was tasked with covering the trial of the "Keating Five," a quintet of senators—including John McCain and John Glenn—accused of improperly intervening on behalf of Charles Keating, chairman of a savings and loan who was convicted of fraud. Simpson also co-authored a 1996 book on politics called *Dirty Little Secrets* that took note of the growing field of opposition research and delivered a prescient warning: "While the use of opposition research to launch unfair, scurrilous, or irrelevant allegations is deplorable, snooping gets a lot more hair-raising the deeper the digging goes."[4]

Simpson's work caught the attention of the editors at *The Wall Street Journal*, who invited him to join the newspaper's Washington bureau as a staff reporter, a post he would fill for the next 15 years. While covering Capitol Hill, Simpson became intrigued by the Russian Mafiya and in 2007, he co-published with his wife and *Journal* colleague, Mary Jacoby, an investigative report on the Russian Mafiya's influence on global trade and Washington lobbyists. Seeking ways to make his career more lucrative, Simpson and another writer, Sue Schmidt, left the aegis of the *Journal* in 2009 to form SNS Global LLC, an entrepreneurial firm that specialized in a "hybrid" model of investigative reporting for private clients, who could use that material to silence corporate critics, win a lawsuit, or even win an election. "Journalism for rent," he called it.[5]

The transition from journalism to private investigations has tempted many reporters who fail to realize that they are completely different worlds. Through California Strategies, an influential public affairs firm in Sacramento, SNS Global received a commission to help bring an exiled prince back to his throne. Sheikh Khalid al Qasimi was an Emirati royal living in exile. He was the eldest son of the emir of Ras al Khaimah, the seventh and final emirate to join the United Arab Emirates. The monarch had dismissed Sheikh Khalid over his opposition to the Gulf War and elevated his younger half-brother to crown prince. Sheikh Khalid had spent a half-dozen years and millions of dollars hiring lobbyists to wage an international campaign against his half-brother, accusing him of sympathizing with Iranian extremists and using Ras al Khaimah as a convenient crack in the sanctions wall against Iran. SNS Global was paid £40,000, or roughly $65,000, for its work, but the firm dissolved only a year after launch.

In 2010, Simpson partnered with a former *Journal* colleague named Peter Fritsch to form another private-investigation firm, Fusion GPS.

Unlike SNS Global, Fusion GPS was able to successfully build a confidential and diverse client list that would include Planned Parenthood,
Herbalife, investors in an Antigua resort, and a construction company
in Venezuela called Derwick Associates. Clients often hired Fusion GPS
through an intermediary, usually a large law firm with an international
practice such as BakerHostetler. A typical client fee was $50,000 for a
month's work, which put Fusion GPS at the high end of the opposition
research spectrum, although it was on par with private intelligence firms
like Kroll, IGI, and K2, staffed with ex-CIA and FBI agents. Fusion GPS
remained a smaller, boutique operation, headquartered in Washington's
Dupont Circle neighborhood. Its employees worked out of a small office
above a Starbucks. Cluttered with computers and cables, it carried the
air of a covert operation. Calling Simpson or Fritsch got you an anonymous message that made no mention of the company or its business.
Fusion GPS maintained a staff of a dozen or so ex-journalists and spe-
cialists like Nellie Ohr, an expert on Russian current affairs and the wife
of a senior Justice Department official. Banking records obtained by the
House Intelligence Committee also revealed a network of active journalists that Fusion GPS had hired around the country, reporters much
like myself. In fact, in 2012, Simpson had reached out to me via email to
see if I might be interested in working with them: "Seth—I'm a former
investigative reporter for the WSJ. I now run a research firm in DC. We
do financial/legal research and I was wondering if you do any freelance
research for firms such as mine." I told him I remembered his work from
the *Journal* and that I was indeed interested in his offer. I suggested we
speak by phone, but he didn't respond. I never heard back from him or
anyone else at Fusion GPS again.

While Simpson called his line of work "hybrid journalism," some
of the targets of his investigations accused Fusion GPS of plain old
mudslinging—trolling through divorce records of the national finance
co-chairman of Mitt Romney's presidential campaign, or snooping
through the domestic disputes of a former Beverly Hills mayor.[6] This
was the journalistic equivalent of peeking into someone's medicine cabinet or their underwear drawer in order to win an election campaign.

In the fall of 2015, the *Washington Free Beacon*, a privately owned, for-profit conservative news website hired Fusion GPS to research Donald Trump, then a few months into his presidential campaign. *The Washington Free Beacon* was funded in large part by hedge-fund billionaire Paul Singer, a "Never Trump" Republican and the second-wealthiest donor to Senator Marco Rubio's run. When the *Free Beacon* seemed to realize that Trump might have a better chance at victory than most people were affording him at the time, Singer hired Fusion GPS to find information that could run Trump right off the campaign trail.

Simpson took on the commission, codenaming it "Bangor," and he began by diving into the bountiful information other journalists had published on Trump.[7] One piece in particular caught his eye, *The New York Times* profile of Felix Sater that cost Sater his job and seemingly his close relationship to Trump. The deeper Simpson's investigations of Sater went, the more troubling Sater's association with Trump became. (Simpson believed that Sater was connected to the Brainy Don, Semion Mogilevich.) Tevfik Arif, Sater's boss at Bayrock, seemed to have a source of funds in the former Soviet Union that was murky at first until it became evident that Arif was a major figure in central-Asian organized crime. But Simpson noticed that despite Trump's repeated efforts to downplay his connection to Sater, there were pictures of the two together. Sater continued to work for the Trump Organization long after Trump had learned about Sater's criminal past. Simpson couldn't figure out if Trump had stopped caring or if the continued relationship hinted at something more sinister. "I concluded that he was okay with that," Simpson said, referring to Trump's public relationship with Sater, "and that was a troubling thing."[8]

Another clue that jumped out at Simpson was the number of former Soviet criminals who had purchased or used Trump's real estate properties. He uncovered the dealings of David Bogatin, Vyacheslav Ivankov, Vadim Trincher, Dmitry Rybolovlev, and Alimzhan Tokhtakhounov. The list went on as did the Trump-Russia spider chart. Then there were transactions in Trump properties in Toronto and Panama that smacked of fraud. Both of the Trump buildings had wound up in bankruptcy, but not before someone affiliated with Russian crime had gotten to them first.

Fusion GPS even examined Trump's golf courses in Ireland and Scotland, which were run by Trump's son Eric. Unlike Trump's U.S. golf courses, the Scottish and Irish courses were required to make public disclosures. What they showed were that the courses were money pits. Trump's golf club in Scotland was losing nearly £2 million a year, yet hundreds of millions of dollars appeared to be flowing into the UK courses. The trouble was, no one knew whose money that was. The golf writer James Dodson said that he, too, wondered about who was funding Trump's golf courses, especially in 2008 when no bank would touch a golf course in the wake of the financial crisis. During a visit to Trump National Golf Club Charlotte, Dodson asked Eric Trump about it. "He said, 'Well, we don't rely on American banks. We have all the funding we need out of Russia.' I said, 'Really?' And he said, 'Oh, yeah. We've got some guys that really, really love golf, and they're really invested in our programs. We just go there all the time.'"[9]

A pattern soon emerged that suggested Trump was deeply tied to Russian money and the Russian Mafiya. Early in Trump's career, he had connections to La Cosa Nostra, but during the 1990s he became increasingly associated with Russian Mafiya figures. "As we've got deeper and deeper into understanding, you know, Donald Trump's business career and his history, it gradually reached a point where it seemed like most of the people around Trump had a connection to Russian organized crime or Russia in one way or another," Simpson told committee members. Christopher Steele, the former British spy who produced the dossier Simpson had been called before the House to testify about, echoed that line when he told friends, "it was as if all criminal roads led to Trump Tower."[10]

If Trump had never done business with Russia, as he claimed, it seemed bizarre for him to pay regular visits to Moscow that often ended in public failures. After several months of research, Simpson's investigative project had evolved into a sprawling examination of Trump's relationships with Russian organized crime, a matter that could compromise national security were he to be elected. Though Simpson had uncovered no smoking gun, there were just too many unanswered questions about Trump and Russia for the matter to be left alone. But Simpson had run out of public documents to go through; to continue with the investigation he would need someone who was not only an expert in Russia, but who also had the right kind of deep, inside sources. Simpson knew "the perfect person" for the job.

CHRISTOPHER DAVID STEELE HAD THE kind of personality you might expect from a veteran British intelligence officer. He was someone who did things by the book, who was scrupulous in his acquisition of information, and who was professionally admired and trusted by his colleagues. Upon his graduation from Cambridge University in 1986, Steele had been recruited by MI6, who put him in their intensive Russian-language program before sending him into the Soviet Union in 1990. Steele was assigned to the British Embassy in Moscow, where he worked under a diplomatic cover and witnessed firsthand the calamitous fall of the USSR and the rebirth of Russia as an independent democratic republic. In 1993, Steele was reassigned to Paris, where he continued to monitor Russian figures of interest, though this assignment would end abruptly when a list of British intelligence agents appeared anonymously online. His cover blown, Steele could no longer work undercover and was sent to MI6's headquarters, where he was made head of the Russia desk.

Steele left the service and entered the private sector in 2009, the same year Simpson departed the *Journal*. Like Simpson, Steele also founded an investigative firm with a former colleague called Orbis Business Intelligence. Orbis made its reputation early on by delivering to the FBI incriminating evidence against Chuck Blazer, the Russian-connected American soccer official who took enough bribes to be able to afford a Trump Tower apartment to house his cats. After that, Orbis quickly grew a clientele that included multinational firms and business titans, including a few Russian oligarchs. Steele worked for a law firm representing Oleg Deripaska, the Russian aluminum tycoon who was once Manafort's wealthy patron. If Fusion GPS was journalism for rent, then Steele's Orbis was intelligence to charter. And with the Russian Mafiya now a pressing preoccupation for Simpson, it seemed inevitable that he would end up meeting the man described by Sir Richard Dearlove, the former head of MI6, as the reputable and respectable "go-to person on Russia in the commercial sector."[11]

While professionally collegial, Steele and Simpson made for an odd couple. The former intelligence officer was much more reserved than the former muckraking journalist, which was a personality trait exacerbated by a personal tragedy. In 2009, the same year he left MI6, Steele's wife, Laura, died after a long illness, leaving the ex-spy a single parent of three until his remarriage six years later. Steele and Simpson were introduced by a mutual friend that same year. Simpson described Steele as a "Boy Scout," albeit one in bespoke suits. The two hit it off. When Simpson was in London, they would meet and talk shop about Russian oligarchs and corruption, and over the next seven years, Fusion GPS would hire Orbis for specialized work. There were many people in Simpson's business who delivered baloney; Steele was a professional who delivered the goods. And Simpson knew that this 51-year-old ex-spy was the only person qualified to help Fusion GPS understand what had really happened on Trump's visits to Russia.

There was only one holdup. By this time in March 2016, Senator Rubio had been eliminated in the Republican primaries and Paul Singer's monthly payments to Fusion GPS came to an end. Simpson's investigation would have run out of fuel had a new client not arrived to pick up the tab. In looking for funding, Simpson had reached out to Marc Elias, the Clinton campaign's general counsel, who was a partner at Perkins Coie, a Seattle-based law firm. Simpson persuaded Elias to hire Fusion GPS to "perform a variety of research services" before the election, including continuing the investigation of Donald Trump.[12] Bank records subpoenaed by the House Intelligence Committee show Perkins Coie paid Fusion GPS more than a million dollars in 2016. It was undoubtedly a huge payday for Fusion GPS, though as a veteran political opposition researcher told me, "Whenever you're offered a lot of money, better save some for legal fees."

Opposition research is very much a partisan game, and working for both Republicans and Democrats in the same election cycle was not usually how the business model worked. Democrats typically hired firms that only worked for Democrats, and vice versa. In fact, the DNC and the Democratic Congressional Campaign Committee kept a list of approved opposition researchers that a campaign needed to use if it wanted the party's money. Fusion GPS, however, swung both ways— Republican and Democrat—because they could offer an international reach that few competitors could match. Clients of Fusion GPS were sold a promise that they would have access to international intelligence networks, something considered out of the league of run-of-the-mill political operatives.

But if working across party lines was taboo, continuing the research that a Republican had initiated for a Democratic firm was unheard of. Opposition research firms working on a presidential campaign usually signed contracts filled with dense language about confidentiality and copyrights. Singer said he was not made aware of Fusion GPS's relationship to Perkins Coie, the DNC, or the Clinton campaign. Since Elias was only orally providing information secondhand from what he had received from Fusion GPS, Hillary Clinton could not be liable for breaching copyright laws. Nor did Singer ever attempt to sue the DNC. But even this conundrum paled when compared to the bombshell that would land in the lap of Congress.

In the spring of 2016, Simpson offered Steele a commission to work on the Trump investigation. Take 20 or 30 days, Simpson told him, and see if you can figure out what Trump's been up to in Russia. Steele turned to his network of "collectors"—sources who gathered material from others, often without their realizing it.[13] Simpson declined to go into detail on Steele's sources, but he indicated that these sources were often selected from a vast diaspora of Russian émigrés who not only had noteworthy ties to people back in Moscow, but maintained them on a frequent basis as well.

Steele's first report, dated June 20, 2016, arrived at Fusion GPS's offices via commercial courier. Calling it explosive is an understatement. Steele had been too nervous to send it electronically; he told friends he felt like he was "sitting on a nuclear weapon."[14] What emerged were reports of Trump's sordid behavior at the 2013 Miss Universe pageant, in particular the golden-showers show performed by prostitutes at the Ritz in Moscow. It was common knowledge among intelligence professionals like Steele that Moscow hotel rooms had hidden cameras to collect its *kompromat*, and if Steele's sources were correct, there was no doubt that the Russians were in possession of material that could impact Trump's behavior toward them. According to Simpson, it wasn't all that hard to gather this information. At the time Steele submitted his first report, no one was really concerned about whether Trump did or did not have a relationship with the Kremlin. "When Chris started asking around in Moscow about this the information was just sitting there," Simpson said. Not only were the allegations of Trump's behavior in Russia not much of a secret but as Simpson later said, "People were talking about it freely." It was only later, after Russia became a big story in the presidential campaign, that people clammed up. "We threw a line in the water and Moby Dick came back," Simpson said.

What people failed to realize when the dossier was made public was that sordid allegations like the one in Steele's report are a dirty secret of the world of private investigations. Several people familiar with this world told me that reports by companies like Kroll, K2, Mintz Group, IGI, and others were often littered with tawdry allegations. "Yes, sex stuff comes up a lot and it's often nonsense," a DC attorney who often hires private investigators told me. One veteran opposition researcher told me he has seen the same thing so often that he has detected a pattern: when the subject of the investigation was connected to Latin America, drugs were involved; when the connection was Russia or Eastern Europe, it was usually sex. "Every single one of their reports has something like that," the opposition researcher said. "That's what they pitch the client to keep them on the hook. They then spend months trying to confirm it." After all, the investigators working for these firms were often, like

Christopher Steele, ex-CIA and MI6 spies, people in the deception business. How much of their reports reflected what the client wanted to hear? What was real and what was total bullshit? Steele himself told friends that his work on the Trump dossier was 70- to 90-percent accurate.[15]

A later Steele report detailed the existence of a "well-developed conspiracy" between Russian leadership and the Trump campaign. In return for hacking the DNC, the Trump campaign had agreed to sideline Russian intervention in Ukraine in the campaign. At a Republican National Committee meeting in Cleveland a week before the GOP convention, Trump campaign staffers had lobbied to exclude language from a party platform that called for the United States to provide "lethal defensive weapons" for Ukraine to defend itself against Russian invasion.

Later, Steele learned that another researcher working independently had developed similar information. Cody Shearer, a freelance journalist who was friendly with Bill and Hillary Clinton, claimed that a source inside the Russian intelligence service, the FSB, had evidence of Trump engaging in compromising personal behavior and had financial ties to influential Russians. Shearer had given the report to a friend of the Clintons, Sidney Blumenthal, who passed it to Jonathan Winer, a State Department employee, who then gave it to Steele. The Shearer report was described in Steele's October 19, 2016, report to Fusion GPS—neither of which at the time of this writing, have yet been made public. Steele included it because it was independent corroboration, but, to some members of Congress, it was a sign that Steele's motives were not so pure. In a memo to the Department of Justice, Republican senators Chuck Grassley and Lindsey Graham wrote: "It is troubling enough that the Clinton Campaign funded Mr. Steele's work, but that these Clinton associates were contemporaneously feeding Mr. Steele allegations raises additional questions about his credibility."

Meanwhile, Steele continued to file reports to Fusion GPS, each one deepening the picture of collusion between the Trump campaign and Russia, while detailing the triad between the Kremlin, the oligarchy, and the Russian Mob. The memos described power struggles among major players who were running the covert effort behind the hacked emails from the DNC and the Clinton campaign. The emails, hacked by Russian intelligence and posted by WikiLeaks, were the subject of constant attention in the press. One of Steele's sources alleged that the entire hacking operation "had been conducted with the full knowledge and support of TRUMP and senior members of the campaign team."[16]

Steele immediately realized that the FBI needed to know what he had uncovered. In assembling what would become the now-infamous "Steele Dossier," the former intelligence officer would submit every memo that he had sent Simpson prior to the election, 17 in all, to the FBI. At great risk to his reputation, he had decided to include everything, even the more scurrilous reports of the golden shower. Whatever the dossier looked like to civilians, to an intelligence officer like John Sipher, a retired Central Intelligence agent who once headed the agency's Russia desk, it looked very familiar. In a report published by Just Security, a national law, rights, and security forum, Sipher found several of Steele's allegations to be "stunningly accurate." Steele was reporting that Russia stole information from Hillary Clinton and was considering how to weaponize it before it became public knowledge. "One large portion of the dossier is crystal-clear, certain, consistent and corroborated," Sipher wrote. "Russia's goal all along has been to do damage to America and our leadership role in the world."[17]

———

AS STEELE PREPARED HIS FIRST bombshell dossier, the Trump campaign was meeting in Trump Tower with the lawyer Natalia Veselnitskaya, the woman described to Don Jr. as a "Russian government lawyer" who promised "dirt" on the Clinton campaign. Simpson knew Veselnitskaya. He worked for her, and when her name appeared in the papers in connection with the Trump Tower meeting it did not bode well for him and Fusion GPS.

Two years before Fusion GPS began investigating Trump, Simpson had been hired to help defend Prevezon Holdings, a Russian-owned

Cyprus-based company that held a large portfolio of U.S. real estate assets. U.S. Attorney Preet Bharara in Manhattan had filed a civil forfeiture complaint that accused Prevezon of laundering $14 million stolen from the Russian Treasury into Prevezon's Manhattan properties. Prevezon's sole shareholder was Denis Katsyv, a wealthy and politically connected Russian oligarch whose father was a former minister of transport in the Moscow region. Veselnitskaya was in-house counsel for the Katsyv family, and the case put Fusion GPS in the impossible position of simultaneously working in support of and against the Kremlin's interests in the United States.

As he got to work on the Prevezon case, Simpson said his first order of business was to investigate where the claims against Prevezon had originated. And the answer to that question led Fusion GPS to the investor Bill Browder. Browder was the driving force behind the Magnitsky Act, the 2012 measure that was designed to punish Russian officials responsible for the death of his lawyer Sergei Magnitsky, who was beaten with rubber batons and left to die in a Moscow prison after exposing a fraudulent $230 million tax-refund scam. According to the U.S. Justice Department, some of the money stolen in the tax scam Magnitsky had uncovered was being laundered by Prevezon in Manhattan. Though the Magnitsky Act initially only barred 18 Russian individuals accused of human rights abuses from entering and banking on U.S. soil, it sent a loud and clear message to the Kremlin. Russia's kleptocrats, some of whom were high-ranking Kremlin officials, including the president himself, could no longer use the West to store their looted assets. It was the first time the corrupt individuals at the top of Russian society had even been slapped on the hand, so to speak, for stealing money from their own country.

Getting rid of this meddlesome law was a key objective of Yuri Chaika, the general prosecutor of the Russian Federation. Chaika had repeatedly prosecuted Browder in absentia and now, it appeared, he had tasked the Katsyv family with the job of undermining the Magnitsky Act in the United States. Katsyv directed Veselnitskaya to register a nonprofit company in Delaware in February 2016 to lobby for the repeal of the American law. The Human Rights Accountability Global Initiative was run by Veselnitskaya, who set up offices in the same Dupont Circle neighborhood as Fusion GPS and hired Rinat Akhmetshin, the former Soviet military counterintelligence officer turned Russian-American lobbyist, to advocate on its behalf.

It was Veselnitskaya who had indirectly hired Fusion GPS to investigate Browder, and who made sure its bills, which totaled more than a half-million dollars, were paid. And it was the material that Fusion GPS had dug up and put into a four-page memo—a memo that claimed Browder himself was in partnership with the Ziff brothers, who supposedly used ill-gotten funds to make donations to the Clinton Foundation—that Veselnitskaya had brought with her to the Trump Tower meeting.

Simpson said he was stunned when news of the Trump Tower meeting broke. He felt used by Veselnitskaya, and yet he had no idea just how deep the rabbit hole went. In another sign of how hopelessly intertwined these matters were, Simpson and Veselnitskaya had attended a court hearing on the Prevezon case that occurred *the same day* as the Trump Tower meeting. Veselnitskaya and Simpson even saw each other at client dinners the day before and the day after the Trump Tower meeting. It was as if Veselnitskaya had come to embody the endless levels of Russian intrigue, where no one was who they appeared to be.

Simpson used his considerable talents on an investigation that penetrated the deep secrets of the Putin regime and uncovered a potential crime that impacted national security. At the same time, Fusion GPS had been paid by a wealthy and politically connected Russian who was running an influence campaign aligned with the Kremlin's interests. (Bill Browder believed the campaign was being funded and directed by the Russian government.) Simpson said his firm took pains, much as a law firm would, to insulate clients from each other, but this was a clear conflict of interests that no ethical lawyer could stomach. "I certainly am not happy to do anything that anyone would think was helping

Vladimir Putin," he said. "And to the extent that this has subjected me to an unfair accusation that I was engaged in some kind of Kremlin operation, I find that very regrettable."[18]

This mess of conflicts has provided fertile ground for the Trump administration's defense of accusations of Russian collusion. As White House Press Secretary Sarah Huckabee Sanders noted, "The Democrat-linked firm, Fusion GPS, actually took money from the Russian government while it created the phony dossier that's been the basis for all of the Russia scandal fake news." President Trump echoed that line. In an interview with *The New York Times*, the president stated:

> Well, I thought originally it might have had to do something
> with the payment by Russia of the D.N.C. Somewhere I heard
> that. Like, it was an illegal act done by the D.N.C., or the Demo-
> crats. That's what I had heard. Now, I don't know where I heard
> it, but I had heard that it had to do something with illegal acts
> with respect to the D.N.C. Now, you know, when you look at the
> kind of stuff that came out, that was, that was some pretty horrif-
> ic things came out of that. But that's what I had heard. But I don't
> know what it means. All I know is this: When somebody calls up
> and they say, "We have infor—" Look what they did to me with
> Russia, and it was totally phony stuff.[19]

"There has been no collusion between us and the Russians," the president told reporters at Camp David. "Now there has been collusion between Hillary Clinton, the DNC, and the Russians. Unfortunately, you people don't cover that very much. But the only collusion is between Hillary and the Russians, and the DNC and the Russians."[20]

—

IT TAKES A LOT TO shock an ex-spy, but for Steele, his findings shook him to his very core. If what his sources were telling him was true, Trump himself was a threat to national security, and the Russian meddling was a crime of the highest order. Steele knew that what he had gathered went beyond politics, beyond his contract with Fusion GPS. This would be a test of his character, and it could have a lasting impact on his career and life. Yet Britain was America's closest ally, and Steele believed he had a duty to report it. Steele and his partner in Orbis, Christopher Burrows, had made a pact when they left MI6: "We both agreed it was a duty to alert U.K. and allied authorities if we came across anything with national-security dimensions. It comes from a very long government service. We still have that ethos of wanting to do the right thing by our authorities," Burrows told Jane Mayer of the *New Yorker*.[21]

Speaking with Simpson over an encrypted line, Steele told him he felt professionally obligated to pass his findings along to the FBI. Simpson wasn't sure about this. This was an area way out of his expertise. He had a duty of confidentiality to his clients and this might compromise it. Simpson said he needed to think about it. He wasn't convinced, at that point, that any crime had been committed. Steele pressed the issue again in another call in early July. How would you even report something like this to the FBI? Simpson had asked. "Don't worry about that," Steele told him. He had the perfect person in mind, a contact he knew at the FBI and who knew him. "I'll take care of it," Steele told him. Finally Simpson relented and told him to go ahead with his decision.

Steele had worked with the FBI before on the FIFA case, and his contact in the bureau, Michael Gaeta, was in Rome. At the time Steele was preparing to notify the FBI of his findings, Gaeta was in Rome working as a legal attaché to the U.S. embassy. Steele reached out and anxiously informed Gaeta that he had "some material" to show him, but that he had to come to London to see it. Gaeta sought and received clearance to do so. On July 5, 2016, Gaeta met with Steele in Orbis's London offices, a five-story building in Westminster, a posh neighborhood not far from Buckingham Palace. Gaeta had one damning conclusion to Steele's dossier: "I have to report this to headquarters."[22]

That initial meeting led to a request to have a formal meeting with three more agents that September who flew to Rome for a full debriefing of Steele. The ex-spy informed Simpson that a full debriefing meant that he would be required to divulge everything: the identity of his sources, how he had obtained his information, and the identity of his client. Once again, Simpson gave him his OK.

The September meeting lasted hours. Steele went over everything he had, including the report by Cody Shearer on Trump's compromising and perverse behavior during the Miss Universe pageant. During their discussions, Steele took detailed notes as the FBI told him that his information appeared to corroborate information the bureau had independently gathered from a source close to Trump. He reported this back to Simpson. "Essentially what he told me was they had other intelligence about this matter from an internal Trump campaign source," Simpson testified. "My understanding was they believed Chris at this point—they believed Chris's information might be credible because they had other intelligence that indicated the same thing."[23]

The other intelligence involved a young member of Trump's foreign policy advisory board named George Papadopoulos. A 2009 graduate of DePaul University, Papadopoulos's career consisted of little more than an internship at the Hudson Institute, a Washington-based conservative think tank. He was later brought on board Ben Carson's presidential campaign as a foreign policy advisor. He headed to London after Carson dropped out, where he had the fancy title of director of the centre for international energy and natural resources law and security for the London-based Centre of International Law Practice. Trump's campaign co-chair Sam Clovis had evidently hired Papadopoulos without conducting much of a background check, as it later came to light that the résumé of Trump's new foreign policy advisor had been inflated. The only traceable work Papadopoulos seemed to have done on energy or foreign policy was a few op-eds written in Israeli newspapers.

During his very short tenure at the Centre for International Law Practice, Papadopoulos had come into contact with Joseph Mifsud, a Maltese professor tied to the institution who took great interest in Papadopoulos's new position with the Trump campaign. During a breakfast meeting at a London hotel on April 26, Professor Mifsud told Papadopoulos that he had just returned from a trip to Moscow where he had met with high-level Russian government officials who passed along some information on Hillary Clinton. "[The Russians] have dirt on her," Mifsud told Papadopoulos, as Papadopoulos later recounted to the FBI. "The Russians had emails of Clinton . . . they have thousands of emails."[24]

Mifsud was apparently a regular attendee of the Valdai Discussion Club, a think tank conference held annually in Sochi, Russia, where Vladimir Putin was known to be a regular. Mifsud reportedly introduced Papadopoulos to some of his notable friends, including a Russian connected to the Ministry of Foreign Affairs and a woman Papadopoulos later described in a campaign email as "Putin's niece." Papadopoulos repeatedly sought to use the woman's connections to arrange a meeting between the Trump campaign and Russian officials, even emailing Paul Manafort, Trump's campaign manager. Manafort forwarded Papadopoulos's email to his deputy Rick Gates (without including Papadopoulos). "We need someone to communicate that DT [Trump] is not doing these trips," Manafort wrote, before adding that someone should take the Russians up on the offer. "It should be someone low-level in the campaign so as not to send any signal."

Though he never succeeded in making this connection, Papadopoulos's new position as a foreign policy advisor for the Trump campaign had the benefit of allowing him to throw a few back with some high-level plenipotentiaries. Over many evening drinks with an Australian diplomat named Alexander Downer at a London pub in May 2016, Papadopoulos drunkenly bragged that Russia had "dirt" on Hillary Clinton. Downer reported it to his superiors, but it wasn't until the Clinton campaign's emails began appearing online that the Australians passed that information along to their American counterparts.

Papadopoulos was one of the first people targeted in Special Counsel Robert Mueller's collusion investigation. In an interview with the FBI just after Trump's inauguration, Papadopoulos claimed that the mysterious Professor Mifsud was "a nothing." A follow-up interview with the FBI caused Papadopoulos to delete his Facebook account, which contained postings about Professor Mifsud, and switch cell phone numbers. When Papadopoulos returned to the country on July 27, 2017, he was arrested at Washington Dulles Airport and in exchange for leniency gave a guilty plea and became a cooperating witness to the investigation. He holds the honor of being the first person to be formally charged by Mueller of lying to the FBI about his contacts with Russian officials. Meanwhile, Professor Mifsud apparently vanished without a trace.

———

BY OCTOBER 2016, TRUMP WAS using his rallies to inflict increasingly barbarous slander against his rival: "Hillary Clinton is the most corrupt politician ever to seek the office of the presidency," he declared before a North Carolina crowd before leading them into the by-then familiar chants of "Lock her up." That same day in Washington, however, the FBI took a monumental step in its investigation of the Trump campaign. The FBI and Justice Department sought and received permission from a secret court to investigate a member of the Trump campaign. The U.S. Foreign Intelligence Surveillance Court, otherwise known as FISA, tasked with reviewing applications to surveil suspected terrorists and spies, granted a request to eavesdrop on another little-known former member of Trump's foreign policy team.

Few had ever heard of Carter Page when Trump uttered his name seven months earlier as part of the same foreign policy advisory board as Papadopoulos. ("An excellent guy," Trump had said of Papadopoulos.) To most observers, nobodies like Papadopoulos and Page were another sign of the Trump campaign's utter cluelessness when it came to foreign affairs. But Trump's wildly inconsistent policies, his hateful, anti-Muslim rhetoric, and his admiration for foreign dictators, not to mention his fundamental dishonesty led more than 50 conservative foreign policy experts, including former top officials in the George W. Bush administration, to sign an open letter stating their opposition to Trump. That opened the door for oddballs and neophytes like Papadopoulos and Page.

A bullet-headed New York energy consultant prone to logorrhea, Page had a résumé that included a stint as an investment banker for

Merrill Lynch in Moscow, where he lived for a few years, and a doctorate from the University of London (where he accused his advisors of "anti-Russian" bias after they twice rejected his vague and verbose thesis).[25] Throughout his career, he eagerly associated himself with Russia, going so far as to describe himself as an "informal advisor to the staff of the Kremlin" in a letter urging an academic press to publish his thesis.[26] Although Page never met or spoke with Trump, he described his time on the campaign as one of the greatest experiences of his life. "The half year I spent on the Trump campaign meant more to me than the five years I spent in the Navy," he said.[27]

Page may not have been known in foreign policy circles, but he showed up on the radar of both Russian intelligence and U.S. counterintelligence in 2013 when he was targeted for recruitment as an intelligence source by a Russian spy. Victor Podobnyy, an undercover operative with Russia's foreign intelligence service who was under surveillance by the FBI, had approached Page at a conference in New York. FBI agents overheard Podobnyy describing an individual identified as "MALE-1"—later confirmed as Page—as an "idiot" whom he intended to feed empty promises, use, and then discard. "He flies to Moscow more often than I do," Podobnyy said, "He got hooked on Gazprom thinking that if they have a project, he could be rise up. May he can. I don't know, but it's obvious that he wants to earn lots of money." The FBI's FISA warrant detailed suspicious behavior by Page after he joined the Trump campaign, according to a memo by House Intelligence Committee Democrats. Agents interviewed Page about his contacts with Russian intelligence in March 2016, one of several such interviews that he has had over the years with the bureau.

While the Washington establishment turned up its nose at Page and the rest of Trump's foreign policy team, Russia was paying close attention. Page soon received an invitation to speak in July 2016 at the New Economic School in Moscow, where he gave a speech criticizing U.S. policy toward Russia, noting that Washington and the West had a "hypocritical focus on ideas such as democratization, inequality, corruption and regime change." Katehon, an influential, conservative Russian think tank, warmly welcomed Page's visit, publishing excerpts of his speech and describing his visit in glowing terms in a post headlined, "Trump's Advisor in Moscow: An Alternative for the US."[28]

Steele's sources told him that something else occurred during this trip. He produced a report on July 19 titled "Russia: Secret Kremlin Meetings Attended by Trump Advisor, Carter Page." According to Steele's report, Page had met earlier that month with Igor Sechin, who headed the Russian oil giant Rosneft. Sechin, a longtime associate of Russian president Vladimir Putin, was the subject of U.S. sanctions following the Russian invasion of Crimea in 2014. Steele's sources informed him that Sechin was so desperate to have sanctions lifted, he offered Page the opportunity to broker the sale of a large portfolio of Rosneft stock to investors. In his testimony before the House Intelligence Committee, Page at first insisted he had not met any Russian officials during his July visit to Moscow. According to a memo by committee Democrats, Page was "forced to admit" not to meeting Sechin, but one of his executives, a man named Andrey Baranov. Asked if he and Baranov discussed the "potential sale of a significant percentage of Rosneft," Page gave an evasive answer. "I don't believe so. He may have mentioned it in passing."[29] Democrats on the Intelligence Committee say still-classified evidence contradicts Page's testimony.

The Steele Dossier and the role it played in the FBI's investigation of the Trump campaign's ties to Russia became the subject of a lengthy and highly contentious investigation by the House Intelligence Committee. Some of the information Steele provided to the FBI was incorporated into the classified application for a FISA court warrant on Page. The question of whether the information provided by Steele—who ultimately was being paid by the Democratic Party—tainted the entire application prompted the release of an extraordinary report by the GOP-controlled House Intelligence Committee led by its chairman, Representative Devin Nunes of California, a member of Trump's transition team.

The "Nunes Memo," as it came to be called, was released in February 2018 with the president's blessing. Over the objection of Democrats, the GOP majority on the committee employed a never-before-used procedure designed for only the most extraordinary of cases to make public the existence of the previously classified FISA warrant on Carter Page. The Nunes Memo stated that Christopher Steele's information formed "an essential part" of the application for the FISA warrant on Carter Page. In addition, the memo stated that Andrew McCabe, the former deputy director of the FBI, told the House Intelligence Committee that a FISA warrant would not have been sought without the information in the Steele Dossier (Democrats on the panel said McCabe's statement was taken out of context). At the same time, the memo made clear that the FBI's investigation had begun with George Papadopoulos's drunken boasts about Russian "dirt" on Hillary Clinton, two months before Steele came forward with his dossier. In addition, FBI Assistant Director Bill Priestap said that corroboration of the Steele Dossier was in its "infancy" at the time of the initial Page FISA warrant application.

The problem with the FISA warrant application, according to the Nunes Memo, was that it did not reveal the political nature of Steele's work, and that it failed to disclose or reference "the role of the DNC, Clinton campaign, or any party/campaign in funding Steele's efforts." This claim lay at the heart of the attack by the GOP on the FBI's investigation of the Trump campaign. While it was superficially true, it was deeply misleading. As the Democratic memo written in response showed, the FISA warrant application indicated that the FBI believed Steele's research was politically motivated and "could be used to discredit [Trump's] campaign." Even Nunes later appeared to acknowledge this. "A footnote saying something may be political is a far cry from letting the American people know that the Democrats and the Hillary campaign paid for dirt that the FBI then used to get a warrant on an American citizen to spy on another campaign," Nunes said on *Fox & Friends*.

In a reflection of the hyper-partisan politics of Washington, the Nunes Memo was both denounced and praised before its release. The FBI went so far as to issue a statement ahead of time announcing that the bureau had "grave concerns" about the memo's accuracy. Trump supporters pushed for the memo in the hopes it would prove that the FBI was corrupt and could destroy the credibility of Special Counsel Robert Mueller's investigation. Chairman Nunes moved on to phase two of his investigation, examining what role, if any, the State Department played in the Steele Dossier and the FISA warrant. Congressman Adam Schiff, ranking minority member on the House Intelligence Committee, said something else had driven what he called the extraordinarily reckless disclosure of classified information: the president's hunger "for valida-tion."[30] Trump proved the point when he took a premature victory lap on Twitter after the release of the Nunes Memo: "This memo totally vindi-cates 'Trump' in probe. But the Russian Witch Hunt goes on and on."[31]

—

IN THE FALL OF 2016, Christopher Steele and Glenn Simpson decided to blow the whistle on what they saw as a sinister plot by Vladimir Putin to alter the outcome of an American election. FBI Director James Comey, who years before as a U.S. attorney had attempted to bring Tokhtakhounov to justice for the Winter Olympics scandal, wasn't letting the public know about the bureau's investigation, so Simpson began talking to reporters throughout the summer, filling them in on his findings about Trump's connections to Russia. At the end of September, he took Steele with him to provide off-the-record briefings at the Tabard Inn in Washington for leading journalists at *The New Yorker*, ABC, *The New York Times*, and *The Washington Post*—where Steele talked for almost two hours.

It's a safe bet that the Clinton campaign was in some way behind these efforts, or at the very least signed off on them. The law firm that hired Simpson and Steele for the research, Perkins Coie, was aware of the media approach, and Perkins Coie would not have authorized the contacts without consulting its client. The initial media outreach yielded a single story: a September 23 report by *Yahoo News*'s Michael Isikoff on Carter Page's meetings in Moscow, which cited "a well-placed Western intelligence source."[32] That story would also find its way into the application for a FISA warrant on Page.

As time ticked by and the election approached, Steele grew increasingly frustrated. He told Bruce Ohr, an associate deputy attorney general at the Justice Department (whose wife, Nellie, worked at Fusion GPS), that he "was desperate that Donald Trump not get elected and was passionate about him not being president." In October, Steele revisited reporters at *The Washington Post*, this time visibly agitated.[33] Steele also met with David Corn at *Mother Jones* magazine, which published a story on October 31 with the headline "A Veteran Spy Has Given the FBI Information Alleging a Russian Operation to Cultivate Donald Trump." The story stayed a safe distance away from the dossier's most explosive allegations, and, without naming Steele, Corn reported his claims that Russian intelligence had "compromised" Trump during his visits to Moscow and could blackmail him.[34] The FBI had been unaware of Steele's media contacts, but now the secret was out. The bureau suspended and then terminated Steele as a source. After Steele's termination, a report conducted by an independent unit in the FBI assessed the ex-spy's reporting in the dossier as "minimally corroborated," according to the Nunes Memo.

As for Steele, the break with the FBI was on mutual terms. Steele was deeply troubled when FBI Director James Comey announced on October 28 that he was reopening the investigation into Hillary Clinton's emails, according to Simpson, who shared the ex-spy's concerns. Both men knew the bureau was running a serious counterintelligence investigation into Trump's links to Russia. Yet, Steele couldn't believe that the FBI was going public with the Clinton email investigation while sitting on the Russia investigation. In addition, *The New York Times* published a story on October 31—"a real Halloween special," Simpson called it—that reported the FBI had found no links between Trump and Russia.[35] What was happening? "Chris was a little scared," Simpson said. "He didn't really understand what was going on with the FBI."

No one had yet touched the dossier's most shocking allegations. If Trump lost, as the Washington establishment expected him to, then perhaps the dossier would have faded away. But if he won, there was zero chance that the explicit language and tawdry allegations on the very first page about the president of the United States would stay confidential. Simpson, of all people, knew what a gossipy bunch journalists were.

The story of Trump cavorting with prostitutes in Russia began to circulate like a Washington version of *samizdat*, the underground literature that was passed hand-to-hand in the Soviet Union. Lobbyists began to hear about it in the summer. The Senate minority leader, Harry Reid, knew of it and publicly urged FBI Director James Comey to share it with the American people. Senator John McCain handed a copy to the FBI after obtaining it through a series of cloak-and-dagger meetings with Steele and his intermediaries abroad. Washington loved elitist games like this, where insider knowledge showed who the real players were.

Sometime in the winter, the dossier fell into the hands of the online media site *BuzzFeed*, then an upstart on the Beltway journalism scene. *BuzzFeed* did not play by the same rules as the old guard in the Washington media (it has also declined to reveal how it obtained the dossier). On January 10, 2017, after CNN disclosed that U.S. officials had briefed Trump on the dossier, *BuzzFeed* did what no other journalism organization dared to do: it printed all 17 of Steele's memos. Noting that the memos were "unverified, and potentially unverifiable," *BuzzFeed* published them nonetheless "so that Americans can make up their own minds." This was journalism in the Internet age. The "elaborate rituals" Simpson had practiced were giving way to a radical new ethos where transparency trumped truth. It was the equivalent of tossing a hand grenade into the public sphere.

The move was greeted with disdain by Capitol Hill journalists. NBC's Chuck Todd summed up the view of the journalism establishment when he told *BuzzFeed* editor Ben Smith on the air, "I've known you a long time, but you just published fake news. You made a knowing decision to put out an untruth."[36] Subjects of the dossier, including Carter Page and Trump attorney Michael Cohen, later sued *BuzzFeed* and *Yahoo News* for defamation. Glenn Simpson was upset as well. "I thought it was a very dangerous thing and that someone had violated my confidences," he said. Steele and his family suddenly vanished from their London home. He reemerged weeks later, only to say that he wouldn't be making any public comments.

Trump reacted immediately to the dossier's publication by decrying it on his Twitter feed as "fake news—a total political witch hunt."[37] Labeling Steele "a failed spy," the president-elect stated what would become a familiar refrain of his presidency. He had nothing to do with Russia. There was no collusion, no deals with Russia, no nothing. At a press conference, Trump referred to the golden showers allegations in the Steele Dossier by noting wryly, "Does anybody really believe that story? I'm also very much of a germaphobe, by the way. Believe me."[38]

INFORMATION WARFARE

I N MAY 2017, DONALD TRUMP, NOW president of the United States, traveled to North Atlantic Treaty Organization (NATO) headquarters in Brussels for the annual summit held by the organization's member nations. Trump was in top form. During a photo shoot with other heads of state, he muscled his way past Montenegro's prime minister, Duško Marković, and later nearly yanked French president Emmanuel Macron's arm off in an absurdly aggressive handshake. Trump didn't pause his bullish personality when he stood before a podium and addressed NATO's leaders. "NATO members must finally contribute their fair share and meet their financial obligations. But twenty-three of the twenty-eight member nations are still not paying what they should be paying and what they are supposed to be paying for their defense. This is not fair to the people and taxpayers of the United

States and many of these nations owe massive amounts of money from past years, and not paying in those past years."[1] Even before the accusation had a chance to sink in, Trump, ever the real estate developer, couldn't help but highlight the newly built NATO headquarters in which he stood. "I never asked once what the new NATO headquarters cost," Trump said. "I refuse to do that. But it is beautiful."

NATO is perhaps Russia's biggest adversary, and not surprisingly, America foots much of the NATO bill. America, which spends more on defense than the next seven countries combined, pays nearly a quarter of NATO's $1.7 billion annual budget, followed by Germany, France, and Britain. The rest of NATO's members weren't paying enough in Trump's view. An example is the Netherlands, which has been singled out for criticism by NATO for its weak defense spending. Holland's army has long been the butt of jokes. In the 1970s, Dutch soldiers were famous for their long hair, leading one defense official to describe the army as a "glorified Scout movement." The hair may be cropped these days, but a recent shortage of ammunition forced bullet-less Dutch soldiers to shout "bang, bang" during training drills. Its army consists of three land brigades and its air fleet would fit on one U.S. aircraft carrier.

While the Netherlands lacks military firepower, it punches well above its weight when it comes to technological savvy. As one of the most connected nations in the world, Holland's intelligence services can draw from a highly educated, talented pool of homegrown computer hackers. No NATO nation could beat America in a conventional armed conflict, but as Russia proved, America was completely vulnerable to a computer attack on its democratic institutions. And it owes the discovery of that breach to an alarm sounded by the Dutch.

It started, as many things do in the intelligence world, with a tip. The Dutch intelligence agency, the AIVD, had received word about a group of Russian hackers working in a university building adjacent to Red Square. And sometime in the summer of 2014, with most of the world distracted by the finals of the World Cup soccer tournament, a hacker from the Dutch Joint Sigint Cyber Unit penetrated the building's network. This was a major coup. The hacker had taken his team inside the network of the Russian hacking group known to computer security professionals as "Cozy Bear."[2]

In the universe of hackers trying to break into the U.S. government's and businesses' systems—a constellation of criminals, hacktivists, terrorists, and nation-state hackers—Cozy Bear was one of the best. "Their tradecraft is superb, operational security second-to-none," wrote Dmitri Alperovitch on the website for CrowdStrike, a California cybersecurity firm that has gone up against Cozy Bear, among others.[3] Cozy Bear had many names: the Dukes, CozyDuke, Advanced Persistent Threat 29 (APT-29). It was an arm of the FSB, the Russian Federal Security Service, which specialized in cybersecurity and offensive operations of every kind. Of all the various Russian intelligence agencies, the FSB had the closest ties to Vladimir Putin, who ran the agency before he became Russia's president.

According to an account in the Dutch newspaper *de Volkskrant*, the Cozy Bear team worked in a highly secure space with cameras that tracked the movements of everyone who entered and exited. The one thing that wasn't secure was the camera itself. When Dutch hackers gained access to it, they were able to determine the faces behind the 13-member Cozy Bear team. Using photo analysis and intelligence databases, the AIVD team was able to turn these faces into traceable identities. Not only that, but AIVD was able to discern what was on the screens of the Cozy Bear team, and what they discovered was a preparation for a major hacking attempt into the U.S. State Department.

The backdrop to this attack was the fraying relations between the United States and Russia. Not long after the conclusion of the 2014 Winter Olympics in Sochi, President Vladimir Putin had annexed Crimea, a Russian-speaking region in Ukraine. Putin warned that Russia would no longer tolerate NATO's efforts to strong-arm his country into submission, as he believed had happened in Ukraine. "If you press a spring too hard," he said, "it will recoil." In response, President Obama punished the Kremlin's inner circle by imposing sanctions. And in response to that, the Kremlin had Cozy Bear step up its covert cyberattacks on the United States.

From its headquarters in the Dutch city of Zoetermeer, the AIVD team monitored Cozy Bear, which had gained access to an unsecure computer of a State Department employee that had been hooked up to the department's unclassified network. From this "perch" inside the State Department computer system, the Russian hackers were able to send malware, disguised as an email from the department employee, to one of the employee's contacts, a White House staffer. The email contained a link to a video of monkeys dressed in white collared shirts and ties working at an office. While the staffer viewed it, the video slipped a malicious code into the staffer's computer that bypassed the White House's secure network. This allowed Cozy Bear to gain access to the White House's email servers, which contained President Obama's sent and received emails and the real-time non-public details of his schedule. In the meantime, it appeared to the AIVD that Cozy Bear was getting ready to mount a second attack.

In early November 2014, AIVD and its military counterpart, the MIVD, notified the liaison for the National Security Agency (NSA) that Cozy Bear was preparing for an all-out attack on the State Department. Acting immediately, on the weekend of November 15–16, the State Department sent out a notice that it would shut down its network for maintenance purposes. But what really happened was nothing short of an epic 24-hour cyber battle between rival and powerful state intelligence services—"hand-to-hand combat," as NSA Deputy Director Richard Ledgett put it—between the NSA, aided by the FBI and the AIVD, and Cozy Bear. Whenever the NSA cut Cozy Bear's link to a server in the State Department's computer system, Cozy Bear would set up a new one. Using a direct line with the AIVD, the NSA was able to watch Cozy Bear as it worked out its next move. Ledgett hinted that the State Department system was used as a "honeypot" to lure in the Russian hackers so the NSA could learn how they operated. "We were able to see them teeing up new things to do," Ledgett said. "That's a really useful capability to have."[4]

—

WHILE THE COZY BEAR HACKERS battled the NSA, another covert, high-tech Russian effort aimed at the United States was getting underway in St. Petersburg. A Russian computer firm carrying the bland name of the Internet Research Agency took up offices in a nondescript four-story office building at 55 Savushkina Street in the old imperial city's northwestern Primorsky District, a suburban neighborhood of towering Soviet apartment buildings. In many ways it resembled an Internet marketing firm, with departments specializing in graphics, data analysis, and search-engine optimization.

Yet, from the start, the agency harnessed these modern tools to promote pro-Russian agendas and spread the Kremlin's influence. Yevgeny V. Prigozhin, a convicted criminal whose connections ran all the way to the top of Russia's chain of command, was its founder and CEO. An oligarch known as "Putin's chef," Prigozhin was found guilty of robbery and was a member of an organized-crime group that practiced fraud and involved "minors in prostitution."[5] He served nine years in prison and was released in 1990, opening a hot dog stand as the Soviet Union collapsed around him. He then managed a chain of grocery stores and in 1997 opened a restaurant in an old ship called New Island, becoming one of St. Petersburg's most popular restaurants. And it was through that restaurant that Prigozhin not only became wealthy, but fell into Putin's inner circle.

In the summer of 2001, Russian president Vladimir Putin dined at New Island with French president Jacques Chirac. Prigozhin personally served the two heads of state. Not only did Putin become a regular, but Prigozhin became the Russian president's favored caterer, which earned him his derisive nickname. He was awarded lucrative contracts to provide lunches to Moscow schoolchildren and feed Russian soldiers. In return, the Kremlin called on him to perform jobs that it did not want attributed to the state. U.S. intelligence officials believe he controlled an Argentinian company called Wagner PMC that employed Russian mercenaries in Syria who fought on behalf of President Bashar al Assad.[6] But it wasn't until Prigozhin started running what would become known as the St. Petersburg "troll factory" that the former hot dog vendor would cook up some particular nastiness.

The Internet Research Agency's first activities in 2014 were tentative and experimental, mostly relegated to tracking and studying politically active groups in America. They tested the effectiveness of their messages by tracking audience engagement and watching the average number of comments on or responses to a post. Two employees, Aleksandra Krylova and Anna Bogacheva, traveled around the United States in June 2014, stopping in Nevada, California, New Mexico, Colorado, Illinois, Michigan, Louisiana, Texas, and New York to gather intelligence. Another employee traveled to Georgia later in the year. By May 2014, the agency had a strategic goal of "spread[ing] distrust towards the candidates and the political system in general."[7] The key to this effort was a department that went by many names, one of which was the "Translator Project."[8] This project concentrated on the U.S. population, which it targeted through influence operations on social media, including YouTube, Facebook, and Twitter. To show their boss just how effective their tactics could be, Prigozhin's employees organized a special birthday surprise, duping an American into posing in front of the White House with a sign that read, "Happy 55th Birthday Dear Boss." The limited details supplied in court documents state that the sign holder was told that the message was for "our boss . . . our funder."[9]

On September 11, 2014, the Internet Research Agency showed how much it had learned and how dangerously effective it was at manipulating Americans. Residents of St. Mary Parish in Louisiana began receiving alarming text messages about a toxic plume from a nearby Columbian Chemicals plant. On Twitter, a man named Jon Merritt reported a powerful explosion at a chemical plant, and other users shared images that appeared to show a plant in flames and surveillance footage from a local helicopter. A woman named Anna McClaren tweeted at Karl Rove: "Karl, Is this really ISIS who is responsible for #ColumbianChemicals?"[10]

But it was fake news, for real. As an article in *The New York Times*

Magazine revealed, there was no explosion at Columbian Chemicals, no Jon Merritt, no Anna McClaren. The entire affair was a carefully crafted hoax, complete with carbon copies of local news sites promoting fake news stories about the explosion. The Internet Research Agency had pulled off something akin to a military intelligence operation, one designed to instill fear in a civilian population. "Information warfare against the United States of America," the agency called it.[11] This was a modern twist on an old spy game, one that was very familiar to the Office of Strategic Services (OSS), the World War II predecessor of the Central Intelligence Agency.

The OSS didn't have the benefit of social media, but the operatives in its Morale Operations branch used what they called "rumors" as weapons of war against Nazi Germany. According to a now declassified 1943 field manual, the OSS developed a special class of gossip called "subversive rumors." This form of scuttlebutt could be used "to cause enemy populations to distrust their own news sources" and "to create division among racial, political, [and] religious" groups within a country. Subversive rumors could be used to "create confusion and dismay with a welter of contradictory reports." The OSS believed that the best fake gossip was simple, plausible, and vivid, the more "strong emotional content" the better. "Rarely can [rumors] by themselves change basic attitudes," the OSS field manual declared in highlighting the limits of their new word-of-mouth weapon. "Their function is to confirm suspicions and beliefs already latent; to give sense and direction to fears, resentments, or hopes that have been built up by more materialistic causes; to tip the balance when public opinion is in a precarious state."[12]

The Soviet KGB also understood the nature of rumors. The KGB's Service A unit was tasked with running *aktivnye meropriiatiia*—covert "active measures" designed to sow distrust against the West. One example included developing fraudulent info about FBI and CIA involvement in the assassination of President John F. Kennedy. Another was Operation Infektion, a KGB-planted rumor that the AIDS virus had escaped from a biological weapons lab in Fort Detrick, Maryland. Thousands of people were involved in the active measures operations, which were integrated into the whole of the Soviet government, and the measures surely would have been familiar to Vladimir Putin, who was just beginning his KGB career in 1980, a time when the CIA estimated that the annual cost of the Soviet Union's active measures program was no less than $3 billion a year.[13] In the 1990s, the United States asked Russia to stop these rumor campaigns, but Sergei Tretyakov, a high-ranking Russian spy who defected to the United States in 2000, said nothing changed. "Russia is doing everything it can today to embarrass the U.S.," Tretyakov said in a 2008 book, *Comrade J.* "Let me repeat this. Russia is doing everything it can today to undermine and embarrass the U.S."[14] What the Internet Research Agency really represented was a modern Russian version of the old OSS rumor factory and KGB active measures division. Social media gave the St. Petersburg operatives a power the likes of which neither the OSS nor the KGB could have imagined. The OSS had to send operatives into enemy territory to plant rumors; the KGB planted the AIDS rumor in a newspaper in India. The modern influence operative didn't have to leave his or her desk in St. Petersburg. In the hands of a spy, Facebook, Twitter, and YouTube were machines for the rapid transmission of rumors. Flip through the musty pages of the OSS field manual and see how well their creed holds up today, and just how effectively the St. Petersburg troll factory was able to wreak havoc on the American public during the 2016 presidential election.

—

IN SEPTEMBER 2015, THE COMPUTER support staff at the Washington, DC–based Democratic national headquarters, home to the Democratic Party and the Democratic National Committee (DNC), received some troubling news. An FBI agent named Adrian Hawkins called the DNC switchboard asking to speak to the person in charge of its computers. Hawkins was transferred to the office of Yared Tamene, the DNC's director of information systems. According to Tamene's memo, which was obtained by *The New York Times*, Agent Hawkins explained that at least one DNC computer on its network had been compromised. The FBI wanted to know if the DNC was aware of this. If so, what were they doing about it? Agent Hawkins told Tamene to be on the lookout for a specific type of malware—a computer program that works behind the scenes to perform malicious and potentially destructive tasks—that the U.S. intelligence community called "dukes."[15]

Tamene wasn't sure what to make of this conversation. He wasn't even sure if he was talking to a real FBI agent. When Tamene asked Hawkins to verify himself, he did not get an "adequate response." As he put it in his memo, "I had no way of differentiating the call I just received from a prank call." Tamene Googled "dukes," and based on the information he obtained, performed a scan of the DNC system using security programs that found nothing. Agent Hawkins, however, kept calling and leaving voicemail messages about the status of the supposed malware program. Amazingly, Tamene did not even bother to return some of his calls, believing there was "nothing to report." In November, Hawkins informed Tamene the compromised DNC computer was now "calling home, where home meant Russia." Agent Hawkins added that the FBI "thinks that this calling home behavior could be the result of a state-sponsored attack," Tamene noted in his memo.[16]

Cozy Bear's hack of the DNC had begun in the summer of 2015, as part of what FBI Director James Comey called a "massive effort" to target hundreds of governmental and "near-governmental" agencies.[17] The Russian hacking team sent emails to more than 1,000 people, emails that appeared to be legitimate messages sent from American organizations and educational institutions, but in fact contained malicious links. And like what had happened at the State Department a year prior, it wasn't long before someone at the DNC had clicked on one. Within nanoseconds, the system was infected by a malware program called "SeaDaddy" and a single line of code that was "ingenious in its simplicity and power."[18] SeaDaddy embedded itself deep inside the network, where it unlocked the DNC's Windows-based systems and gave Cozy Bear hackers the run of the house. Cozy Bear figured out where the important files were and began spiriting away huge volumes of Democratic Party emails and documents from several accounts through encrypted connections, which it sent "back home."

What the Cozy Bear operatives were quietly trying to do was hoover up as much political intelligence as they could, in the hopes that they could find something useful. This was standard practice in the intelligence world. Cyber operations were cheap and low-risk, and could be plausibly denied, yet they sometimes yielded entire databases and megabytes of emails from powerful origins, especially if they were left undisturbed for long periods of time. In retrospect, the FBI's response to the DNC hack and the ambivalent—at best—response by Tamene and the DNC would prove disastrous. Several critical months would go by before the DNC concluded that Agent Hawkins was, in fact, a 13-year FBI veteran who specialized in computer forensics. So why didn't the DNC take his warnings more seriously? Jeh Johnson, the secretary of Homeland Security, had also extended his agency's assistance but said his offers were rebuffed.[19] FBI Director James Comey said he had made "multiple requests at different levels" to have his agents perform a forensic examination of the DNC servers. Those requests too were rejected.[20] While the DNC dithered, the Russians were gathering up material for an even more audacious attack.

SIX MONTHS AFTER THE FBI first contacted the DNC, yet *another* Russian digital espionage unit targeted one of the major spoils of its DNC hack, the computers of Hillary Clinton's presidential campaign. Beginning on March 10, the first of scores of emails went out addressed to Clinton staffers. In this "phishing" attack, the emails were carefully crafted so as to appear as legitimate messages from Google, which provided the campaign's email infrastructure. Staffers were directed to change their email passwords through a fake Google login site. More than 100 Clinton staffers were targeted. Jake Sullivan, Clinton's foreign policy advisor, was the subject of 14 separate attempts, and Hillary Clinton herself was a target on two occasions (although she did not fall for the trick). On 36 other occasions, however, Clinton staffers did click on the treacherous "Reset Password" link. So did three DNC staffers.[21]

This second group of Russian government hackers was known to computer security experts as "Fancy Bear," aka "Strontium," "Sednit," "Sofacy," and "APT28." Fancy Bear hackers were affiliated with the Main Intelligence Directorate of the General Staff of the Russian Armed Forces, also known as the GRU, which handled military intelligence.[22] In contrast to Cozy Bear's elite hacker aesthetic, Fancy Bear's attack on the DNC reflected the GRU's aggressive and ruthless culture, exercised through the considerable autonomy it was afforded within the state security services.[23]

That two teams of Russian government hackers converged on the DNC might seem excessive, but it was not unusual in Russia, where intelligence services not only worked separately but competitively. The Russian intelligence agencies don't act as a coordinated front, but rather what Mark Galeotti, a leading expert on the Russian security services and underworld, described as "a many-headed hydra." "The agencies often replicate each others' work, engaging in bloody competition rather than sharing intelligence," Galeotti wrote. Putin has encouraged these rivalries as a way to control them, as these groups subvert one another to curry favor with the president.[24]

Fancy Bear's Clinton campaign hack reflected Putin's bold new plan to sway the presidential election away from a surefire victory for Hillary Clinton, whom he loathed. Putin publicly blamed Clinton for inciting mass protests against his regime in late 2011 and early 2012, and U.S. intelligence believed he held a grudge against her for comments he almost certainly saw as disparaging him. According to the findings of the U.S. intelligence community, Putin ordered "an influence campaign"—a hybrid of hacking and social media—aimed at the two major U.S. political campaigns. "Russia's goals were to undermine public faith in the U.S. democratic process, denigrate Secretary Clinton, and harm her electability and potential presidency," the heads of the FBI, CIA, and NSA concluded in a joint report on Russia's intentions. "We further assess Putin and the Russian Government developed a clear preference for President-elect Trump."[25]

Finally, seven months after it received its first warning from the FBI, the DNC in mid-April installed a "robust set of monitoring tools," Tamene wrote in his internal memo. The new monitoring system allowed Tamene to examine who had access to the network and what systems they could access. He found that an unauthorized person, who had the network privileges of a system administrator, had penetrated the DNC's network.[26] The DNC immediately hired CrowdStrike, a cybersecurity firm. CrowdStrike confirmed the DNC's worst fears: the hack had originated in Russia.

By then it was too late. Fancy Bear had already claimed a big fish and duped Clinton's campaign chairman, John Podesta, with this email:

Hi John
Someone just used your password to try to sign in to your
Google Account
john.podesta@gmail.com
Details: Saturday, 19 March, 8:34:30 UTC
IP Address: 134.249.139.239
Location: Ukraine
Google stopped this sign-in attempt. You should change your
password immediately.
CHANGE PASSWORD <https://bit.ly/1PibSU0>
Best,
The Gmail Team[27]

Podesta's team checked with Charles Delavan, the campaign's information technology consultant. In a response that he would deeply regret, Delavan replied, "This is a legitimate email."[28] And just like that, Fancy Bear had 50,000 of Podesta's emails stretching back 10 years. The hack was not only shocking, it became a source of deep humiliation and distrust within the Clinton campaign.

—

TO BE FAIR, MANIPULATING ELECTIONS is a game the Americans and the Russians have played for decades. Dov Levin, a postdoctoral fellow at Carnegie Mellon University, counted 117 instances where the United States or the Soviet Union intervened in foreign elections during the Cold War, through campaign funding, assistance, dirty tricks, promises, and, in some cases, plain old threats. By Levin's count, the United States was the bigger offender, intervening 81 times in foreign elections—more than twice as often as the Soviet Union—in a time period that stretched from the 1946 election in Argentina to the 2000 election in Serbia. And Levin's research found that these efforts by both countries yielded an average of a 3 percent change in vote share, enough to sway a close election, especially one where Russia was doing its best to turn the tide. And now, through its Cold War rival, the United States was about to get a taste of its own medicine.[29]

As Election Day approached, activity ramped up at the Internet Research Agency in St. Petersburg, which now led the social media arm of the Russian influence operation. The Translator Project, the division that concentrated on the U.S. election, grew to a staff of more than 80 people working 12-hour shifts as they furiously cranked out angry, divisive messages on Facebook and Twitter. At the height of the U.S. presidential campaign, the budget for the Internet Research Agency's operations reached more than $1.25 million a month, with payments disguised as software support and development funneled through companies related to Prigozhin's catering business.[30]

On February 10, 2016, staff at the Internet Research Agency circulated an internal memo spelling out the themes of the campaign the Russians would be waging on social media accounts in the coming months. The memo instructed staff to post content that focused on "politics in the USA" and to "use any opportunity to criticize Hillary and the rest (except Sanders and Trump—we support them)." Agency hashtags, the thematic names for online content, were a good indication of how it carried out those orders: #Trump2016, #TrumpTrain,

#MAGA, #IWontProtectHillary, and #Hillary4Prison. Pro-Trump social media accounts created by the agency gave no indication that Russians were behind them. These included the Facebook accounts Clinton FRAUDation and Trumpsters United and the Twitter account "March for Trump"—complete with a red-white-and-blue Trump silhouette, apparently produced by the Internet Research Agency's graphics team.[31]

Twitter identified 3,814 accounts that were linked to the Internet Research Agency, and more than 50,000 automated accounts linked to the Russian government that generated more than a million election-related tweets.[32] One agency Twitter account, @TEN_GOP, which billed itself as the "Unofficial Twitter account of Tennessee Republicans," attracted more than 130,000 followers with its anti-immigrant, anti-Muslim posts. @TEN_GOP content was shared by Trump campaign officials, including Kellyanne Conway, Michael Flynn, and the campaign's digital media director, Brad Parscale. The president's son Don Jr. followed the account, and on Twitter in September 2017, President Trump publicly thanked an account thought to be associated with @TEN_GOP after the account tweeted, "We love you, Mr. President." Many members of the far right reacted angrily when Twitter shut down @TEN_GOP.[33]

Facebook also has been the subject of fierce criticism for allowing its platform to be abused by the Internet Research Agency. After months of denials by the company, Facebook's chief security officer, Alex Stamos, conceded that roughly 3,000 ads were purchased by 470 bogus accounts that likely operated out of Russia and were linked to one anothre. The ads, which ran from June 2015 to May 2017, cost approximately $100,000. (Another $50,000 was spent on 2,200 ads that "might have originated in Russia," Stamos wrote.[34]) Facebook estimated that 11.4 million people viewed the ads, half of which were purchased for less than three dollars each. Russian-based trolls leveraged the ads to promote roughly 120 Facebook pages set up by the troll factory itself. These pages posted more than 80,000 pieces of content between January 2015 and August 2017, according to Facebook. In that time frame, according to a U.S.

Senate document, an estimated 126 million Americans—roughly half the U.S. population—were exposed to Facebook content generated by Putin's chef's trolling company.[35]

By exploiting a quirk in how social media platforms work, the Internet Research Agency got a huge return for their ruble by posting divisive content. Facebook and Twitter, like all social media sites, employs algorithms, a set of rules, to determine what you see and what you don't. And what you see first tends to be content calculated to grab your attention. The problem with these algorithms is that anger and fear is what largely drive them. Thus, the unintended but very real consequence was that Facebook and Twitter put a premium on the divisive Russian content that pitted Americans against one another. The sites also inadvertently prioritized fake Russian content over real news. They were perfect weapons of information warfare.

Even still, the Russian social media campaigns were easily dismissed as small potatoes. Two days after the election, Facebook Chief Executive Mark Zuckerberg said it was "crazy" to think fake Russian content influenced the election. Zuckerberg later said he regretted the comment, but it was true that the amount of content the Russians posted on Facebook and Twitter was a tiny fraction of the billions or even trillions of posts on the sites during the election.[36] The total amount Russians spent amounted to 0.1 percent of Facebook's daily advertising revenue and an even smaller fraction of the estimated $2 billion (or more) in free TV that Trump is estimated to have received during the 2016 campaign.[37] But Facebook's and Twitter's algorithms allowed the Russian trolls to specifically target select audiences in malicious and divisive ways that TV could not.

Just as the OSS had trained its employees to create divisions along racial lines, the Russian information warriors—and the Trump campaign—began to pick the scabs on America's deepest wounds. The Internet Research Agency began to craft messages aimed at black voters, who overwhelmingly supported Hillary Clinton, that were designed to keep them away from the polls. Facebook's platform gave advertisers the flexibility to specifically target "Jew haters" if they so wished, as the online investigative site ProPublica discovered.[38] One of the Internet Research Agency's first ads, posted on social media on April 6, read, "You know, a great number of black people support us saying that #HillaryClintonIsNotMyPresident." As the election approached, the agency redoubled its efforts to dissuade African Americans from voting via Facebook accounts like United Muslims for America and Blacktivist as well as launching Instagram accounts like @Woke_Blacks. It was on this latter account, one of 170 Russian-controlled accounts on Instagram (which is owned by Facebook), that the following message appeared on October 16: "[A] particular hype and hatred for Trump is misleading the people and forcing Blacks to vote Killary. We cannot resort to the lesser of two devils. Then we'd surely be better off without voting AT ALL."[39]

Coincidentally or not, the Trump campaign was pursuing the same line. A senior Trump campaign official told *Bloomberg* that an effort to suppress the black vote in Florida was one of "three major voter suppression operations under way." On October 24, eight days after the Woke Blacks message appeared on Instagram, Trump's team began placing similar spots on select radio stations that catered to black audiences. In addition, the Trump campaign used a Facebook "dark post"—negative ads that were visible only to the person who received them—to remind black voters that in 1996 Hillary Clinton described some young black men as "super predators." The message, like the goal of the Russians, was designed to keep black voters at home. "We know because we've modeled this," the anonymous campaign official said. "It will dramatically affect her ability to turn these people out."[40] Trump was clearly very satisfied with this effort, for the campaign's director of digital operations, Brad Parscale, has already been named manager for Trump's 2020 reelection campaign.[41]

By the summer, the Internet Research Agency was becoming more than a troll factory. From its headquarters in St. Petersburg, Russia, the agency began to organize political rallies in the United States. The Facebook group United Muslims of America promoted a pro-Clinton rally on July 9, 2016, in Washington, DC, even going so far as to recruit an American to hold a sign with a picture of Clinton and a quote falsely attributed to her that stated, "I think Sharia Law will be a powerful new direction of freedom." Later that month, the agency organized and promoted two rallies in New York that summer, one titled "March for Trump" and the other called "Down with Hillary." At a Florida Goes Trump rally held in August, the Russians paid an American to build a cage on a flatbed truck and another to dress up like Hillary Clinton in prison stripes. According to data Facebook provided the U.S. Senate, a total of 129 real-world gatherings had originated from 13 social media pages, each run by an employee at the Internet Research Agency. Approximately 338,300 unique accounts viewed these events; another 25,800 accounts marked that they were interested in an event; and about 62,500 marked that they were going to an event, although it is not known if they followed through.[42]

Fancy Bear, the Russian hacking group linked to Russian military intelligence, also began exploiting Facebook during the election. Facebook disclosed that Fancy Bear used accounts to target major U.S. political parties with offensive cyber operations, although it declined to provide details. Facebook said it warned targets "at highest risk" and was in contact with law enforcement about the activity. Later in the summer of 2016, Fancy Bear created fake personas that were used to seed stolen information to journalists. Facebook said it removed the accounts.[43]

ON JUNE 15, 2016, AN email arrived in the inbox of the editor of the online news site the Smoking Gun. "Hi. This is Guccifer 2.0 and this is me who hacked Democratic National Committee." The hacker claimed he had been inside the system for more than a year and had made off with thousands of documents. Attached to the email were an assortment of stolen DNC documents, including a donor list, internal memos, and a 237-page opposition research file on Trump. "The main part of the papers, thousands of files and mails, I gave to WikiLeaks," the hacker wrote ominously. "They will publish them soon."[44]

U.S. intelligence was confident that "Guccifer 2.0" was little more than a thinly veiled cover, or legend, for Russian military intelligence, the GRU. The hacker's choice of pseudonym was a subtle dig at Hillary Clinton. The original Guccifer was a Romanian hacker named Marcel Lazăr Lehel, who had hacked Clinton confidant Sidney Blumenthal's email, where he had retrieved evidence that Clinton had used a private email account while serving as secretary of state in 2012. (The FBI launched an investigation in 2015 after Clinton's private email server became front-page news in *The New York Times*.)

By leaking the documents to the press, Russian intelligence had turned what had begun as an intelligence-gathering operation into an active measures or covert action campaign. Guccifer 2.0 was the second attempt by Russia to release documents hacked out of the Democratic Party. A website called DCLeaks.com began posting stolen documents from the media office of the Hillary Clinton campaign on June 8, along with emails stolen from accounts of Republican congressional officials. (The Associated Press traced DCLeaks.com to a Romanian Internet company on a former Communist-era chicken farm.) The stolen documents were pushed to journalists via Facebook accounts linked to Russian foreign intelligence, but neither Guccifer 2.0 nor DCLeaks.com had the desired impact. The third release via WikiLeaks would be a game-changer.

What WikiLeaks knew how to do well was grab the media spotlight. Founded in 2006 by an Australian computer programmer turned international fugitive named Julian Assange, WikiLeaks didn't just publish classified or private information; it sought to ensure that the information got attention. That is what Assange had done in 2010 when he released "Collateral Murder," a video shot from the gunsight of an Apache attack helicopter in Iraq that showed American soldiers killing more than a dozen people, including two journalists for Reuters news agency. But the publication of the video and the release of an enormous trove of classified material supplied by an army private named Chelsea Manning sent Assange into hiding. Beginning in 2012, Assange was granted refuge by the government of Ecuador to reside within its embassy in London to avoid extradition to Sweden, where he was sought for alleged sexual offenses.

On July 22, just three days before the kickoff of the Democratic National Convention in Philadelphia, WikiLeaks began releasing its cache of more than 44,000 hacked DNC emails, some of which were only 58 days old. The embarrassing revelations showed that the DNC had helped sideline Clinton's rivals and it forced the resignation of Chairwoman Debbie Wasserman Schultz of Florida. Roger Stone bragged about his contact with WikiLeaks, and seemed to have an idea of what was coming next. "Trust me," he mused on Twitter, "it will soon be Podesta's time in the barrel." Sure enough, WikiLeaks released thousands more emails hacked from John Podesta, Clinton's campaign chairman.

Trump loved it. His speeches were filled with material gleaned from the hacked emails. During a press conference in July, Trump crept dangerously close to treason when he called on America's adversary to help dig up even more Clinton emails. "Russia, if you're listening, I hope you're able to find the 30,000 emails that are missing. I think you will probably be rewarded mightily by our press," Trump said. The GOP candidate cheered as John Podesta's hacked emails rolled out. "WikiLeaks, I love WikiLeaks," Trump crowed on October 10. Indeed, his son Don Jr. had been in secret contact with WikiLeaks over the summer, though proof that Don Sr. was privy to that line of communication has not, at the time of this writing, been ascertained.

The unremitting stream of leaked emails received far more media coverage than any other single issue during the campaign, including Trump's numerous scandals. To be sure, the Clinton campaign bears blame for this. So does FBI Director James Comey, who reopened an investigation into Clinton's emails 11 days before the election—only to swiftly close it as unfounded. But it's the role of WikiLeaks, far from a disinterested party, that the U.S. government found deeply troubling.

Only three days after Trump declared his love for WikiLeaks, Director of National Intelligence James Clapper released a statement that Russian intelligence services were likely behind the disclosures of hacked emails that had appeared on the website. In fact, all three American intelligence services—the FBI, CIA, and NSA—had jointly concluded with "high confidence" that Russia military intelligence, the GRU, used WikiLeaks to release the hacked emails. The CIA even managed to identify the Russians who supplied the emails, which laid "a circuitous route" from the GRU to WikiLeaks.[45] This is standard intelligence tradecraft, designed to obscure the original source. (Indeed, Julian Assange has said that the Russians were not his source nor was any other "state party.") CIA Director Mike Pompeo announced in April 2017 that "it is time to call out WikiLeaks for what it really is—a non-state hostile intelligence service often abetted by state actors like Russia."

Russian hackers also targeted the nation's election infrastructure. A top-secret document obtained by *The Intercept* revealed that the GRU had also hacked a U.S. voting software supplier and sent phishing emails to more than 100 local election officials days before the election.[46] And Russian hackers appeared to have targeted Internet-connected election-related networks in 21 states, according to the Department of Homeland Security, and penetrated one voter election database.[47] Things got so bad that President Obama pulled Vladimir Putin aside at a meeting of the Group of 20 in China and told him "to cut it out," warning that there would be serious consequences if he didn't.

IT IS IMPOSSIBLE TO SAY with certainty that Russian meddling carried Trump to victory in the 2016 election. There is no evidence that any votes were tampered with and amid the fusillade of information from all sources that bombarded American voters throughout the campaign it is hard to single out one single piece of it that tilted the balance. However, the converse is also true: it is impossible to say with certainty that Russian meddling *didn't help* Trump win the presidency. In an election that was decided by less than 80,000 votes in three states, Michigan, Pennsylvania, and Wisconsin, even a small number of votes impacted or changed could have made the difference.

As a candidate and as president, Trump repeatedly downplayed, doubted, and diminished the conclusion of his intelligence community that Russia meddled in the U.S. election. Trump was far more willing to believe a former high-ranking spy from a former police state where deception is an art form. After a meeting with Vladimir Putin in Da Nang, Vietnam, the president told reporters on Air Force One in November 2017, "He said he didn't meddle. I asked him again. You can only ask so many times. But I just asked him again, and he said he absolutely did not meddle in our election." Trump continued, "I really believe that when he tells me that, he means it. But he says, 'I didn't do that.' I think he's very insulted by it, if you want to know the truth."

This is outrageous, of course, but the country has spent far too much time reacting to each and every outrageous thing the president has said or done. What has largely gone unnoticed is what the president has failed to do. As of the time of this writing, Trump has only partially complied with a law passed overwhelmingly by Congress that required him to impose fresh sanctions on Russian corruption and individuals operating in the country's intelligence and defense sectors. Trump has failed to give Pentagon's Cyber Command the authority to use its awesomely powerful cyber tools to respond to the Russian hackers of Fancy Bear and Cozy Bear. The president is dithering, and the stakes are high.

Trump has ignored the dire warnings of his own intelligence community that Russia will be back in force in the 2018 and 2020 elections unless something is done. Admiral Mike Rogers, the head of the NSA and U.S. Cyber Command, sounded the alarm in February 2018. "President Putin has clearly come to the conclusion that there's little price to pay and that therefore 'I can continue this activity,'" Admiral Rogers told senators. "Clearly, what we have done hasn't been enough."[48] Dan Coats, the director of national intelligence, practically pleaded for presidential leadership on this issue. "We need to inform the American public that this is real," said Coats, who leads the nation's 17 intelligence agencies.

"That this is going to happen, and the resilience needed for us to stand up and say we're not going to allow some Russian to tell us how to vote, how to run our country," Coats then added, "I think there needs to be a national cry for that."

A little over a year after the election, the identity of one of the hackers behind the DNC assault came to light. A hacker named Konstantin Kozlovsky, prosecuted in Russia for breaking into bank computer systems, confessed in December 2017 that he had hacked the DNC at the direction of Russian intelligence. "I fulfilled various tasks under the leadership of employees of the FSB, including the hacking into the National Democratic Committee of the USA and the electronic correspondence of Hillary Clinton," Kozlovsky told a Moscow judge, according to court documents. "I also hacked into very substantial military entities of the USA and other organizations."[49]

In February 2018, an additional 13 Russian hackers, all working for the Internet Research Agency, and including "Putin's chef" and organized-crime member Yevgeny Prigozhin, were indicted by Special Counsel Robert Mueller's investigation. Prigozhin answered to the accusations, if only to defy them. "The Americans are really impressionable people, they see what they want to see," Prigozhin said, speaking to RIA Novosti, a Russian state news agency. "If they want to see the devil—let them see him." In March 2018, the Trump administration, under pressure for its weak response to Russia's active measures campaign, sanctioned Prigozhin and other members of the Internet Research Agency for their meddling in the 2016 U.S. election.

12.

THE PROSECUTOR AND
THE PRESIDENT

ROBERT MUELLER DID NOT CHOOSE PUBLIC service. Rather, he explained, he fell into it early on. Like his father, an executive at DuPont, Mueller attended Princeton University. He set out to be a doctor, but organic chemistry derailed his plans. He found himself moved by the example of a teammate on the lacrosse team, an upperclassman named David Hackett. After graduation, Hackett joined the Marine Corps and was killed by a sniper on his second tour of duty in Vietnam. Rather than being dissuaded, Mueller was inspired. One year after graduation, Mueller followed Hackett's footsteps and received his commission as a Marine officer. After Second Lieutenant Mueller had spent two months in the punishing U.S. Army Ranger school, the Marines put him charge of a platoon patrolling the jungles of Quang Tri, the northernmost province of South Vietnam.

Not long after Donald Trump was declared medically unfit to serve in combat due to a diagnosis of bone spurs in his heels—a malady he described to *The New York Times* as "temporary" and "minor"— Mueller's platoon came under attack by a North Vietnamese army company.[1] Mueller's swift, aggressive response defeated the attack and earned him a Bronze Star with a "V" device for valor. "With complete disregard for his own safety, he then skillfully supervised the evacuation of casualties from the hazardous area and, on one occasion, personally led a fire team across the fire-swept area terrain to recover a mortally wounded Marine who had fallen in a position forward of the friendly lines," the citation stated. This was the Marine ethos of no man left behind—*nemo resideo*. Even from a young age, Robert Mueller spoke with his actions, not words. Commitments mattered.

Back home, Mueller earned his law degree from the University of Virginia and started out in private practice, but he grew bored. He found his life's passion as a federal prosecutor, first in San Francisco, then in Boston. The two years he spent as partner at the law firm of Hale and Dorr were two years too many. A friend told *The Washington Post* that Mueller hated the idea of protecting criminals for money.[2] In 1995, he took an enormous pay cut to be a run-of-the-mill homicide prosecutor at the U.S. Attorney's office in Washington, DC, while the city was in the midst of a crack cocaine epidemic. "In his heart of hearts, he's a prosecutor," said the late Lee Rawls, Mueller's former chief of staff and a classmate at Princeton.[3]

When President George W. Bush nominated Mueller, a lifelong Republican, in 2001 to serve as FBI director, the bureau had been rocked by a string of high-profile scandals, including the arrest earlier in the year of Robert Hanssen, an agent who had spied for Russia over the course of 15 years. One week into Mueller's term, terrorists loyal to Osama bin Laden hijacked four planes and crashed two of them into the World Trade Center and one into the Pentagon.

The next day, Mueller had his very first presidential briefing at the White House. He began by telling President George W. Bush that the FBI had begun to identify the individuals responsible for the attack by identifying their seat numbers. About two minutes into his briefing, the president stopped him. "Bob, that's all well and good," Bush told him. "That's what I expected the bureau to do. That's what the bureau has been doing well for the last 100 years. What I want to know from you is, what are you doing to prevent the next terrorist attack?" Mueller, to his embarrassment, did not have an answer, but by the next day he did, and he led the FBI in a dramatic change of priorities to not just solve crimes but prevent them. Mueller's term at the FBI lasted 12 years. Only J. Edgar Hoover served longer.

Russian organized crime was a focus of Mueller's tenure at the FBI. And one Russian organized-crime figure loomed large in Mueller's FBI: Semion Mogilevich. The Brainy Don had landed on the FBI's 10 Most Wanted list in 2009 after a yearlong internal discussion. Few Americans had ever heard of Mogilevich. Then again, few Americans had ever heard of another 10 Most Wanted figure named Osama bin Laden before the September 11 attacks.

The FBI's investigation into Mogilevich had centered on Budapest, Hungary, which had been the Brainy Don's base of operations. Mueller visited the city in 2005, shortly after the bureau received approval to station agents permanently in Budapest. "As soon as the task force began investigating his activities, Mogilevich realized he could no longer use Budapest as his base of operations," Mueller said. "He immediately fled the country, and is now hiding in Moscow." Under Mueller, Budapest became an even larger priority. That made the Hungarian capital "the only place in the world outside of the Iraqi and Afghanistan war zones where the FBI is fully operational on the ground in a foreign country," Garrett Graff wrote in his book on Mueller's tenure at the FBI, *The Threat Matrix*.[4] The bureau also created a "threat fusion cell" to "target, dismantle, disrupt, neutralize, and render impotent" Mogilevich's organization. The fusion cell was staffed with agents from the FBI and officials from the NSA, giving the bureau access to the spy agency's powerful eavesdropping tools. The FBI declined to discuss the cell, saying it remains an ongoing investigative matter.

WHAT BROUGHT TOGETHER ROBERT MUELLER and Donald Trump—
two sons of prominent families whose lives had widely diverged, one
toward public service, another toward greed—on the world stage not
long after Trump's most victorious hour was another FBI director, the
one who may have helped Trump inadvertently win the election. James
R. Comey cast an imposing figure, as tall as LeBron James, and nearly as
commanding in meetings as the basketball star was on court. He was a
former religion major at the College of William and Mary, fond of quoting spiritual figures (his Twitter account briefly took the pseudonym of
the American theologian Reinhold Niebuhr). Like Mueller, Comey, too,
had given up a high-paying partnership at a law firm to serve as a federal
prosecutor in Richmond, Virginia.

He went on to serve as deputy attorney general under President
George W. Bush where he and Mueller had made common cause. "I
know Jim Comey," Mueller had told a group of alumni from his alma
mater on the evening before he was named special counsel. "He's a very
good man." Both men were united in their opposition to the reautho-
rization of the highly classified Terrorist Surveillance Program, which
they each felt was unconstitutional and illegal. Working in tandem, they
mounted a dramatic stand in then Attorney General John Ashcroft's
hospital room as the Bush White House pressured Ashcroft to reautho-
rize the program while he recovered from gallbladder surgery. Mueller
and Comey threatened to resign over the issue, and, in the end, Bush
backed down and assented to the changes they requested.

Comey was in the fourth year of his 10-year term at the FBI when
he earned the ire of President Trump, who viewed him as disloyal. The
FBI director had told Trump privately on three separate occasions that
the president was not under investigation in the bureau's Russia probe.
And yet Comey had refused the president's request to, as Trump put it,
"get that fact out." (Comey testified that the FBI had been reluctant to
do so because it would pose a problem if the situation changed.) Trump
was also mad that Comey had said there was no evidence to support the

president's claim that he had been wiretapped by then President Obama.

In early May, Trump brooded over what he saw as Comey's betrayal, before urging his staff to draw up what was described to *The New York Times* as a multi-page "screed" against Comey.[5] But that did little to sate his fury and on May 9, Trump dispatched his longtime bodyguard, Keith Schiller, to FBI headquarters with a toned-down letter relieving Comey of his job. "While I greatly appreciate you informing me, on three separate occasions, that I am not under investigation," Trump wrote, "I nevertheless concur with the judgment of the Department of Justice that you are not able to effectively lead the Bureau." Comey wasn't even in Washington to defend himself when the letter arrived, a fact that Trump used to his advantage to humiliate him.

The president seemed very pleased with himself the next day as he warmly welcomed two top Russian diplomats to the Oval Office. One was the wily Russian foreign minister Sergey Lavrov, and the other was Sergey Kislyak, the Russian ambassador to the United States who had recently come under fire for his clandestine meetings with Michael Flynn and Jared Kushner. "I just fired the head of the FBI. He was crazy, a real nut job," Trump told them, according to a record of the meeting shared with *The New York Times*. "I faced great pressure because of Russia. That's taken off."[6] Trump then went off script. The president told the Russians about highly classified information provided by Israel. It involved a plot by ISIS to build laptop computer bombs that could pass undetected through airport security. Trump did not name Israel as the source, but he did reveal an extremely sensitive detail that "could jeopardize modus operandi of Israeli intelligence," according to Ronen Bergman, who covers intelligence for *Yedioth Ahronoth*, Israel's largest daily newspaper.[7]

Israeli intelligence had been warned before Trump took office by their counterparts at Langley. During a meeting in early January at CIA headquarters, a group of Mossad officers were told by the CIA that Russia had "leverages of pressure" on Trump, according to Bergman's reporting.[8] Israel, which had some of the best human sources of intelli-

gence in the Middle East, was told to "be careful" after Trump's inauguration about what information it chose to share with the White House
and the National Security Council, to be headed by Michael Flynn.[9]

The president continued to vent his fury at his ex-FBI director.
"Look, he's a showboat. He's a grandstander," Trump told NBC's Lester
Holt on May 11. "The FBI has been in turmoil. You know that, I know
that, everybody knows that."[10] In a cryptic threat the following day,
Trump tweeted out, "James Comey better hope that there are no 'tapes'
of our conversations before he starts leaking to the press!"[11] Once again,
Trump precipitated another crisis of his own making. Comey had been
keeping detailed, contemporaneous notes on his interactions with the
president from the moment they met. He woke up in the middle of the
night on May 15 and, spurred by Trump's tweet, decided to share them.
He asked Daniel Richman, a friend and former federal prosecutor, to
share the details of his memos with a reporter. And those memos, now
in the hands of Special Counsel Mueller, may yet prove to be evidence
of obstruction of justice by the forty-fifth president. "I've seen the tweet
about tapes," Comey later told the Senate. "Lordy, I hope there are
tapes."[12]

COMEY'S FIRST MEETING WITH TRUMP took place on January 6, 2017,
in a conference room at Trump Tower in New York. He was there to
brief the president-elect on the findings of the intelligence community
concerning Russian efforts to interfere in the election. At the end of
the briefing, Comey remained alone with Trump to alert him to what
Comey called "the salacious and unverified" allegations in the Steele
Dossier. The FBI and the rest of the intelligence community knew the
media were about to make it public and Comey briefed the president
alone to minimize potential embarrassment.

Trump expressed his disgust at the allegations that he cavorted with
prostitutes in the Moscow Ritz in 2013 and strongly denied them. Without being directly asked, Comey offered Trump the assurance that he

was not the subject of an FBI counterintelligence investigation. Something the president-elect said or did during that meeting—we don't know yet exactly what—deeply troubled the FBI director. As soon as he left Trump Tower, Comey documented his meeting with Trump. This was something he had never done before, but going forward, Comey would keep a record of each and every interaction he had with the president. "I was honestly concerned he might lie about the nature of our meeting so I thought it important to document," Comey later told the Senate.

The FBI director would go on to document a private dinner on January 27 in the Green Room of the White House. Comey's instincts told him that the president was trying to create some sort of patronage relationship. "I need loyalty, I expect loyalty," Trump told him. At the end of the dinner, Trump again demanded Comey's loyalty.

"You will always get honesty from me," the FBI director replied.

Trump paused, and then said, "That's what I want, honest loyalty."

"You will get that from me," Comey replied.

On February 14, Comey found himself alone again with the president, this time in the Oval Office after a counterterrorism briefing. A day earlier, Michael Flynn, the national security advisor, had resigned after just 23 days on the job. Flynn had lied to Vice President Mike Pence and other top White House officials about his conversations with Ambassador Kislyak shortly after Trump's election victory. Pence had then gone on CBS's *Face the Nation* and said there had been no contact between the Trump team and Russian officials. "I think to suggest that is to give credence to some of these bizarre rumors that have swirled around the candidacy," Pence said.

Comey's FBI knew that wasn't true. Not only had Flynn lied to Pence, he had also lied to FBI agents. He falsely told them that he did not ask Kislyak to hold off on retaliating against sanctions imposed by President Obama for Russia's meddling in the election, when in fact he had. U.S. officials had been listening in on the calls with Kislyak— as Flynn, a former head of the Defense Intelligence Agency (DIA)— surely knew they would be. This was a measure of Flynn's hubris. Before that, Flynn had ignored the advice of his former DIA colleagues and accepted an all-expenses-paid trip to Moscow, where he sat next to Vladimir Putin at the tenth anniversary banquet of the Russian state-funded channel RT, formerly known as Russia Today.

The Justice Department had alerted White House officials that Flynn's attempts to cover his tracks about his lies to Pence made him susceptible to blackmail. As Comey met alone with the president in the Oval Office, Trump told him, "I hope you can see your way clear to letting this go, to letting Flynn go. He is a good guy. I hope you can let this go." Comey said he took it to mean the president was asking him to drop the Flynn investigation. Comey promised nothing. As the FBI director and former prosecutor surely knew, the president's words were potentially grounds for a charge of obstruction of justice.

On March 20, Comey publicly confirmed what many had long suspected. The FBI was investigating the nature of any links and any coordination between the Trump campaign and the Russian government's efforts to interfere in the 2016 presidential election. Two days later, the new director of national intelligence, Dan Coats, told associates that the president asked him whether he could intervene with Comey and get the bureau to back off on its investigation of former national security advisor Michael Flynn as part of its Russia investigation, according to *The Washington Post*. Trump called Comey at the FBI a week later.[13] The Russia investigation was "a cloud" that was impairing his ability to act on behalf of the country, the president told him. Trump asked what the FBI could do to "lift the cloud." Trump also told Comey to get word out that the FBI was not personally investigating him. The president repeated that request in another phone call the following month, along with further complaints about "the cloud."

"I've been very loyal to you, very loyal," Trump told Comey. "We had that thing, you know"—an apparent reference to the dinner where the president had asked for his loyalty. *I've been good to you,* Comey believed the president was telling him. *You should be good to me.* That was the last time he spoke to President Trump.

With Comey's sudden dismissal, which took most of the White House by surprise, the pressure to appoint a special counsel, which had been building all year, grew to a fever pitch. The decision over whether or not to appoint one fell to Rod Rosenstein, who was two weeks into the job as deputy attorney general. His boss, former Alabama senator Jeff Sessions, had recused himself from the Russia investigation in March because of his role in the Trump campaign, earning the attorney general a permanent spot in Trump's doghouse. Trump publicly chastised his attorney general's actions as "DISGRACEFUL!" on Twitter and mocked Sessions privately as "Mr. Magoo," a blind, bumbling cartoon character.[14]

Rosenstein told the Senate during his confirmation hearing in March 2017 that two conditions had to be met for him to name a special counsel. First, he would have to determine that a crime had been committed, and, second, that the investigation of that crime would pose a conflict of interest for the Justice Department. On May 12, three days after Comey's dismissal, CNN reported that Rosenstein thought nothing had changed and he saw no need to appoint a special counsel.[15] Five days later, a little more than a week after Trump dismissed his FBI director, Rosenstein changed his mind and Robert Mueller was named special counsel. The reason why has not been explained, but it's quite possible that someone brought Comey's memos to Rosenstein's attention.

Rosenstein's announcement brought an end to a discussion within the White House about returning Mueller to his old job as FBI director. According to *The Washington Post*, Mueller had met with Trump for 30 minutes and impressed him with his no-nonsense, straightforward manner. Trump was surprised when he heard the news. "Wasn't that guy just in here interviewing for the FBI?" he asked one of his aides.[16]

ROBERT MUELLER IS NOT THE kind of prosecutor who tries his case in public. "I abhor leaks," he said during his confirmation hearing to be FBI director. "I think you set a standard of very harsh treatment when an investigation is conducted and somebody is determined to have leaked." As a result, the Mueller investigation was one of Washington's better-kept secrets. Even the precise location where Mueller runs his investigation has not yet been disclosed.

As he had before in his career, Mueller once again gave up a lucrative job, a $3.4 million partnership at the DC powerhouse firm WilmerHale, to take on the position of special counsel. Mueller's team includes several attorneys he brought with him from WilmerHale, including Assistant Special Counsel James L. Quarles III, a former assistant special prosecutor for the Watergate Special Prosecution Force, who served as Mueller's main point of contact with the White House; Jeannie S. Rhee, a former attorney in the Justice Department's Office of Legal Counsel; and Aaron Zebley, who was Mueller's chief of staff at the FBI. Other attorneys were detailed to the special counsel's office from various posts inside the Justice Department, including Andrew Weissmann, a veteran prosecutor and former general counsel of the FBI. Interestingly, Weissmann's signature appears on the cooperation agreement that Felix Sater signed with the federal government back in 1998.

The special counsel's staff grew into what amounted to a boutique law firm with 17 attorneys. The investigation was run out of a suite of offices in a business district somewhere in southwest Washington, DC, about a mile from the Justice Department. The office contained a secure space for reading top-secret information, known in DC-speak as a Sensitive Compartmented Information Facility, or SCIF. Witness interviews were conducted in a windowless conference room with FBI agents carrying armfuls of documents and prosecutors rotating in and out. Mueller himself appeared on occasion for key portions of the interviews, sitting quietly against the wall.[17]

The Mueller investigation had barely gotten started when President Trump ordered the firing of the special counsel in early June. Trump's move came amid reports that Mueller was examining whether the president attempted to obstruct justice. According to *The New York Times*, the president argued that Mueller had a conflict of interest because, among other things, there was a dispute over membership fees when Mueller resigned in 2011 as a member of the Trump National Golf Club in Northern Virginia. ("Mr. Mueller left the club in October 2011 without dispute," said Peter Carr, a spokesman for the special counsel's office.) The White House counsel, Donald McGahn, refused to order Mueller's firing and threatened to quit instead. The president then backed down. (Trump called the *Times* report "fake news.")[18]

One of Mueller's first targets was Paul Manafort, Trump's campaign chairman. Leading the investigation were a team of prosecutors led by Weissmann, who was joined by Kyle Freeny, an expert on money laundering, and Greg Andres, who specialized in foreign bribery. With the Manafort inquiry barely two months old, Mueller made his first public move when in the early hours of July 26, he had FBI agents raid Manafort's home in Alexandria, Virginia. In a sign of how tight a ship Mueller runs, word of the Manafort raid did not leak out for 10 days. It was to be one of what would later be revealed to be 15 warrants in the Manafort case, all of which required Mueller's team to comb through more than half a million records and the scanned contents of 87 computers, phones, and thumb drives.

The timing of the raid was curious. Manafort had testified in a closed-door interview with the Senate Intelligence Commission the day before. Had Manafort said something to the Senate that prompted the raid? The day after the raid of Manafort's home, George Papadopoulos was met by FBI agents upon arrival at Dulles International Airport. The agents confiscated his passport and arrested him on charges of lying to federal officials and obstruction of justice. In earlier interviews with the FBI, Papadopoulos claimed that his interactions with Professor Mifsud, the shadowy London-based professor with connections to the Russian government, had occurred before he joined the Trump campaign. Likewise, Papadopoulos claimed to have met the woman he described in campaign emails as "Putin's niece" long before he joined the Trump ticket. After his arrest, however, Papadopoulos changed his story and revealed the truth: the only reason the professor took an interest in him was because of his status with the Trump campaign.

By the end of September, the special counsel's office had spent $3.2 million getting itself up and running, with salaries accounting for slightly more than half that amount. The Justice Department spent an additional $3.5 million to support the Mueller investigation. That money would have been spent on the investigation "irrespective of the existence of the [special counsel's office]," according to a summary released by the Justice Department.

Mueller's special counsel office filed the first criminal charges against Paul Manafort and his right-hand man, Rick Gates, in October 2017. A Washington, DC, grand jury indicted the two men on six counts, including a money-laundering conspiracy and other crimes, and sought to seize four of Manafort's properties (which did not include his Trump Tower apartment). Trump's name did not appear once in the 31-page indictment, which was widely seen as an effort to pressure the two men into cooperating with the special counsel's office. Mueller's prosecutors appear to view Manafort as a path to an even bigger fish, possibly Trump himself. Months later, Gates pleaded guilty and agreed to cooperate with Mueller's investigators, leaving Manafort alone to face two separate indictments brought by the special counsel. Manafort has vowed to fight, but as the 68-year-old's assets have dwindled away and the reality of a dozen years in federal prison for the money-laundering count alone sets in, it seems like it's only a matter of time before he, too, will agree to cooperate.

The Washington press corps had known for days that Manafort's arraignment was coming. Cable news had started their coverage hours before he strode into the courthouse, but before Trump's defenders could utter the words "no collusion," the special counsel released an even bigger bombshell. George Papadopoulos's guilty plea made it clear that there had been some collusion, albeit at a low level, with Russia. "There's a large-scale, ongoing investigation of which this case is a small part," Aaron Zelinsky, one of Mueller's prosecutors, said during Papadopoulos's plea hearing. Trump's defenders dismissed Papadopoulos, much as he had dismissed Professor Mifsud, as a nothing. "He was the coffee boy," Michael Caputo, a former Trump campaign spokesman, told CNN. Trump agreed. "Few people knew the young, low-level volunteer named George, who has already proven to be a liar," the president said via Twitter.[19]

If there was one thing that was proven by the Papadopoulos plea, it was how little the Washington press corps knew about the Mueller investigation. It was certainly true that no one in the media knew that the 30-year-old former Trump campaign aide had flipped back in July and entered his plea nearly a month earlier. Even Michael Flynn, Trump's former national security advisor, had entered a plea bargain with Mueller who was now running an operation so silent that no one had any idea what was coming next. Feeling the heat, President Trump replaced his longtime counsel Marc Kasowitz with veteran Washington lawyers John Dowd and Ty Cobb, who, instead of fighting the Mueller probe, tried to cooperate with it. By the end of 2017, Dowd said in a memo, the Trump campaign had turned over 1.4 million documents to the special counsel and the White House handed over an additional 20,000 pages to the special counsel on issues regarding Michael Flynn and James Comey. In addition, 20 White House personnel voluntarily gave interviews to the special counsel, including eight members of the White House Counsel's office, with Donald McGahn, the president's chief legal advisor, appearing on November 30, 2017. Jared Kushner, the president's son-in-law, also spoke with the special counsel's office in November. Kushner's interview lasted less than an hour.

The desire to be as transparent as possible led to tensions between Trump's legal team and the White House. While Dowd and Cobb discussed the tensions over lunch, Ken Vogel, a reporter for *The New York Times*, happened to be sitting nearby. "The White House counsel's office is being very conservative with this stuff," Cobb told Dowd, according to Vogel. "Our view is we're not hiding anything." Referring to White House counsel Don McGahn, Cobb added, "He's got a couple documents locked in a safe."[20] This was potentially a clever way to reveal sensitive attorney-client information to a reporter without getting disbarred.

The job of fighting the Mueller inquiry was left to members of the president's party in Congress. Just as Democrats did during the Clinton years, congressional Republicans began to investigate the investigators, searching for conflicts of interest. In an early embarrassment, Congress made public text messages between two FBI agents assigned to Mueller's investigation who were having an affair. In the texts, each of the agents had referred to the future president as an "idiot" and agreed Hillary Clinton deserved to win "100,000,000-0."

Mueller reacted swiftly. One of the agents was Peter Strzok, a top FBI counterintelligence official. Republicans viewed it as no coincidence that Strzok opened the bureau's investigation into the Trump campaign in July 2016. Immediately upon learning of the allegations, the special counsel's office removed Strzok from the investigation, according to Mueller's spokesman. The other, Lisa Page, was an attorney brought on through a short-term detail from the FBI's Office of the General Counsel, and she returned to the bureau in mid-July. Page reportedly had worked on the FBI task force in Budapest that investigated Semion Mogilevich and Russian organized crime. Republicans made much of a cryptic reference in the Page-Strzok texts to an "insurance policy" in the event Trump won and a meeting with FBI Deputy Director Andy McCabe, whom, the president repeatedly suggested, was close with the Clintons.

"America will get what the voting public deserves," Strzok texted during a Republican debate.

"That's what I'm afraid of," Page replied.

Republican lawmakers kept finding conflicts of interest in Mueller's team. While at WilmerHale, Mueller prosecutor Jeannie Rhee had, the Republicans noted, represented the Clinton Foundation. Judicial Watch, a conservative watchdog group, unearthed an email Mueller prosecutor Andrew Weissmann wrote to Sally Yates, the acting attorney general, the night Yates was fired by President Trump for refusing to defend his executive order closing the nation's borders to refugees and people from predominantly Muslim countries. The email read: "I am so proud. And in awe. Thank you so much. All my deepest respects, Andrew Weissmann."[21]

On February 16, Mueller unsealed perhaps his biggest surprise to date: the indictment of 13 Russians involved in the Internet Research Agency. The indictment was based in part on information from the CIA, NSA, and FBI, and it read like a spy novel, too. The indictment was replete with undercover visits to the United States, stolen identities, and rallies and actions plotted from their headquarters in St. Petersburg, Russia. The indictment also left a few tantalizing clues that some of the individuals involved in the agency may now be cooperating with Mueller's investigation.

With no extradition treaty between the United States and Russia, the Internet Research Agency indictment was unlikely to put anyone behind bars, but it exposed the lie behind Trump's many attempts to claim that Russia didn't meddle in the U.S. election. Indeed, Trump's unease was palpable in a bizarre string of tweets he issued the day after the indictment. The president espoused a theory from the fringes of the right wing that linked the FBI's Russia investigation to the February 14 shooting at Stoneman Douglas High School in Parkland, Florida, that killed 17 students and staff. "Very sad that the FBI missed all of the many signals sent out by the Florida school shooter. This is not acceptable. They are spending too much time trying to prove Russian collusion with the Trump campaign—there is no collusion. Get back to the basics and make us all proud!"[22]

Yet Mueller's investigation was only just getting started. The special counsel's office was said to be preparing a similarly revealing indictment of the Russians who carried out the hacking and leaking of emails stolen from the Democratic National Committee during the 2016 election. Any hacking case would likely involve Ryan Dickey, an expert in computer crimes who prosecuted "Guccifer," the extradited Romanian hacker Marcel Lazăr Lehel, who pleaded guilty in 2016 to unauthorized access to a protected computer and aggravated identity theft. No indictment had been filed at the time of this writing.

Trump was said to have expected a swift end to Mueller's investigation, but if the past is any indication, the special counsel's probe of Russia will weigh on his presidency for years, just as earlier investigations of past presidents have. The independent counsel inquiry led by Kenneth Starr and three other independent counsels into President Bill Clinton dragged on for six years at a cost of nearly $80 million before ultimately concluding that there was insufficient evidence to show that any crimes were committed. Independent counsel Lawrence E. Walsh's

Iran-Contra investigation also lasted six years at a cost of more than $47 million.

Without fanfare, Mueller has begun slowly unwinding the many layers of conspiracy involving Trump and Russia. Donald Trump has promised he would build a "big, beautiful wall" along the U.S.-Mexican border as part of his plan to make America great again. But so far, the only wall that is being built is the legal one that Special Counsel Robert Mueller is erecting around the White House, and it increasingly seems too high for America's forty-fifth president to escape.

ACKNOWLEDGMENTS

THIS BOOK STARTED AS AN OUTPOURING of frustration about a story no one seemed to be paying much attention to: the frightening implications of the relationship between our newly elected president, Donald J. Trump, and Russia.

I began writing a blog, trump-russia.com, to help myself think through these issues. I thought no one was paying attention, but it turned out that people were. It was my agent, Scott Mendel, who found me, and had the vision to see what became this book. I can't thank Scott enough for his steady hand in guiding me through this process and his sage advice. He is a man of his word.

President Trump has reinvigorated America's journalists. *The New York Times* and *The Washington Post* and other news outlets have risen to the challenge, as have venerable magazines like *The Atlantic Monthly* and *The New Yorker*. This book relies heavily on their work and would not have been possible without it. Special thanks go out to David Cay Johnston and Jane Mayer for their support.

Despite what the president says, the FBI is a wonderful institution and I am fortunate to have the opportunity to get to know them. Of the many former federal agents I spoke with I would like to thank Ray Kerr and Jim Moody, who spent hours helping me understand Russian organized crime. There are many others, inside and outside the government, who helped me understand Russia, hacking, opposition research, social media, and information warfare. Valerie Wattenberg provided research and translation. Phyllis Schultze, a criminal justice librarian at Rutgers Law School, found me several needles in the haystack. There are some who I cannot acknowledge, but they know who they are.

I was doubly lucky to find my fearless publisher, Melville House, co-founded by Dennis Johnson with Valerie Merians. Melville House treated me like family. My editor, Michael Barron, has worked tirelessly to help make me a better writer than I actually am. The Trump-Russia story is a complex, sprawling one and this book would not be what it is without the seamless narrative Michael helped me create. Managing Editor Susan Rella kept the book on schedule and provided excellent edits as well. Thanks also goes to my publicists, Stephanie DeLuca and Alexandra Primiani, and to Ian Dreiblatt, digital marketing manager; Peter Clark, sales manager; Dylan Soltis, direct sales manager; and, Simon Reichley, rights manager. Marina Drukman designed the cover. Katie Haigler did a terrific job copyediting the manuscript. Michael Moglia, Molly Mellott, Andy Tang, and Sarah Robbins also helped with the enormous amount of endnotes.

Encouragement along the way came from many sources. My father-in-law, Gerald Lubensky, was my biggest fan and his enthusiasm was contagious. Greg Bull believed this book would happen even when I didn't. Alex Roth and Mike Cormack helped assure me I was on the right track by reading early drafts. I am very proud to call Amy Knight a friend; not only is she an expert on the KGB but she has championed this project from the beginning. The marketing and design dynamic duo of Dean & Nathalie Lubensky provided excellent advice and support along the way. Also inspiring were the early readers of my website—Yvonne, Terry, Don, Marty, and others whom I now consider my friends.

Most of all I would like to thank my wife, Anita. This book would not have been possible without her. For the past 15 years, I have aspired to be the man that she sees in me. I don't know if I succeeded, but I am a far better person for trying.

NOTES

INTRODUCTION

1 Alexander Smith, "Putin on U.S. election interference: 'I couldn't care less,'" NBC News, March 10, 2018, https://www.nbcnews.com/news/world/putin-u-s-election-interference-i-couldn-t-care-less-n855151.

2 "Remarks by President Trump in Press Gaggle Aboard Air Force One en route Hanoi, Vietnam," whitehouse.gov, November 11, 2017. https://www.whitehouse.gov/briefings-statements/remarks-president-trump-press-gaggle-aboard-air-force-one-en-route-hanoi-vietnam/.

3 Bill Littlefield, "A Day (and a Cheeseburger) with President Trump," WBUR, May 5, 2017, http://www.wbur.org/onlyagame/2017/05/05/james-dodson-donald-trump-golf.

4 Donald Trump (@realDonaldTrump), "Russia has never tried to use leverage over me. I HAVE NOTHING TO DO WITH RUSSIA - NO DEALS, NO LOANS, NO NOTHING!," Twitter, January 11, 2017, https://twitter.com/realDonaldTrump/status/819159806489591809.

5 Jose Maria Irujo and John Carlin, "The Spanish Connection with Trump's Russia Scandal," El País, April 3, 2017, https://elpais.com/elpais/2017/03/31/inenglish/1490984556_409827.html; Sebastian Rotella, "Russian Politician Who Reportedly Sent Millions to NRA Has Long History in Spain," ProPublica, January 19, 2018, https://www.propublica.org/article/russian-politician-who-reportedly-sent-millions-to-nra-has-long-history-in-spain.

6   Rosalind S. Helderman and Tom Hamburger, "Guns and religion: How American conservatives grew closer to Putin's Russia," *The Washington Post*, April 30, 2017, https://www.washingtonpost.com/politics/how-the-republican-right-found-allies-in-russia/2017/04/30/e2d83ff6-29d3-11e7-a616-d7c8a68c1a66_story.html.

7   Katie Pavlich, "Part 1: Meet the Woman Working with the NRA and Fighting for Gun Rights in Russia," TownHall.com, May 6, 2014, https://townhall.com/columnists/katiepavlich/2014/05/06/meet-the-woman-fighting-for-gun-rights-in-russia-n1830491.

8   Ralph Benko, "'Clinton Beats Trump' Is the Real 'Fake News' Scandal," Forbes.com, December 12, 2016, https://www.forbes.com/sites/ralphbenko/2016/12/12/clinton-beats-trump-is-the-real-fake-news-scandal/#1b7bb40d130d.

9   Articles of Organization, Bridges LLC, South Dakota, 2016. It is unclear what this company was formed to do.

10 Maria Butina (@Maria_Butina), "спросила кандидата в президенты США Дональда Трампа о позиции в отношении России.Трамп говорит о смягчении санкций," Twitter July 11, 2015, https://twitter.com/Maria_Butina/status/619961053170958336; "Donald Trump handles questions at Freedom Fest July 11, '15 Las Vegas," YouTube video, 14:45, posted by "Demo Cast" July 12, 2015, https://www.youtube.com/watch?time_continue=2&v=nP8xogCIGXw.

11 Matt Apuzzo, Matthew Rosenberg, and Adam Goldman, "Top Russian Official Tried to Broker 'Backdoor' Meeting Between Trump and Putin," *The New York Times*, November 17, 2017, https://www.nytimes.com/2017/11/17/us/politics/trump-russia-kushner.html.

12 Nicholas Fandos, "Operative Offered Trump Campaign 'Kremlin Connection' Using N.R.A. Ties," *The New York Times*, December 3, 2017, https://www.nytimes.com/2017/12/03/us/politics/trump-putin-russia-nra-campaign.html.

13 Peter Stone and Greg Gordon, "FBI investigating whether Russian money went to NRA to help Trump," *McClatchyDC*, January 18, 2018, http://www.mcclatchydc.com/news/nation-world/national/article195231139.html.

14 Embassy Madrid, "Spain Details Its Strategy to Combat the Russian Mafia," 10MADRID154_a, February 8, 2010, accessible at WikiLeaks, https://wikileaks.org/plusd/cables/10MADRID154_a.html.

CHAPTER 1: THE WORLD'S MOST TALKED ABOUT ADDRESS

1   Dee Wedemeyer, "Bonwit Teller Building to Be Sold," *The New York Times,* January 26, 1979, http://www.nytimes.com/1979/01/26/archives/bonwit-teller-building-to-be-sold-genesco-owns-bonwit-chain.html.

2   David W. Dunlap, "Meet Donald Trump," *Times Insider,* October 16, 1973, https://www.nytimes.com/times-insider/2015/07/30/1973-meet-donald-trump/.

3   Wayne Barrett. *Trump: The Deals and the Downfall* (New York: HarperCollins, 1992), pp. 188–89.

4   Michael Franzese's account is taken from: *Russian Organized Crime in the United States: Hearing before the Permanent Subcommittee on Investigations of the Committee on Governmental Affairs*, U.S. Senate, 104th Congress, 2nd sess. (May 15, 1996) (Michael Franzese testimony).

5   Michael Franzese and Dery Matera. *Quitting the Mob: How the "Yuppie Don" Left the Mafia and Lived to Tell His Story* (New York: HarperCollins, 1992).

6   Roy Rowan, "The 50 Biggest Mafia Bosses," *Fortune*, November 10, 1986, http://archive.fortune.com/magazines/fortune/fortune_archive/1986/11/10/68275/index.htm.

7 Federal Bureau of Investigation, "Overview of Russian/Eurasian Criminal Activities in the United States: A Preliminary Report," July 1993.

8 Alan Block, *Red Notice*, unpublished manuscript in the author's possession. The late criminologist Alan Block wrote an entire book about the Russians involved in the gas-tax scam and interviewed Bogatin in prison. I am indebted to Phyllis Schultze of Rutgers University for her assistance. Moschella confirmed the quote for me in an online interview.

9 Nicholas Horrock and Linnet Myers, "Extradition Target Says His Real Crime Is Success," *Chicago Tribune*, April 3, 1992, http://articles.chicagotribune.com/1992-04-03 /news/9201300839_1_extradition-poland-evasion.

10 Justice Department, "Former Organized Crime Figure Sentenced in Million-Dollar Fuel Tax Fraud Scheme," News Release, June 7, 1996, https://www.justice.gov/archive/opa /pr/1996/Jun96/261.tax.htm.

11 Allan Dodds Frank, "See No Evil," *Forbes*, October 6, 1986.

12 David Cay Johnson. *The Making of Donald Trump* (Brooklyn: Melville House, 2016), loc. 1427 of 3406, Kindle.

13 Dominick Dunne, "The Fall of Roberto Polo," *Vanity Fair*, October 1988, https://www .vanityfair.com/magazine/1988/10/dunne198810.

14 "Dan Dorfman, "On the Trail of Baby Doc," *New York*, July 14, 1986.

15 Block, *Red Notice*.

16 Robert I. Friedman, "The Money Plane," *New York*, January 22, 1996, http://www.unz .com/print/NewYork-1996jan22-00024/.

17 Ibid.

18 Wayne Barrett. *Trump*, p. 203

19 Malcolm Nance. *The Plot to Hack America: How Putin's Cyberspies and WikiLeaks Tried to Steal the 2016 Election* (New York: Skyhorse Publishing, 2016), loc. 123 of 3865, Kindle.

20 Donald Trump, "There's nothing wrong with America's Foreign Defense Policy that a little backbone can't cure," *The New York Times*, September 2, 1987.

21 *Soviet Active Measures: Hearings before the Permanent Select Committee on Intelligence*, U.S. House, 97th Congress, 2nd sess. (July 14 and 18, 1982).

22 Michael Oreskes, "Trump Gives Vague Hint of Candidacy," *The New York Times*, September 2, 1987.

23 Selwyn Raab, "Mob-Linked Businessman Killed in Brooklyn," *The New York Times*, May 3, 1989, https://www.nytimes.com/1989/05/03/nyregion/mob-linked-businessman -killed-in-brooklyn.html.

24 Horrock and Myers, "Extradition Target Says His Real Crime Is Success."

25 Alan A. Block. *Russian Organized Crime: The New Threat?*, ed. Phil Williams (London: Taylor & Francis, 1997), p. 168.

26 Foreign Broadcast Information Service, "JPRS Report: East Europe," May 6, 1992.

27 Robert I. Friedman, "The Most Dangerous Mobster in the World," *Village Voice*, May 26, 1999, https://www.villagevoice.com/1998/05/26/the-most-dangerous-mobster-in-the -world/.

28 Wayne Barrett. *Trump: The Deals and the Downfall* (New York: HarperCollins, 1992), p. 203.

29 An attorney for the agency declined my request for a copy of Trump's sworn statement, citing an exemption under New Jersey's Open Public Records Act for records involving the criminal background of applicant.

CHAPTER 2: MAFIYA TAJ MAHAL

1 David Cay Johnston, "Trump's Taj Opens for Business," *The Philadelphia Inquirer*, April 6, 1990.

2 Lenny Glynn, "Trump's Taj—Open at Last, with a Scary Appetite," *The New York Times*, April 8, 1990, https://www.nytimes.com/1990/04/08/business/trump-s-taj-open-at-last-with-a-scary-appetite.html.

3 John Curran, "Trump Taj Mahal Fined $477,000 By Fed'l Banking Regulators," Associated Press, January 28, 1998; "Trump's Taj Mahal Pays $477,000 Penalty For Money Violations," *The Wall Street Journal*, January 29, 1998.

4 U.S. Treasury Department, "FinCEN Fines Trump Taj Mahal Casino Resort $10 Million for Significant and Long Standing Anti-Money Laundering Violations," March 6, 2015, https://www.fincen.gov/news/news-releases/fincen-fines-trump-taj-mahal-casino-resort-10-million-significant-and-long.

5 *Implementation of Indian Regulatory Gaming Act: Oversight Hearing before the Subcommittee on Native American Affairs of the Committee on Natural Resources*, U.S. House, 103rd Congress, 1st sess. (October 5, 1993).

6 Robert I. Friedman. *Red Mafiya: How the Russian Mob Has Invaded America* (Boston: Little, Brown and Company, 2000), p. 133.

7 *Asian Influenced Crime: Influence in the Asian Entertainment Industry: Hearings before the Permanent Subcommittee on Investigations*, U.S. Senate, 103rd Congress, 1st sess. (June 18 and August 4, 1992).

8 Molly Gordy, "Trump Supports Casino Suspect," New York *Daily News*, September 25, 1995, http://www.nydailynews.com/archives/news/trump-supports-casino-suspect-article-1.692948.

9 There was a mishap during the show. Kirkorov pushed a 70-year-old security guard who fell, hit his head on the concrete floor, and lost consciousness. He sued Kirkorov and died shortly before trial. A jury found that Kirkorov was not responsible.

10 Steve Rosenburg, "Why Donald Trump Strikes a Chord with Russians," BBC, September 7, 2016, http://www.bbc.com/news/world-europe-37286988.

11 Ibid.

12 Oleg Karmaza, "Interview with Vyacheslav Ivankov," *Komsomolskaya Pravda*, April 23, 1997.

13 Paul Klebnikov. *Godfather of the Kremlin: The Decline of Russia in the Age of Gangster Capitalism* (Boston: Harcourt, 2000), p. 17.

14 Friedman, *Red Mafiya*, p. 114.

15 Friedman, *Red Mafiya*, p. 115.

16 Friedman, *Red Mafiya*, p. 119.

17 Ibid.

18 Federal Bureau of Investigation, "Eurasian Organized Crime: Extortion, Murder, Tax Fraud, Credit Fraud, Robbery and Drug Trafficking Activities in the New York Metropolitan Area," December 22, 1993.

19 Declaration of Robert Levinson, Davis International v. New Start Group (U.S. Dist. Ct. D. Del.), filed May 31, 2005.

20 Friedman, *Red Mafiya*, p. 132

21 Later that year, *La Presse*, a Montreal newspaper, reported that Slava Fetisov was paying Russian gangsters to ensure his family's safety—an allegation the hockey star

denied; Joe LaPointe, "Russian Crime Groups Harassing Expatriates," *The New York Times*, December 24, 1993, https://www.nytimes.com/1993/12/24/sports/hockey-russian -crime-groups-harassing-expatriates.html.

22 Friedman, *Red Mafiya*, p. 132.

23 William Sokolic, "Casino Is a Soviet Film Set," *The Philadelphia Inquirer*, October 26, 1996.

24 Friedman, *Red Mafiya*, p. 132.

25 Douglas Birch, "Fearful Russian Lawmaker Flees to US," Associated Press, February 6, 2011.

26 Megan K. Stack, "Putin foe speaks out from rural self-exile," *Los Angeles Times*, March 21, 2010, http://articles.latimes.com/2010/mar/21/world/la-fg-russia-putin21 -2010mar21.

CHAPTER 3: A MILLIONAIRE WITHOUT A DOLLAR

1 Rachel L. Swarnes, "Unlikely Meeting of Minds: Lebed Meets The Donald," *The New York Times*, January 23, 1997, http://www.nytimes.com/1997/01/23/world/unlikely-meeting-of -minds-lebed-meets-the-donald.html.

2 Mark Singer, "Trump Solo," *The New Yorker*, May 19, 1997, https://www.newyorker.com /magazine/1997/05/19/trump-solo.

3 Singer, "Trump Solo."

4 Timothy O'Brien. *TrumpNation: The Art of Being the Donald* (New York: Warner Books, 2005), p. 146.

5 Mark Bowden, "The Art of the Donald," *Playboy*, May 1, 1997, http://www.playboy.com /articles/the-art-of-the-donald.

6 Sean Langille, "Never Forget Donald Trump's Cameo in 'Home Alone 2,'" *Washington Examiner*, December 23, 2016, https://www.washingtonexaminer.com/never-forget -donald-trumps-cameo-in-home-alone-2/article/2610290.

7 Jeff Grocot, "Trump Tours Sites for Luxury Towers," *The Moscow Times*, November 6, 1996.

8 The building was financed with a $20.4 million loan from the Kremlin-connected VTB Bank.

9 Bowden, "Art of the Donald."

10 Grocott, "Trump Tours."

11 Anne Farris, "Visa Revoked, Ukrainian Still Attended Event," *The Washington Post*, December 19, 1997, https://www.washingtonpost.com/archive/politics/1997/12/19/visa -revoked-ukrainian-still-attended-event/61a731ab-3b4e-4220-8791-a3a1ae823be0/.

12 Daniel Kadlec, "Populist Hero or Bottom Feeder?" *Time*, March 31, 1997, http://content .time.com/time/magazine/article/0,9171,986113,00.html.

13 "Smoke and Fire," *Newsweek*, March 24, 1996, http://www.newsweek.com/smoke-and -fire-175840.

14 Brooke International Ltd., headquartered in London, traded commodities from the former Soviet Union. Brooke Irkutsk Inc. was involved in a joint venture that milled logs in Siberia. Mil-Brooke Ltd., registered in Cyprus, provided parts and services worldwide for Russian Mil helicopters.

15 Geoff Winestock, "Ducat Factory Fracas Cools Off, Somewhat," *The Moscow Times*, March 10, 1993, http://old.themoscowtimes.com/sitemap/free/1993/3/article/ducat-factory -fracas-cools-off-somewhat/219157.html.

16 "Up in Smoke? Venture Partners Fume," *The Moscow Times*, February 12, 1993, http://old
   .themoscowtimes.com/sitemap/free/1993/2/article/up-in-smoke-venture-partners
   -fume/219392.html; Rob Williams, "No butts about it, capitalism falters," *News and Observer*,
   March 7, 1993; Beth Knobel, "How a Dream Deal Turned into a Russian Nightmare: U.S.
   Cigarette Company's Joint Venture Got Bogged Down in Disputes," *Los Angeles Times*, April
   11, 1993, http://articles.latimes.com/1993-04-11/business/fi-21547_1_joint-venture/2.

17 Buried in an annex to Brooke Group's 1995 annual report was an unusual agreement.
   LeBow's company agreed to purchase 84,540 shares of the Russian joint venture (or
   12 percent of the company) in which Vladimir Tyumentsev—the manager of the factory
   that had given Brooke Group so much trouble—"had an interest." The price was $15 a
   share, or nearly $1.27 million in total. In addition, millions more would be paid to Bel-
   grave Ltd., a Gibraltar company owned by a Russian émigré art dealer named Eduard
   Nakhamkin, as an "inducement" for Tyumentsev to turn over the shares. Belgrave,
   with an address in Mallorca, Spain, was to receive a fee of more than $5.2 million (plus
   another $1 million or more in interest payments). All told, the firing of Tyumentsev cost
   LeBow's shareholders more than $10 million. The agreement says that Belgrave Ltd. and
   LeBow's company were involved in "some of the same investments" in Russia. Belgrave
   "has accumulated experience in Russia and elsewhere," which LeBow's company thought
   would be of value. The agreement has bound all parties to never speak to the press.

18 Embassy Moscow, "The Luzhkov Dilemma," 10MOSCOW317_a, February 12, 2010,
   accessible at WikiLeaks, https://wikileaks.org/plusd/cables/10MOSCOW317_a.html.

19 Michael Schwirtz, "$30,000 Watch Vanishes Up Church Leader's Sleeve," *The New
   York Times*, April 5, 2012, http://www.nytimes.com/2012/04/06/world/europe/in-russia
   -a-watch-vanishes-up-orthodox-leaders-sleeve.html.

20 Jeff Grocott, "Trump Lays Bet on New Moscow Skyline," *The Moscow Times*, November
   12, 1996, http://old.themoscowtimes.com/news/article/tmt/316249.html.

21 "Trump Eyes Moskva," *Moscow News*, February 1, 1997.

22 Carey Scott, "Trump Tower for Red Square?" *The Times* (London), December 22, 1996.

23 Andrew Kramer, "Detectives Fight Odds in Contract Hit Cases," *The Moscow Times*,
   November 27, 1996, http://old.themoscowtimes.com/sitemap/free/1996/11/article/detectives
   -fight-odds-in-contract-hit-cases/315522.html/.

24 Trump, however, wasn't the only investor to show interest. Two oligarchs would later
   wage a battle for control over the Moskva, and one would flee to the United States, where
   he claimed that his stake in the hotel made him a target for assassination. The hotel would
   end up under the ownership of the Canadian Four Seasons luxury chain.

25 Alessandra Stanley, "Moscow's Seedy Monster Hotel Is Told to Clean Up Its Act," *The
   New York Times*, June 22, 1994, https://www.nytimes.com/1994/06/22/world/moscow-s
   -seedy-monster-hotel-is-told-to-clean-up-its-act.html.

26 Klebnikov, *Godfather of the Kremlin*, p. 15.

27 "New Valley Purchases Russian Real Estate Development Company," *Business Wire*,
   January 31, 1997.

28 Jeffrey Toobin, "Trump's Miss Universe Gambit," *The New Yorker*, February 26, 2018,
   https://www.newyorker.com/magazine/2018/02/26/trumps-miss-universe-gambit.

29 "Donald Trump to modernise two of the biggest Moscow hotels," *Agence France-Presse*,
   January 29, 1997; "Report: Moscow near deal with Trump on Moskva Hotel," Associated
   Press, January 23, 1997.

30 "Dark Deeds on Moscow Nights," *The Washington Times*, March 2, 2006, https://www
.washingtontimes.com/news/2006/mar/2/20060302-092217-3041r/.

31 Deposition of Donald J. Trump, December 19, 2007, Donald J. Trump v. Timothy L.
O'Brien, Doc. No. A-6141-08T3, Sup. Ct. of NJ (App. Div. 2007).

32 Singer, "Trump Solo."

33 Helen Kohen, "Columbus & Controversy . . . Again," *The Miami Herald*, December 23, 1992.

34 Don Terry, "Columbus Divides Ohio's Capital City," *The New York Times*, December 26,
1993, https://www.nytimes.com/1993/12/26/us/columbus-divides-ohio-s-capital-city.html.

35 Grace Marston, "Andy Warhol Talks about Donald Trump throughout the Mid-1980s,"
Warhol, January 21, 2016, https://www.warhol.org/andy-warhol-talks-about-donald
-trump-throughout-the-mid-1980s/.

36 Tsereteli owned 9.5 percent of a U.S. company called Optical Basics Inc., with an address
in Beverly Hills, California. Optical Basics owned two lucrative casinos in Moscow,
Kristall and Golden Palace. The casino came under the control of Zakhary Kalashov,
whom the U.S. government has since sanctioned as a key member of a Mafiya group
known as the "Brothers' Circle." Tsereteli says the investment was made through his
lawyer, who disappeared and was never found. The casinos were shut down in what Russian state press described as an action against the Georgian Mafiya in 2006, during a time
of rising tensions between Georgia and Russia.

37 Alexander Sirotin, "Breakfast with Trump," *Seagull*, September 1, 2008, https://www
.chayka.org/node/2010.

38 U.S. Geological Society, Bureau of Mines, "Minerals yearbook: Mineral industries of
Europe and central Eurasia," 1993.

39 S. C. Gwynne and Larry Gurwin, "The Russia Connection," *Time*, July 8, 1996.

40 "Rich linked to money laundering," *The Washington Times*, June 21, 2002, https://www
.washingtontimes.com/news/2002/jun/21/20020621-032133-6702r/.

41 Fritz Ermath, the CIA's former national intelligence officer for the USSR, made this claim
at a congressional hearing in 1999. At a 1996 Senate hearing, then CIA director John
Deutsch said Nordex was associated with Russian criminal activity moving out of Russia
and establishing itself in Vienna. A year later, FBI Director Louis J. Freeh was asked at a
House hearing whether there was any evidence that former KGB officials were involved
in the Russian organized-crime syndicates. "Yes, sir, there is; both in investigations in
Russia, as well as in other parts of Europe, in companies such as Nordex, which is a
Vienna-based company, a multinational company. There are strong indications of former
KGB officers working directly with some of these organized crime groups, and that poses
an additional level of threat and sophistication," Freeh replied.

42 "R3.5 Billion and $100,000 Worth of Strategic Materials Went through Nordex. But This
Was Not the Only Scandal at the Center of which Loutchanksy's Company Found Itself,"
Kommersant, August 20, 1996.

43 "Millionaire wants to erect huge Columbus statue in Miami Beach," United Press International, March 26, 1992, https://www.upi.com/Archives/1992/03/26/Millionaire-wants
-to-erect-huge-Columbus-statue-in-Miami-Beach/8718701586000/.

44 Gregg Fields, "The New Barbarian," *The Miami Herald*, November 13, 1995.

45 "From Russia with 'ugh': Columbus statue: Work is too big, price is too high and many
think it is abominable," *The Baltimore Sun*, May 12, 1997, http://articles.baltimoresun
.com/1997-05-12/news/1997132065_1_columbus-statue-statue-of-liberty-tsereteli.

46 Michael Gordon, "Russia's New Court Sculptor: Only the Colossal," *The New York Times*, January 25, 1997, http://www.nytimes.com/1997/01/25/world/russia-s-new-court -sculptor-only-the-colossal.html.

CHAPTER 4: POST-SOVIET PAYOUTS

1 Candice Hughes, "Yeltsin: Russia a 'Superpower of Crime,'" Associated Press, June 7, 1994.

2 Phil Williams. *Russian Organized Crime: The New Threat?* (London: Frank Cass, 1997), p. 136.

3 Luke Harding, "The Richer They Come . . ." *The Guardian*, July 2, 2007, https://www.the guardian.com/world/2007/jul/02/russia.lukeharding1.

4 Jay McKenzie, "Trump, Putin and the mob. Research collection. Part 4: Paul Manafort was the Kremlin's point man on the Trump campaign," *Medium*, September 14, 2017, https://medium.com/@JamesFourM/trump-putin-and-the-mob-part-4-paul-manafort -was-the-kremlins-point-man-on-the-trump-campaign-9943c44c34a8.

5 Stephen Handelman. *Comrade Criminal* (New Haven, CT: Yale University Press, 1997), p. 23.

6 Alan A. Block, *All Is Clouded by Desire: Global Banking, Money Laundering and International Organized Crime* (Santa Barbara, CA: Praeger, 2004), p. 155.

7 Cal Millar and Jack Lakey, "Corruption Charges Swirling in Moscow," *The Toronto Star*, August 23, 1993.

8 Michael Posner, "The Invisible Man," *The Globe and Mail*, May 27, 2005, https://www .theglobeandmail.com/report-on-business/rob-magazine/the-invisible-man/article1 8228210/; Charles Clover, "Questions over Kuchma's Advisor Cast Shadows," *Financial Times*, October 29, 1999.

9 Matthew Bodner, "Russia's 8 Most Memorable Davos Moments," *The Moscow Times*, January 23, 2014, https://themoscowtimes.com/articles/russias-8-most-memorable-davos -moments-31309.

10 Indictment, United States v. Semion Mogilevich, Igor Fisherman, Jacob Bogatin, and Anatoly Tsoura (US Dist. Ct. E. Penn., n.d.), http://online.wsj.com/public/resources /documents/ruslobby-mogilevich-04172007.pdf.

11 Larry McCrary, "Stock Sensation's Trappings of Success Shape Up as a Sham, YBM Magnex, a Bucks Magnet Firm, Put Up Numbers that Were too Good to be True," *The Philadelphia Inquirer*, January 15, 1999.

12 Paul Lashmar and Andrew Mullins, "How Wall Street Was Fleeced by the Most Evil Gangster in the World," *The Independent*, August 20, 1999, https://www.independent.co.uk /news/how-wall-st-was-fleeced-by-the-most-evil-gangster-in-the-world-1113929.html.

13 Karen Dawisha, *Putin's Kleptocracy: Who Owns Russia?* (New York: Simon & Schuster, 2015), loc. 3679 of 11966, Kindle.

14 Alexander Litvinenko, "Letter Regarding Mitrokhin Dossier," Litvinenko Inquiry, web-archive.nationalarchives.gov.uk/20160613090305. Archived on June 13, 2016, https://www .litvinenkoinquiry.org.

15 Dawisha, *Putin's Kleptocracy*, loc. 6385 of 11966, Kindle.

16 United Kingdom National Archives, Litvinenko Inquiry, "Letter regarding Mitrokhin Dossier, signed by Alexander Litvinenko," INQ018925, Archived on June 13, 2016.

CHAPTER 5: LITTLE MOSCOW

1 Bill Carter, "Survival of the Pushiest," *The New York Times Magazine*, January 28, 2001, https://www.nytimes.com/2001/01/28/magazine/survival-of-the-pushiest.html.

2 Michael Kranish, "A fierce will to win pushed Donald Trump to the top," *The Washington Post*, January 19, 2017, https://www.washingtonpost.com/politics/a-fierce-will-to-win-pushed -donald-trump-to-the-top/2017/01/17/6b36c2ce-c628-11e6-8bee-54e800ef2a63_story.html.

3 Donald Trump, "What I Saw at the Revolution," *The New York Times*, February 19, 2000, http://www.nytimes.com/2000/02/19/opinion/what-i-saw-at-the-revolution.html.

4 Simon Ostrovsky, "Trump Brings N.Y. to Moscow," *The Moscow Times*, September 26, 2002, http://old.themoscowtimes.com/sitemap/free/2002/9/article/trump-brings-ny -to-moscow/243342.html/.

5 "Russians Will Settle in the House of Donald Trump," *Vedomosti*, September 25, 2002.

6 Ibid.

7 "The Trump Factor," *New York*, December 2, 1991.

8 Caleb Melby and Keri Geiger, "Behind Trump's Russia Romance, There's a Tower Full of Oligarchs," *Bloomberg Businessweek*, March 16, 2017, https://www.bloomberg.com/news /articles/2017-03-16/behind-trump-s-russia-romance-there-s-a-tower-full-of-oligarchs.

9 Witness Statement of Michael Cherney, Cherney v. Deripaska (U.K. H. Ct. of Just., Queen's Bench Division).

10 Royce Knut, "FBI Tracked Alleged Mob Russian Ties of Giuliani Campaign Supporter," Center for Public Integrity, December 14, 1999, available at http://www.freerepublic .com/focus/f-news/1785427/posts.

11 Melby and Geiger, "Behind Trump's Russia Romance."

12 Michael Falcone, "Donald Trump's Political 'Pit Bull': Meet Michael Cohen," ABC News, April 6, 2011, http://abcnews.go.com/Politics/donald-trumps-political-pit-bull -meet-michael-cohen/story?id=13386747.

13 Robert Friedman, "The Organizatsiya," *The New York Times*, November 7, 1994.

14 Jake Pearson, "Notorious Russian Mobster Says He Just Wants to Go Home," Associated Press, January 27, 2018, http://www.businessinsider.com/ap-notorious-russian-mobster -says-he-just-wants-to-go-home-2018-1.

15 Interview with Glenn Simpson before the House Permanent Select Committee on Intelligence, U.S. House of Representatives, November 14, 2017.

16 *Russian Organized Crime in the United States: Hearing before the Permanent Subcommittee on Investigations of the Committee on Governmental Affairs*, U.S. Senate, 104th Congress, 2nd sess. (May 15, 1996).

17 Deposition of Michael Cohen, September 17, 2007, Fomina v. Netscheret, (11th Cir. Ct. Miami Dade County, 2007).

18 Julia March, "Billionaire 'Catwoman' Evades Eviction," *New York Post*, February 2, 2013.

19 Lauren Price, "Upping the Ante," *New York Post*, February 22, 2007, https://nypost .com/2007/02/22/upping-the-ante/.

20 Maggie Haberman, "Michael D. Cohen, Trump's Longtime Lawyer, Says He Paid Stormy Daniels Out of His Own Pocket," *The New York Times*, February 13, 2018, https://www .nytimes.com/2018/02/13/us/politics/stormy-daniels-michael-cohen-trump.html.

21 Melby and Geiger, "Behind Trump's Russia Romance."

22 Ken Silverstein, "Miami: Where Luxury Real Estate Meets Dirty Money," *The Nation*, October 2, 2013, https://www.thenation.com/article/miami-where-luxury-real-estate-meets -dirty-money/.

23 Nathan Layne et. al, "Russian Elite Invested Nearly $100 Million in Trump Buildings," Reuters, March 17, 2017, available at https://www.huffingtonpost.com/entry/report-russian

-elite-invested-nearly-100-million-in-trump-buildings-records-show_us_58c
c8d96e4b0be71dcf50fc6.

24 Ilya Shumanov, Lily Dobrovolakya, and Julia Pavlovskaya, "Miami's Ours: Why bandits and businessmen are moving into Trump's Towers," *Forbes Russia*, November 7, 2016, http://www.forbes.ru/mneniya/332245-mayami-nash-pochemu-rossiyskie-biznesmeny -i-bandity-selyatsya-v-bashnyah-trampa.

25 Nicholas Nehamas, "Before Trump attacked foreigners, he helped them sell condos," *The Miami Herald*, October 14, 2016, http://www.miamiherald.com/news/politics -government/article108150442.html.

26 Interview with Glenn Simpson, Executive Session, House Permanent Select Committee on Intelligence, U.S. House of Representatives, November 14, 2017.

27 Jason Horowitz, "In Taormina, a Playground for the Jet Set, Trump's Worlds Will Col- lide," *The New York Times*, May 25, 2017, https://www.nytimes.com/2017/05/25/world /europe/taormina-sicily-group-of-7-summit-donald-trump.html.

28 Anthony Cormier and Chris McDaniel, "How Trump's Lawyer Placed a Big Casino Bet That Left Dozens Empty-Handed," *BuzzFeed*, March 15, 2017, https://www.buzzfeed .com/anthonycormier/trumps-lawyer-launched-an-offshore-casino-and-left-a-wake.

29 Cindy Boren, "Ex-FIFA official had $6,000-a-month Trump Tower apartment for unruly cats," *The Washington Post*, May 27, 2015, https://www.washingtonpost.com/news/early-lead /wp/2015/05/27/ex-fifa-official-had-6000-a-month-trump-tower-apartment-for-unruly-cats/.

CHAPTER 6: BUILDING TRUMP TOWERS AND HUNTING BIN LADEN

1 Richard Branson, "Meeting Donald Trump," Virgin.com, October 21, 2016, https://www .virgin.com/richard-branson/meeting-donald-trump.

2 Bayrock Group LLC was a tax partnership. Profits passed through to the partners and Bayrock itself did not pay taxes. Initially, Arif was the company's sole managing member and he owned 99 of Bayrock's 100 shares, with the remaining share held by Rif International Group Inc., which Arif controlled. (Operating Agreement, Bayrock Group LLC, dated as of June 1, 2002.)

3 The businessman later sued Sater, claiming that the broker had engaged in margin trad- ing and bought and sold securities without his knowledge. A judge dismissed the case. Paul J. Scotch v. Moseley (Dist. Ct. Mid. Dist. Penn., July 7, 1988).

4 Sal Lauria and David S. Barry, *The Scorpion and the Frog: High Times and High Crimes* (Beverly Hills, CA: New Millenium, 2008), p. 255.

5 Complaint and Affidavit in Support of Arrest Warrants, U.S. v Gennady Klotsman and Felix Sater (E. Dist. Ct. NY).

6 U.S. Attorney, Eastern District of New York, "19 Defendants Indicted in Stock Fraud Scheme that Was Promoted by Organized Crime," March 2, 2000.

7 Felix Sater, Statement, March 3, 2018; Andrew Rice, "Felix Sater: Donald Trump's Original Russia Connection," *New York*, August 3, 2017, http://nymag.com/daily /intelligencer/2017/08/felix-sater-donald-trump-russia-investigation.html.

8 Felix Sater, Statement.

9 Ibid.

10 Eugene Babushkin, "Felix Sater: I advised Trump and Hunted Bin Laden" *Snob*, Novem- ber 15, 2016, https://snob.ru/selected/entry/116532.

11 James Bamford, *The Shadow Factory: The NSA from 9/11 to Eavesdropping on America* (New York: Anchor, 2009), loc. 125 of 6849, Kindle.

12 Nick Fielding and Dipesh Gadhery, "Al-Qaeda's Satellite Phone Records Revealed," *The Sunday Times* (London), March 24, 2002, https://911timeline.s3.amazonaws.com/2002/sundaytimes032402.html.

13 Lauria and Barry, *The Scorpion and the Frog*, pp. 254–55.

14 Timothy O'Brien, "Trump, Russia, and a Shadowy Business Partnership," *Bloomberg*, June 21, 2017, https://www.bloomberg.com/view/articles/2017-06-21/trump-russia-and-those-shadowy-sater-deals-at-bayrock.

15 Sater's account of his work with Trump comes from: Deposition of Felix Sater, Donald Trump v. Timothy L. O'Brien (Sup. Ct. of NJ, April 1, 2008).

16 Gary Silverman, "Trump's Russian Riddle," *Financial Times*, August 14, 2016, https://www.ft.com/content/549ddfaa-5fa5-11e6-b38c-7b39cbb1138a.

17 Deposition of Felix Sater, Trump v. O'Brien.

18 Bayrock Group LLC employment agreement with Felix Sater, November 10, 2005 (effective January 1, 2003).

19 Michael Rothfeld, Bradley Hope, and Alexandra Berzon, "Publicity Over Dispute by Former Trump Partners Could Tarnish President, One Warns," *The Wall Street Journal*, April 20, 2017, https://www.wsj.com/articles/publicity-over-dispute-by-former-trump-partners-could-tarnish-president-one-warns-1492680604.

20 Joseph Tanfani and David Cloud, "Trump business associate led double life as FBI informant—and more, he says," *Los Angeles Times*, March 2, 2017, http://www.latimes.com/politics/la-na-pol-sater-trump-20170223-story.html.

21 Deposition of Felix Sater, Trump v. O'Brien.

22 Moscow was not the only place in the former Soviet Union where Sater was trying to build a Trump Tower. He arrived in Kiev, Ukraine, in the summer of 2005 bearing another letter from Trump. This letter declared, much as the Moscow letter had, that Ukraine also was an ideal location for a signature development of Donald J. Trump. Sater met with Ukraine's minister of transportation, Evhen Chervonenko, who announced on September 12, 2005, that Trump would be investing $500 million to build a hotel and yacht club in the Black Sea port of Yalta. Just like in Moscow, nothing came of this deal.

23 Deposition of Donald Trump, December 17, 2007, Trump v. O'Brien.

24 Ibid.

25 Timothy O'Brien, *TrumpNation: The Art of Being the Donald* (New York: Warner Books, 2005), loc. 79 of 5880, Kindle.

26 Deposition of Donald Trump, Trump v. O'Brien.

27 Deposition of Felix Sater, Trump v. O'Brien.

28 Maria Abakumova and Natalia Kuznetsova, "No Man's Land: Which of the Investors Will Get the Territory of Badaevsky Brewery," *Forbes Russia*, March 11, 2014.

29 Deposition of Felix Sater, Trump v. O'Brien.

30 Ibid.

31 Felix Sater to Michael Cohen, email, November 3, 2015. Ivanka Trump said she did not recall whether she had sat in Putin's chair during her brief tour of Red Square and the Kremlin, although she said it was possible she had.

32 "Sergei Millian: Donald Trump Will Improve Relations with Russia," RIA-Novosti, April 13, 2016.

33 Mark Maremont, "Key Claims in Trump Dossier Said to Come from Head of Russian-American Business Group," *The Wall Street Journal*, January 24, 2017, https://www.wsj

.com/articles/key-claims-in-trump-dossier-came-from-head-of-russian-american-business-group-source-1485253804.

34 Tom Hamburger, "In 'Little Moscow,' Russians helped Donald Trump's brand survive the recession," *The Washington Post*, November 4, 2016, https://www.washingtonpost.com/politics/in-little-moscow-russians-helped-donald-trumps-brand-survive-the-recession/2016/11/04/f9dbd38e-97cf-11e6-bb29-bf2701dbe0a3_story.html.

35 Ned Parker, "Ivanka and the Fugitive from Panama," Reuters, November 7, 2017, https://www.reuters.com/investigates/special-report/usa-trump-panama/.

36 Alexander Sirotin, "Breakfast with Trump," *Seagull*, September 1, 2008, https://www.chayka.org/node/2010.

37 Complaint, Kriss v Bayrock (U.S. Dist. Ct. S. NY).

38 Embassy Vienna, "USG Concerns Over Austrian Banking Operations," 06VIENNA-515_a, February 17, 2008, accessible at WikiLeaks, https://wikileaks.org/plusd/cables/06VIEN NA515_a.html.

39 Rob Barry, "Russian State-Run Bank Financed Deal Involving Trump Hotel Partner," *The Wall Street Journal*, May 17, 2017, https://www.wsj.com/articles/russian-state-run-bank-financed-deal-involving-trump-hotel-partner-1495031708.

40 Charles V. Bagli, "Real Estate Executive with Hand in Trump Projects Rose from Tangled Past," *The New York Times*, December 17, 2007, http://www.nytimes.com/2007/12/17/nyregion/17trump.html.

41 Sentencing, October 23, 2009, U.S. v. Sater (U.S. Dist. Ct. E. NY, 2009).

42 Bagli, "Real Estate Executive with Hand in Trump Projects Rose from Tangled Past."

43 Deposition of Donald J. Trump, Trump v. O'Brien.

44 Deposition of Donald J. Trump, November 5, 2013, Abercrombie v. SB Hotel Associates (17th Jud. Ct. FL, 2013).

45 Jeff Horowitz, "Trump hired $40M stock fraud felon with links to Mafia as senior advisor," Associated Press, December 4, 2015, accessible at https://www.houstonchronicle.com/news/nation-world/nation/article/Trump-hired-40M-stock-fraud-felon-with-links-to-6676615.php.

46 "Felix Sater: I advised Trump and Hunted Bin Laden," *Snob*, November 15, 2016.

47 Trump Acquisition LLC to IC Investment, Letter of Intent, October 13, 2015; Michael Cohen, Statement, August 28, 2017.

48 Matt Apuzzo and Maggie Haberman, "Trump Associate Boasted That Moscow Business Deal 'Will Get Donald Elected,'" *The New York Times*, August 28, 2017, https://www.nytimes.com/2017/08/28/us/politics/trump-tower-putin-felix-sater.html.

49 Anthony Cormier and Jason Leopold, "How a Player in the Trump-Russia Scandal Led a Double Life As an American Spy," *BuzzFeed*, March 12, 2018, https://www.buzzfeed.com/anthonycormier/felix-sater-trump-russia-undercover-us-spy.

50 Megan Twohey and Scott Shane, "A Back-Channel Plan for Ukraine and Russia, Courtesy of Trump Associates," *The New York Times*, February 19, 2017, https://www.nytimes.com/2017/02/19/us/politics/donald-trump-ukraine-russia.html.

51 Republic of Turkey, Antalya City, Supreme Republican Public Prosecutor's Office, Bill of Indictment.

52 Ibid.

53 Richard Orange and Rowena Mason, "ENRC Billionaire Was on 'Sex Yacht' Seized by Turkey," *Telegraph*, October 13, 2010.

54 Deposition of Donald J. Trump, November 16, 2011, Trilogy Partners v. SBC Associates (U.S. Dist. Ct. S. FL, 2011).

CHAPTER 7: THE CONDO CASINO

1 Joyce Libal and Rae Simmons, *Careers with Character: Professional Athlete & Sports Official* (Hashemite Kingdom of Jordan: Mason Crest, 2014), Chapter 4.

2 Indictment, August 21, 2002, U.S. v. Alimzhan Tokhtakhunov (U.S. Dist. Ct. S. NY, 2002).

3 Andrew Kramer and James Glanz, "In Russia, Living the High Life; in America, a Wanted Man," *The New York Times*, June 1, 2013, https://www.nytimes.com/2013/06/02/world/europe/tokhtakhounov-says-criminal-charges-are-just-a-misunderstanding.html.

4 Peter Baker, "A Player on Russia's Cutting Edge," *The Washington Post*, August 9, 2002, https://www.washingtonpost.com/archive/politics/2002/08/09/a-player-on-russias-cutting-edge/61949f0f-0728-4ea1-93cd-dec2df863453/.

5 "Interview: Alleged Russian Crime Boss Says Russian Mafia Is 'A Necessary Myth,'" Radio Free Europe / Radio Liberty, June 22, 2011, https://www.rferl.org/a/interview_tokhtakhtunov_russian_mafia/24243385.html.

6 Amy Shipley, "Russian Implicated in Olympic Scandal," *The Washington Post*, August 1, 2002, https://www.washingtonpost.com/archive/politics/2002/08/01/russian-implicated-in-olympic-scandal/845c6aa1-9168-4447-9a8b-dd827c326a55/.

7 Erika Niedowski, "All that glitters for Russia's big spenders," *The Baltimore Sun*, October 2, 2005, http://articles.baltimoresun.com/2005-10-02/news/0510020042_1_millionaire-moscow-russians.

8 Ken Kurson, "Pocket Aces: Tycoons, Celebrities, Oligarchs and Algorithms," *The Observer* (London), April 17, 2013, http://observer.com/2013/04/pocket-aces-tycoons-celebrities-oligarchs-and-algorithms/#ixzz2yVaqdUZU; Ken Kurson, "EXCLUSIVE: A Player Speaks; Molly Bloom Takes On Spider-Man Actor in New Book," *The Observer* (London), May 6, 2014, http://observer.com/2014/05/exclusive-a-player-speaks-molly-bloom-takes-on-spider-man-actor-in-new-book/.

9 William Bastone, "Trump Tower House Arrest for Racketeer," *The Smoking Gun*, March 22, 2017, http://www.thesmokinggun.com/documents/crime/house-arrest-in-trump-tower-378095.

10 Dashiell Bennet, "How Illegal Poker and the Russian Mob Might Have Sunk an Obama Appointee," *The Atlantic Monthly*, April 26, 2013, https://www.theatlantic.com/politics/archive/2013/04/how-illegal-poker-and-russian-mob-might-have-sunk-obama-appointee/315861/.

11 Marc Santora and William K. Rashbaum, "Agents Descend on a New York Gallery, Charging its Owner," *The New York Times*, April 16, 2013, http://www.nytimes.com/2013/04/17/nyregion/agents-raid-upper-east-side-gallery-in-gambling-probe.html.

12 Kaja Whitehouse and Jennifer Gould Kell, "President's pick for French ambassador folded over ties to poker ring: sources," *New York Post*, April 26, 2013, https://nypost.com/2013/04/26/presidents-pick-for-french-ambassador-folded-over-ties-to-poker-ring-sources/.

CHAPTER 8: MISTER UNIVERSE

1 Donald Trump (@realDonaldTrump), "The Miss Universe Pageant will be broad-

cast live from MOSCOW, RUSSIA on November 9th. A big deal that will bring our countries together!," Twitter, June 18, 2013, https://twitter.com/realdonaldtrump /status/347187059653476352.

2 Donald Trump (@realDonaldTrump), "Do you think Putin will be going to The Miss Universe Pageant in November in Moscow—if so, will he become my new best friend?," Twitter, June 18, 2013, https://twitter.com/realdonaldtrump/status/347191326112112640.

3 Shane Harris, "In a personal letter, Trump invited Putin to the 2013 Miss Universe pageant," *The Washington Post*, March 9, 2018, https://www.washingtonpost.com/world /national-security/in-a-personal-letter-trump-invited-putin-to-the-2013-miss-universe -pageant/2018/03/09/a3404358-23d2-11e8-a589-763893265565_story.html.

4 Noah Kirsch, "The Full Exclusive Interview: Emin Agalarov, Russian Scion at Center of Trump Controversy," *Forbes*, July 12, 2017, https://www.forbes.com/sites/noahkirsch/2017/07/12 /the-full-exclusive-interview-emin-agalarov-russian-donald-trump-jr-controversy/.

5 "Emin Agalarov presents to the public Olivia," Turan Information Agency, May 31, 2013.

6 Max Seddon, "The Azeri pop singer who approached Trump for Russia," *Financial Times*, July 11, 2017, https://www.ft.com/content/25c0d7d0-6640-11e7-8526-7b38dcaef614.

7 Evengia Pismennaya, Stepan Kravchenko, and Stephanie Baker, "The Day Trump Came to Moscow: Oligarchs, Miss Universe and Nobu," *Bloomberg*, December 21, 2016, https: //www.bloomberg.com/news/articles/2016-12-21/the-day-trump-came-to-moscow -oligarchs-miss-universe-and-nobu.

8 "Donald Trump plans to build office centre in Russia similar to NY Trump Tower," ITAR-TASS, November 9, 2013.

9 Konrad Putzier, "Hotel trio aims to bring Manhattan to Moscow," *Real Estate Weekly*, November 13, 2013, http://rew-online.com/2013/11/12/hotel-trio-aims-to-bring-manhattan -to-moscow/.

10 "Trump 2014 on Putin, Ukraine, Crimea," C-SPAN video, 1:46. Posted August 1, 2016, https://www.c-span.org/video/?c4616460/trump-2014-putin-ukraine-crime.

11 Putzier, "Hotel trio."

12 Ken Dilanian and Jonathan Allen, "Trump Bodyguard Keith Schiller Testifies Russian Offered Trump Women, Was Turned Down," NBC, November 9, 2017, https://www.nbc news.com/news/us-news/trump-bodyguard-testifies-russian-offered-trump-women -was-turned-down-n819386.

13 "Stormy Daniels' Explosive Full Interview on Donald Trump Affair: 'I Can Describe His Junk Perfectly,'" *In Touch Weekly*, February 14, 2018, http://www.intouchweekly.com /posts/stormy-daniels-full-interview-151788.

14 "US Presidential Election: Republican Candidate Donald Trump' s Activities in Russia and Compromising Relationship with the Kremlin," Company Intelligence Report 2016/080, Steele Dossier, updated June 20, 2016.

15 "Russia/US Presidential Election: Further Indications of Extensive Conspiracy Between Trump's Campaign Team and the Kremlin," Company Intelligence Report 2016/095, Steele Dossier, undated.

16 Memorandum Opinion, May 13, 2003, Comtek v. Commissioner (U.S. Tax Ct., 2003).

17 Donald Trump (@realDonaldTrump), "I just got back from Russia—learned lots & lots. Moscow is a very interesting and amazing place! U.S. MUST BE VERY SMART AND VERY STRATEGIC.," Twitter, November 10, 2013. https://twitter.com/realdonaldtrump /status/399729261684490240?lang=en.

18 Donald Trump (@realDonaldTrump), "I had a great weekend with you and your family. You have done a FANTASTIC job. TRUMP TOWER-MOSCOW is next. EMIN was WOW!," Twitter, November 11, 2013. https://twitter.com/realdonaldtrump/status/3999 39505924628480?lang=en.

19 Emin Agalarov, (@eminofficial), "Mr. Trump thank you for brining #missuniverse to us we had an awesome time TRUMP tower moscow—let's make it happen!,". Twitter, November 12, 2013, https://twitter.com/eminofficial/status/400210760510754816. Retweeted by @AgalarovAras.

20 "Member of the presidential race in the US, Trump does not abandon the draft tower in Russia—Crocus Group," ITAR-TASS, July 3, 2015.

21 Noah Kirsch, "Exclusive: Powerful Russian Partner Boasts of Ongoing Access to Trump Family," Forbes, March 20, 2017, https://www.forbes.com/sites/noahkirsch/2017/03/20 /russian-billionaire-family-trump-ties-ongoing/.

22 Shaun Walker, "The Trumps of Russia? How billionaire Agalarov family ended up in the spotlight," The Guardian, July 15, 2017, https://www.theguardian.com/world/2017 /jul/14/who-are-aras-emin-agalarov-donald-trump-jr-emails.

23 "Russia Corruption Report," GAN Anti-Corruption Business Portal, accessed March 14, 2018, https://www.business-anti-corruption.com/country-profiles/russia.

24 Irina Gruzinova, "Billionaire Aras Agalarov: 'I do not know how to make money on state construction projects,'" Forbes Russia, November 3, 2015, http://www.forbes.ru /milliardery/282185-milliarder-aras-agalarov-ya-ne-umeyu-zarabatyvat-na-gosud arstvennykh-stroikakh.

25 Neil MacFarquhar, "A Russian Developer Helps Out the Kremlin on Occasion. Was He a Conduit to Trump?," The New York Times, July 16, 2017, https://www.nytimes.com /2017/07/16/world/europe/aras-agalarov-trump-kremlin.html.

26 Aras Agalarov, "Personal Opinion," Kommersant, August 12, 2015, https://www.kommer sant.ru/doc/2872472.

27 "Donald Trump Announces a Presidential Bid," The Washington Post, June 16, 2015. https://www.washingtonpost.com/news/post-politics/wp/2015/06/16/full-text-donald -trump- announces-a-presidential-bid/.

28 Irina Reznik and Henry Meyer, "Trump Jr. Hinted at Review of Anti-Russia Law, Moscow Lawyer Says," Bloomberg, November 6, 2017, https://www.bloomberg.com/news /articles/2017-11-06/trump-jr-said-anti-russia-law-may-be-reviewed-moscow-lawyer-says.

29 Michael Wolff, Fire and Fury: Inside the Trump White House (New York: Henry Holt and Co., 2018), p. 254.

30 Katrina Manson, "Russian lobbyist Rinat Akhmetshin on that notorious meeting at Trump Tower," Financial Times, September 1, 2017, https://www.ft.com/content /540354a4-8e4c-11e7-a352-e46f43c5825d.

31 Russian Money Laundering: Hearing before the House Committee on Banking and Financial Services, U.S. House, 106th Congress. 1st sess. (September 21–22, 1999) (Statement by Richard L. Palmer).

32 U.S. General Accounting Office, "Suspicious Banking Activities: Possible Money Laundering by U.S. Corporations Formed for Russian Entities," October 2000.

33 Michael A. Ross to Robert H. Hast, letter, November 28, 2000.

34 U.S. General Accounting Office, "Suspicious Banking Activities."

35 Irakly Kaveladze, "Bank of New York Scandal Turns into Ethnic Witch Hunt," Bridge

News, September 24, 1999, https://www.justsecurity.org/wp-content/uploads/2017/07/Kaveladze-Witch-Hunt-Op-Ed.pdf.

36 Interview with Glenn Simpson before the House Permanent Select Committee on Intelligence, U.S. House of Representatives, November 14, 2017.

37 Dmitri Sibirov, "Agalarov All the 'Crocus'?" *Moscow Post*, August 17, 2016. Also see the website of Russian Alexander Lebedev, billionaire banker and former Russian spy: "Aras Agalarov," lebedev.com, http://www.lebedev.com/persona/?p=agalarov (accessed March 18, 2018).

38 Alexander Zheltov and Andrey Y. Salnikov, "Azerbaijani 'Authority' Killed in Car of Co-Founder of Crocus," *Kommersant*, April 8, 2006, https://www.kommersant.ru/doc/664819.

CHAPTER 9: BLOOD MONEY

1 Stone's account is from Roger Stone, *The Making of the President 2016: How Donald Trump Orchestrated a Revolution* (New York: Skyhorse Publishing, 2017), p. 72.

2 Michael Kranish, "'He's better than this,' says Thomas Barrack, Trump's loyal whisperer," *The Washington Post*, October 11, 2017, https://www.washingtonpost.com/politics/hes-better-than-this-says-thomas-barrack-trumps-loyal-whisperer/2017/10/10/067fc776-a215-11e7-8cfe-d5b912fabc99_story.html.

3 Lewandowski's account of the meeting is from Corey Lewandowski and David Bossie, *Let Trump Be Trump: The Inside Story of His Rise to the Presidency* (New York: Center Street, 2017), pp. 119–23, 145.

4 Art Levine, "Publicists of the Damned," *Spy*, February 1992.

5 Lewandowski and Bossie, *Let Trump Be Trump*, p. 145.

6 Brett Forrest, "Paul Manafort's Overseas Political Work Had a Notable Patron: A Russian Oligarch," *The Wall Street Journal*, August 30, 2017, https://www.wsj.com/articles/paul-manaforts-overseas-political-work-had-a-notable-patron-a-russian-oligarch-1504131910.

7 Landeskriminalamt Baden-Wurtemberg, Ev Jura Az.: 513-04/005, Ordner v Vernehemungen, Hajdarov, Dschalyl. Document in the author's possession.

8 Andreas Ulrich, "Mafia-Prozess rückt Putin-Vertrauten ins Zwielicht," *Der Spiegel*, September 1, 2007, http://www.spiegel.de/wirtschaft/oligarchen-mafia-prozess-rueckt-putin-vertrauten-ins-zwielicht-a-503199.html; First Amended Complaint, August 3, 2001, Base Metal Trading SA v. Russian Aluminum (U.S. Dist. Ct. S. NY).

9 Barry Meier, *Missing Man: The American Spy Who Vanished in Iran* (New York: Farrar, Straus and Giroux, 2016), p. 178.

10 Jeffrey H. Birnbaum and John Solomon, "Aide Helped Controversial Russian Meet McCain," *The Washington Post*, January 25, 2008, http://www.washingtonpost.com/wp-dyn/content/article/2008/01/24/AR2008012403383.html.

11 Embassy Moscow, "United Company Rusal: Making of a National Champion?" 06MOSCOW12713_a, November 30, 2006, accessible at WikiLeaks, https://wikileaks.org/plusd/cables/06MOSCOW12713_a.html.

12 Stratfor, "HUMINT—RUSSIA—my night with Deripaska (part I)," August 15, 2007, accessible at WikiLeaks, https://wikileaks.org/gifiles/docs/54/5467826_humint-russia-my-night-with-deripaska-part-i-.html.

13 Jeff Horowitz and Chad Day, "Before Trump job, Manafort worked to aid Putin," Associated Press, March 22, 2017, https://apnews.com/122ae0b5848345faa88108a03de40c5a.

14 Complaint, May 15, 2017, Deripaska v. The Associated Press (U.S. Dist. Ct. DC).

15 Horowitz and Day, "Before Trump job, Manafort worked to aid Putin."

16 Mark Ames and Ari Berman, "McCain's Kremlin Ties," *The Nation*, October 20, 2008, https://www.thenation.com/article/mccains-kremlin-ties/.

17 Forrest, "Paul Manafort's Overseas Political Work Had a Notable Patron."

18 Ibid.

19 Government's Opposition to the Motion of Defendant Paul Manafort to Modify Conditions of Release, U.S. v. Manafort (U.S. Dist. Ct. DC).

20 Kenneth P. Vogel, "Manfort's Man in Kiev," *Politico*, August 18, 2016, https://www.politico.com/story/2016/08/paul-manafort-ukraine-kiev-russia-konstantin-kilimnik-227181.

21 Embassy Kiev, "Ukraine: Extreme Makeover for the Party of Regions?" 06KIEV473_a, February 3, 2006, accessible at WikiLeaks, https://wikileaks.org/plusd/cables/06KIEV473_a.html.

22 Ashish Kumar Sen, "Paul Manafort's Ukraine Connection," AtlanticCouncil.org, October 30, 2017, http://www.atlanticcouncil.org/blogs/new-atlanticist/paul-manafort-s-ukraine-connection.

23 Franklin Foer, "The Plot Against America," *The Atlantic Monthly*, March 2018, https://www.theatlantic.com/magazine/archive/2018/03/paul-manafort-american-hustler/550925/.

24 Embassy Kiev, "Ukraine: Extreme Makeover for the Party of Regions?"

25 Marc Champion, "In Ukraine, a Friend of Russia Stages Sweeping Political Makeover," *The Wall Street Journal*, May 15, 2007, https://www.wsj.com/articles/SB117919105570402733.

26 Sen, "Paul Manafort's Ukraine Connection."

27 Government's Consolidated Response to Defendant Firtash's and Knopp's Motions to Dismiss Indictment, July 24, 2017, U.S v. Firtash (U.S. Dist. Ct. N. IL).

28 Amended Complaint, December 19, 2011, Yulia Tymoshenko v. Dmitry Firtash et al. (U.S. Dist. Ct. S. NY).

29 In the Matter of Pericles Emerging Market Partners LP, Winding Up Petition, Grand Court of the Cayman Islands, Financial Services Division, December 9, 2014.

30 Ibid.

31 Surf Horizon Limited v. Manafort and Gates (NY Sup. Ct., January 10, 2018).

32 Stephanie Baker, "Manafort's Offer to Russian Oligarch Was Tied to Disputed Deal," *Bloomberg*, September 27, 2017, https://www.bloomberg.com/news/articles/2017-09-27/manafort-s-offer-to-russian-is-said-to-be-tied-to-disputed-deal.

33 Steven Lee Myers, *The New Tsar*, (New York: Vintage, 2015), pp. 361–62.

34 In the Matter of Pericles Emerging Market Partners LP.

35 Simon Shuster, "A Frank Interview with Ukraine's President: 'Politics Is the Ability to Control Your Emotions,'" *Time*, June 14, 2012, http://world.time.com/2012/06/14/a-frank-interview-with-ukraines-president-politics-is-the-ability-to-control-your-emotions/.

36 Foer, "The Plot Against America."

37 Kenneth Vogel and Andrew Kramer, "Skadden, Big New York Law Firm, Faces Questions on Work With Manafort," *The New York Times*, September 21, 2017, https://www.nytimes.com/2017/09/21/us/politics/law-firm-faces-questions-for-ukraine-work-with-manafort.html.

38 Amended Complaint, Tymoshenko v Firtash; Kenneth P. Vogel and Matthew Goldstein, "How Skadden, the Giant Law Firm, Got Entangled in the Mueller Investigation," *The New York Times*, February 24, 2018, https://www.nytimes.com/2018/02/24/us/politics/skadden-law-firm-mueller-investigation.html

39 Indictment, February 23, 2018, U.S. v. Paul J. Manafort (U.S. Dist. Ct. DC., 2018).

40 Alexander Burns and Maggie Haberman, "Mystery Man: Ukraine's U.S. Fixer," *Politico*, March 5, 2014, https://www.politico.com/story/2014/03/paul-manafort-ukraine-104263.

CHAPTER 10: THE DOSSIER

1 Interview with Glenn Simpson before the House Permanent Select Committee on Intelligence, U.S. House of Representatives, November 14, 2017.

2 Opinion of the Lords of Appeal, October 11, 2006, Jameel v. Wall Street Journal Europe (U.K. House of Lords, 2006).

3 Stephen Salisbury, "A Tragedy Underscores an Epidemic of Teen Drinking," *The Philadelphia Inquirer*, April 5, 1982.

4 Larry Sabato and Glenn Simpson, *Dirty Little Secrets: The Persistence of Corruption in American Politics* (New York: Times Books, 1996), p. 186.

5 Sabato and Simpson, *Dirty Little Secrets*, p. 162.

6 Gillum and Boburg, "Journalism for Rent."

7 Ibid.

8 Interview with Glenn Simpson before the House Permanent Select Committee on Intelligence.

9 Littlefield, "A Day (and a Cheeseburger) with President Trump."

10 Jane Mayer, "Christopher Steele, the Man Behind the Trump Dossier," *The New Yorker*, March 12, 2018, https://www.newyorker.com/magazine/2018/03/12/christopher-steele -the-man-behind-the-trump-dossier.

11 Tom Hamburger and Rosalind Helderman, "Hero or Hired Gun? How a British Former Spy Became a Flash Point in the Russia Investigation," *The Washington Post*, February 6, 2018, https://www.washingtonpost.com/politics/hero-or-hired-gun-how-a-british-former -spy-became-a-flash-point-in-the-russia-investigation/2018/02/06/94ea5158-0795-11e8 -8777-2a059f168dd2_story.html.

12 Hamburger and Helderman, "Hero or Hired Gun?"; Matthew J. Gehringer to William W. Taylor III, letter, October 24, 2017, https://www.documentcloud.org/documents /4116755-PerkinsCoie-Fusion-PrivelegeLetter-102417.html.

13 Hamburger and Helderman, "Hero or Hired Gun?"

14 Ibid.

15 Luke Harding. *Collusion: Secret Meetings, Dirty Money, and How Russia Helped Donald Trump Win* (New York: Knopf Doubleday, 2017), loc. 433 of 4503, Kindle.

16 "Russia/US Presidential Election: Further Indications of Extensive Conspiracy Between Trump's Campaign Team and the Kremlin," Company Intelligence Report 2016/095, Steele Dossier, undated.

17 John Sipher, "A Second Look at the Steele Dossier," Just Security, September 6, 2017, https://www.justsecurity.org/44697/steele-dossier-knowing/.

18 Interview with Glenn Simpson before the House Permanent Select Committee on Intelligence

19 "Excerpts From *The Times*'s Interview With Trump," *The New York Times*, July 19, 2017, https://www.nytimes.com/2017/07/19/us/politics/trump-interview-transcript.html

20 "Remarks by President Donald Trump, Vice President Mike Pence, Senate Majority Leader Mitch McConnell, and House Speaker Paul Ryan After Congressional Republican Leadership Retreat," whitehouse.gov, January 6, 2018, https://www.white house.gov/briefings-statements/remarks-president-donald-trump-vice-president -mike-pence-senate-majority-leader-mitch-mcconnell-house-speaker-paul-ryan -congressional-republican-leadership-retreat/.

21 Mayer, "Christopher Steele."

22 Michael Isikoff and David Corn, *Russian Roulette: The Inside Story of Putin's War on America and the Election of Donald Trump* (New York: Hachette, 2018), loc. 2349 of 5007, Kindle.

23 *Interview with Glenn Simpson before the House Permanent Select Committee on Intelligence*, U.S. House, November 14, 2017.

24 Statement of Offense, U.S. v. George Papadopoulous, October 5, 2017 (U.S. Dist. Ct. D. D.C., 2017).

25 Luke Harding and Stephanie Kirchgaessner, "Ex-Trump adviser Carter Page accused academics who twice failed his PhD of bias," *The Guardian*, December 22, 2017, https://www.theguardian.com/world/2017/dec/22/trump-carter-page-phd-thesis-trump.

26 Massimo Calabresi and Alana Abramson, "Carter Page Touted Kremlin Contacts in 2013 Letter," *Time*, February 4, 2018, http://time.com/5132126/carter-page-russia-2013-letter/.

27 Scott Shane, Mark Mazzetti, and Adam Goldman, "Trump Adviser's Visit to Moscow Got the F.B.I.'s Attention," *The New York Times*, April 19, 2017, https://www.nytimes.com/2017/04/19/us/politics/carter-page-russia-trump.html.

28 "Trump's Advisor in Moscow: An Alternative for the US," Katehon, June 7, 2016. http://katehon.com:8080/agenda/trumps-advisor- moscow-alternative-us

29 *The Testimony of Carter Page, The Permanent Select Committee on Intelligence*, U.S. House, November 14, 2017, https://intelligence.house.gov/uploadedfiles/carter_page_hpsci_hearing_transcript_nov_2_2017.pdf.

30 Business Meeting, Permanent Select Committee on Intelligence, U.S. House, February 5, 2018.

31 Donald Trump, (@realDonaldTrump), "This memo totally vindicates 'Trump' in probe. But the Russian Witch Hunt goes on and on.," Twitter, February 3, 2018. https://twitter.com/realdonaldtrump/status/959798743842349056? lang=en.

32 Michael Isikoff, "U.S. intel officials probe ties between Trump adviser and Kremlin," *Yahoo News*, September 23, 2016, https://www.yahoo.com/news/u-s-intel-officials-probe-ties-between-trump-adviser-and-kremlin-175046002.html.

33 Hamburger and Helderman, "Hero or Hired Gun?"

34 David Corn, "A Veteran Spy Has Given the FBI Information Alleging a Russian Operation to Cultivate Donald Trump," *Mother Jones*, October 31, 2016, https://www.motherjones.com/politics/2016/10/veteran-spy-gave-fbi-info-alleging-russian-operation-cultivate-donald-trump/.

35 Eric Lichtblau and Stephen Lee Myers, "Investigating Donald Trump, F.B.I. Sees No Clear Link to Russia," *The New York Times*, October 31, 2016, https://www.motherjones.com/politics/2016/10/veteran-spy-gave-fbi-info-alleging-russian-operation-cultivate-donald-trump/.

36 "Chuck Todd to BuzzFeed editor: You published 'fake news,'" *The Hill*, January 11, 2017, http://thehill.com/homenews/news/313895-chuck-todd-to-buzzfeed-editor-you-published-fake-news.

37 Donald Trump (@realDonaldTrump), "fake news—a total political witch hunt.," Twitter, January 10, 2017. https://twitter.com/realdonaldtrump/status/818990655418617856 ?lang=en

38 "Donald Trump's News Conference: Full Transcript and Video," *The New York Times*, January 11, 2017. https://www.nytimes.com/2017/01/11/us/politics/trump-press-conference-transcript.html.

CHAPTER 11: INFORMATION WARFARE

1 "Remarks by President Trump at NATO Unveiling of the Article 5 and Berlin Wall Memorials—Brussels, Belgium," whitehouse.gov, May 25, 2017, https://www.whitehouse

.gov/briefings-statements/remarks-president-trump-nato-unveiling-article-5-berlin-wall-memorials-brussels-belgium/.

2 The location of Cozy Bear has been assumed to be Moscow State University's journalism department building at 9 Mokhovaya Street. Huib Modderkolk, "Dutch agencies provide crucial intel about Russia's interference in US elections," *de Volkskrant*, January 25, 2018, https://www.volkskrant.nl/tech/dutch-agencies-provide-crucial-intel-about-russia-s-interference-in-us-elections~a4561913/.

3 Dmitri Alperovitch, "Bears in the Midst: Intrusion into the Democratic National Committee," CrowdStrike, June 15, 2016, https://www.crowdstrike.com/blog/bears-midst-intrusion-democratic-national-committee/.

4 Ellen Nakashima, "New details emerge about 2014 Russian hack of the State Department: It was 'hand to hand combat,'" *The Washington Post*, April 3, 2017, https://www.washingtonpost.com/world/national-security/new-details-emerge-about-2014-russian-hack-of-the-state-department-it-was-hand-to-hand-combat/2017/04/03/d89168e0-124c-11e7-833c-503e1f6394c9_story.html.

5 Ilya Zhegulev, "Evgeny Prigozhin's right to be forgotten: What does Vladimir Putin's favorite chef want to hide from the Internet?," *Meduza*, June 13, 2016, https://meduza.io/en/feature/2016/06/13/evgeny-prigozhin-s-right-to-be-forgotten.

6 Karen DeYoung, Ellen Nakashima, and Lizzy Sly, "Putin ally said to be in touch with Kremlin, Assad before his mercenaries attacked U.S. troops," *The Washington Post*, February 23, 2018, https: www.washingtonpost.com/world/national-security/putin-ally-said-to-be-in-touch-with-Kremlin-Assad-before-his-mercenaries-attacked-US-troops/2018/02=22=f4ef050c-1781-11e8-8b08-027a6ccb38eb_story.html.

7 Indictment, February 16, 2018, U.S. v. Internet Research Agency LLC (U.S. Dist. Ct. DC., 2018).

8 Ibid.

9 Ibid.

10 Adrian Chen, "The Agency," *The New York Times Magazine*, June 2, 2015, https://www.nytimes.com/2015/06/07/magazine/the-agency.html.

11 Indictment, U.S. v. Internet Research Agency

12 William J. Donovan, "Morale Operations Field Manual—Strategic Services (Provisional)," Office of Strategic Services, 1943, https://www.cia.gov/library/readingroom/docs/CIA-RDP89-01258R000100010002-4.pdf.

13 Thomas Boghardt, "Soviet Bloc Intelligence and Its AIDS Disinformation Campaign," *Studies in Intelligence*, December 2009, https://www.cia.gov/library/center-for-the-study-of-intelligence/csi-publications/csi-studies/studies/vol53no4/pdf/U-%20Boghardt-AIDS-Made%20in%20the%20USA-17Dec.pdf.

14 Pete Earley. *Comrade J: The Untold Secrets of Russia's Master Spy in America After the End of the Cold War* (Berkley: Berkley Publishing Co., 2009), p. 331.

15 Eric Lipton, David E. Sanger, and Scott Shane, "The Perfect Weapon: How Russian Cyberpower Invaded the U.S.," *The New York Times*, December 13, 2016, https://www.nytimes.com/2016/12/13/us/politics/russia-hack-election-dnc.html.

16 Lipton, "The Perfect Weapon."

17 *Testimony of James Comey: Before the Permanent Select Committee on Intelligence*, U.S. Senate, 115th Congress, 1st sess. (June 8, 2017), https://www.intelligence.senate.gov/sites/default/files/documents/os-jcomey-060817.pdf.

18 Alperovitch, "Bears in the Midst."

19 *Statement of Jeh Johnson: Before the Permanent Select Committee on Intelligence*, U.S. House, 115th Congress, 1st sess. (June 21, 2017), https://intelligence.house.gov/uploaded files/jeh_johnson_-_prepared_statement_to_hpsci_-_6-21-17_hearing.pdf.

20 *Testimony of James Comey: Before the Senate Select Committee on Intelligence*, U.S. Senate, 115th Congress, 1st sess. (Jan. 10, 2017).

21 *Disinformation: A Primer in Active Measures and Influence Campaigns: Hearings before the Select Committee on Intelligence*, U.S. Senate, 115th Congress (March 30, 2017) (Statement of Thomas Rid), https://www.intelligence.senate.gov/sites/default/files/documents /os-trid-033017.pdf.

22 Ellen Nakashima, "Cybersecurity firm finds evidence that Russian military unit was behind DNC hack," *The Washington Post*, December 22, 2016, https://www.washington post.com/world/national-security/cybersecurity-firm-finds-a-link-between-dnc-hack -and-ukrainian-artillery/2016/12/21/47bf1f5a-c7e3-11e6-bf4b-2c064d32a4bf_story.html.

23 Mark Galeotti, "Putin's Hydra: Inside Russia's Intelligence Services," European Council on Foreign Relations, May 11, 2016, http://www.ecfr.eu/publications/summary/putins _hydra_inside_russias_intelligence_services.

24 Ibid.

25 "Assessing Russian Activities and Intentions in Recent US Elections," Office of the Director of National Intelligence, Washington, DC, January 6, 2017, https://www.dni.gov/files /documents/ICA_2017_01.pdf.

26 Lipton, "The Perfect Weapon."

27 mfisher@hillaryclinton.com to slatham@hillaryclinton.com, "Re: Someone Has Your Password," March 19, 2016, accessible at WikiLeaks, https://wikileaks.org/podesta -emails/emailid/36355.

28 delavan@hillaryclinton.com to slatham@hillaryclinton.com, "Re: Someone Has Your Password," March 19, 2016, accessible at WikiLeaks, https://wikileaks.org/podesta -emails/emailid/36355.

29 Don Levin, "Partisan electoral interventions by the great powers: Introducing the PEGI Dataset," *Conflict Management and Peace Science*, 2016. I thank Don for granting me access to his dataset.

30 Indictment, U.S. v. Internet Research Agency.

31 Indictment, U.S. v. Internet Research Agency.

32 "Update on Twitter's Review of the 2016 U.S. Election," Twitter, January 19, 2018, https: //blog.twitter.com/official/en_us/topics/company/2018/2016-election-update.html.

33 Joel Ebert, "Twitter suspends fake Tennessee GOP account later linked to Russian 'troll farm,'" *Tennessean*, October 18, 2017, https://www.tennessean.com/story/news/politics/2017/10/18 /twitter-suspends-fake-tennessee-gop-account-later-linked-russian-troll-farm/776937001/; Phillip Bump, "At least five people close to Trump engaged with Russian Twitter trolls from 2015 to 2017," *The Washington Post*, November 2, 2017, https://www.washingtonpost.com/news /politics/wp/2017/11/02/at-least-five-people-close-to-trump-engaged-with-russian-twitter -trolls-from-2015-to-2017/; Betsy Woodruff, "Trump Campaign Staffers Pushed Russian Propaganda Days Before the Election," *The Daily Beast*, October 18, 2017, https://www.thedaily beast.com/trump-campaign-staffers-pushed-russian-propagand-days-before-the-election.

34 Alex Stamos, "An Update on Information Operations on Facebook," Facebook, September 6, 2017, https://newsroom.fb.com/news/2017/09/information-operations-update/.

35 Colin Stretch to Richard Burr, letter, January 8, 2018.

36 Mark Zuckerberg, Facebook post, September 27, 2017, https://www.facebook.com/zuck /posts/10104067130714241?.

37 Nicholas Confessore and Karen Yourish, "$2 Billion Worth of Free Media for Donald Trump," *The New York Times*, March 15, 2016, https://www.nytimes.com/2016/03/16 /upshot/measuring-donald-trumps-mammoth-advantage-in-free-media.html.

38 Julia Angwin, Madeleine Varner, and Ariana Tobin, "Facebook Enabled Advertisers to Reach 'Jew Haters,'" ProPublica, September 14, 2017, https://www.propublica.org/article /facebook-enabled-advertisers-to-reach-jew-haters.

39 Indictment, U.S. v. Internet Research Agency

40 Joshua Green and Sasha Issenberg, "Inside the Trump Bunker, With Days to Go," *Bloomberg News*, October 27, 2016, https://www.bloomberg.com/news/articles/2016-10 -27/inside-the-trump-bunker-with-12-days-to-go.

41 Issie Lapowsky, "Trump Names Digital Guru Brad Parscale Campaign Director for 2020 Run," *Wired*, February 27, 2018, https://www.wired.com/story/brad-parscale-campaign -manger-trump-2020/.

42 Colin Stretch to Richard Burr, letter, January 8, 2018.

43 Ibid.

44 Guccifer20@gmx.us to Unknown, "new leaks from Democratic National Committee," email, June 15, 2016.

45 "U.S. intel report identifies Russians who gave emails to WikiLeaks officials," Reuters, January 5, 2017, https://www.reuters.com/article/us-usa-russia-cyber-celebrate/u-s-intel -report-identifies-russians-who-gave-emails-to-wikileaks-officials-idUSKBN14P2NI.

46 Matthew Cole, "Top Secret NSA Report Details Russian Hacking Effort Days Before 2016 Election," *The Intercept*, June 6, 2017, https://theintercept.com/2017/06/05/top-secret -nsa-report-details-russian-hacking-effort-days-before-2016-election/.

47 Associated Press, "U.S. Tells 21 States That Hackers Targeted Their Voting Systems," *The New York Times*, September 22, 2017, https://www.nytimes.com/2017/09/22/us/politics /us-tells-21-states-that-hackers-targeted-their-voting-systems.

48 Matthew Rosenberg, "White House Has Given No Orders to Counter Russian Meddling, N.S.A. Chief Says," *The New York Times*, February 27, 2016.

49 Svetlana Reiter, "Jailed Russian Hacker Claimed Responsibility For U.S. Election Cyber-Attacks," thebell.io,https://thebell.io/jailed-russian-hacker-claimed-responsibility-for-u-s-election-cyber -attacks/; Konstantin Kozlovskiy. Facebook Post. September 19, 2017. https://www.facebook .com/permalink.php?story_fbid=1654125991286065&id=1620554077976590

CHAPTER 12: THE PROSECUTOR AND THE PRESIDENT

1 Steve Eder and Dave Philipps, "Donald Trump's Draft Deferments: Four for College, One for Bad Feet," *The New York Times*, August 1, 2016, https://www.nytimes.com/2016/08/02 /us/politics/donald-trump-draft-record.html.

2 Marc Fisher and Sari Horwitz, "Mueller and Trump: Born to wealth, raised to lead. Then, sharply different choices," *The Washington Post*, February 23, 2018, https://www.washington post.com/politics/mueller-and-trump-born-to-wealth-raised-to-lead-then-sharply -different-choices/2018/02/22/ad50b7bc-0a99-11e8-8b0d-891602206fb7_story.html.

3 Garrett M. Graff, "The Ultimate G-Man: Robert Mueller Remakes the FBI," *The Washingtonian*, August 1, 2008.

4   Garrett M Graff. *The Threat Matrix: The FBI at War in the Age of Global Terror* (New York: Little, Brown and Company, 2011), p. 563.

5   Michael S. Schmidt and Maggie Haberman, "Mueller Has Early Draft of Trump Letter Giving Reasons for Firing Comey," *The New York Times*, September 1, 2017, https://www.nytimes.com/2017/09/01/us/politics/trump-comey-firing-letter.html.

6   Matt Apuzzo, Maggie Haberman, and Matthew Rosenberg, "Trump Told Russians That Firing 'Nut Job' Comey Eased Pressure from Investigation," *The New York Times*, May 19, 2017, https://www.nytimes.com/2017/05/19/us/politics/trump-russia-comey.html.

7   Ronen Bergman, interview by Dave Davies, *Fresh Air*, NPR, January 31, 2018, https://www.npr.org/2018/01/31/582099085/journalist-details-israels-secret-history-of-targeted-assassinations

8   Howard Blum, "Exclusive: What Trump Really Told Kislyak After Comey Was Canned," *Vanity Fair*, November 22, 2017, https://www.vanityfair.com/news/2017/11/trump-intel-slip.

9   Ronen Bergman, "US intel sources warn Israel against sharing secrets with Trump administration," *Ynet News*, January 12, 2017, https://www.ynetnews.com/articles/0,7340,L-4906642,00.html.

10 "President Donald Trump on his firing of James Comey," YouTube video, 13:15, posted by "NBC News," May 11, 2017, https://www.youtube.com/watch?v=5Wvuw_Zmubg

11 Donald Trump, (@realDonaldTrump), "James Comey better hope that there are no 'tapes' of our conversations before he starts leaking to the press!," Twitter, May 12, 2017. https://twitter.com/realdonaldtrump/status/863007411132649473?lang=en

12 *Testimony of James Comey: Before the Permanent Select Committee on Intelligence*, U.S. Senate, 115th Congress, 1st sess. (June 8, 2017).

13 Adam Entous, "Top intelligence official told associates Trump asked him if he could intervene with Comey on FBI Russia probe," *The Washington Post*, June 6, 2017, https://www.washingtonpost.com/world/national-security/top-intelligence-official-told-associates-trump-asked-him-if-he-could-intervene-with-comey-to-get-fbi-to-back-off-flynn/2017/06/06/cc879f14-4ace-11e7-9669-250d0b15f83b_story.html?utm_term=.37435ecd79c6.

14 Devlin Barrett, Josh Dawsey, and Rosalind S. Helderman, "Mueller investigation examining Trump's apparent efforts to oust Sessions in July," *The Washington Post*, February 28, 2017, https://www.washingtonpost.com/world/national-security/mueller-investigation-examining-trumps-apparent-efforts-to-oust-sessions-in-july/2018/02/28/909cfa7c-1cd7-11e8-b2d9-08e748f892c0_story.html.

15 Evan Perez and Manu Raju, "Sources: Rosenstein sees no need for special prosecutor in Russia probe," CNN, May 12, 2017, https://www.cnn.com/2017/05/12/politics/rosenstein-special-prosecutor-russia-investigation/index.html.

16 Fisher and Horwitz, "Mueller and Trump."

17 Robert Costa, Carol D. Leonning, and Josh Dawsey, "Inside the secretive nerve center of the Mueller investigation," *The Washington Post*, December 2, 2017, https://www.washingtonpost.com/politics/inside-the-secretive-nerve-center-of-the-mueller-investigation/2017/12/02/e6764720-d45f-11e7-b62d-d9345ced896d_story.html.

18 Michael S. Schmidt and Maggie Haberman, "Trump Ordered Mueller Fired, but Backed Off When White House Counsel Threatened to Quit," *The New York Times*, January 25, 2018, https://www.nytimes.com/2018/01/25/us/politics/trump-mueller-special-counsel-russia.html.

19 Maegan Vazquez, "Ex-Trump campaign adviser: Papadopoulos was just a 'coffee boy,'" CNN, October 31, 2017, https://www.cnn.com/2017/10/31/politics/caputo-papadopoulos -coffee-boy-cnntv/index.html.

20 Peter Baker and Kenneth P. Vogel, "Trump Lawyers Clash Over How Much to Cooper- ate with Russia Inquiry," The *New York Times*, September 17, 2017, https://www.nytimes .com/2017/09/17/us/politics/trump-lawyers-white-house-russia-mcgahn-ty-cobb.html.

21 Email from Sally Yates to Redacted, "FW:I am so proud," email, January 30, 2017. Obtained by Judicial Watch Inc. via FOIA.

22 Donald Trump (@realDonaldTrump), "Very sad that the FBI missed all of the many signals sent out by the Florida school shooter. This is not acceptable. They are spend- ing too much time trying to prove Russian collusion. Get back to the basics and make us all proud!" Twitter, February 17, 2018. https://twitter.com/realdonaldtrump /status/965075589274177536

INDEX